Lecture Notes in Computer Science   1927
Edited by G. Goos, J. Hartmanis and J. van Leeuwen

Springer
Berlin
Heidelberg
New York
Barcelona
Hong Kong
London
Milan
Paris
Singapore
Tokyo

Peter Thomas   Hans-W. Gellersen (Eds.)

Handheld and Ubiquitous Computing

Second International Symposium, HUC 2000
Bristol, UK, September 25-27, 2000
Proceedings

Springer

Series Editors

Gerhard Goos, Karlsruhe University, Germany
Juris Hartmanis, Cornell University, NY, USA
Jan van Leeuwen, Utrecht University, The Netherlands

Volume Editors

Peter Thomas
Middlesex University, School of Computing Science
Bounds Green Road, London, N11 2NQ, UK
E-mail: pjt@cableinet.co.uk

Hans-W. Gellersen
University of Karlsruhe, Telecooperation Office (TecO)
Vincenz-Priessnitz-Str. 1, 76131 Karlsruhe, Germany
E-mail: hwg@teco.uni-karlsruhe.de

Cataloging-in-Publication Data applied for

Die Deutsche Bibliothek - CIP-Einheitsaufnahme

Handheld and ubiquitous computing : second international symposium ;
proceedings / HUC 2000, Bristol, UK, September 25 - 27, 2000.
Peter Thomas ; Hans W. Gellersen (ed.). - Berlin ; Heidelberg ; New York ;
Barcelona ; Hong Kong ; London ; Milan ; Paris ; Singapore ; Tokyo :
Springer, 2000
  (Lecture notes in computer science ; Vol. 1927)
  ISBN 3-540-41093-7

CR Subject Classification (1998): C.2, K.8, K.4, H.5, H.4, D.2, C.3

ISSN 0302-9743
ISBN 3-540-41093-7 Springer-Verlag Berlin Heidelberg New York

This work is subject to copyright. All rights are reserved, whether the whole or part of the material is concerned, specifically the rights of translation, reprinting, re-use of illustrations, recitation, broadcasting, reproduction on microfilms or in any other way, and storage in data banks. Duplication of this publication or parts thereof is permitted only under the provisions of the German Copyright Law of September 9, 1965, in its current version, and permission for use must always be obtained from Springer-Verlag. Violations are liable for prosecution under the German Copyright Law.

Springer-Verlag Berlin Heidelberg New York
a member of BertelsmannSpringer Science+Business Media GmbH
© Springer-Verlag Berlin Heidelberg 2000
Printed in Germany

Typesetting: Camera-ready by author, data conversion by PTP Berlin, Stefan Sossna
Printed on acid-free paper   SPIN 10722882   06/3142   5 4 3 2 1 0

Preface

The papers collected here are those selected for presentation at the Second International Symposium on Handheld and Ubiquitous Computing 2000 (HUC 2000) held in Bristol, UK in September 2000. The symposium was the second in a series of symposia which explores new research in the area of emerging mobile, personal, and handheld technologies.

The first event, HUC'99, was held in Karlsruhe (Germany), organised by the Telecooperation Office (TecO) of the University of Karlsruhe in close collaboration with the Center for Arts and Media Technology (ZKM). This previous event, the first of its kind in the world, attracted a large number of paper submissions, was attended by over 200 international delegates, and demonstrated the growing international interest in the area with contributions from the United States, Japan and Europe.

The 18 papers collected here were chosen from 70 submissions to HUC 2000, and represent a valuable resource for those wishing to understand the themes being pursued in this vibrant and exciting area of technology. The papers range from work on intelligent environment and devices, user experience, and interface design, to research in context aware systems, wearable computing, and location-based services. Together, the papers represent a snapshot of the state of the art in research in handheld and ubiquitous computing. The symposium also attracted a large number of short paper submissions, and these are available in the Springer journal *Personal Technologies* volume 4, number 4, which was published in tandem with these proceedings.

The HUC 2000 symposium was organised in collaboration with HP Laboratories, Bristol, where the event was held, and supported by a number of commercial, academic, governmental and professional society sponsors including Nokia Mobile Phones (Finland), Microsoft (USA), HP Laboratories (Great Britain), British Telecom (Great Britain), the Institute of Electrical Engineers (Great Britain), ACM (USA), British Computer Society (Great Britain), and the Engineering and Physical Sciences Research Council (Great Britain). We would like to thank these organisations for their interest in and support for the event.

We would like also to thank the reviewers who offered insightful comments on the papers submitted to the symposium, and the programme committee for their assistance in compiling the technical symposium programme. In particular, we would like to thank Dr. Phil Stenton for his support in securing the involvement of HP Laboratories.

September 2000   Peter Thomas
                                                                                                  Hans-W. Gellersen

Symposium Organisation

Supporting Societies

Association for Computing Machinery (ACM) with the special interest groups:
 SIGCHI (Computer-Human Interaction)
 SIGMOBILE (Mobile Computing)

The Institute of Electrical Engineers (GB)
The British Computer Society (GB)

Sponsors

HP Laboratories (GB), Nokia (FI), BT (GB), Microsoft (US), The Appliance Studio Ltd (GB), the Engineering and Physical Sciences Research Council (GB).

Symposium Chair

Peter Thomas   University of the West of England (GB)

Programme Committee

Peter Thomas (chair)   University of the West of England (GB)
Gregory Abowd   Georgia Institute of Technology (US)
Hans-W. Gellersen (past chair)   TecO, University of Karlsruhe, (D)
Tom Moran   Xerox (US)
Jun Rekimoto   Sony CSL (JP)
Chris Schmandt   MIT Media Laboratory (US)
Phil Stenton   HP (GB)

Invited Speakers

Niels Ole Bernsen   Odense University (DK)
Tim Kindberg   HP Laboratories (US)
David May   University of Bristol (GB)

List of Reviewers

David Benyon, Napier University (GB)
Staffan Björk, Viktoria Institute (S)
Marie-Luce Bourguet, Canon Research Centre Europe Ltd (GB)
Stephen Brewster, University of Glasgow (GB)
Keith Cheverst, Lancaster University (GB)
Mary Czerwinski, Microsoft Research (US)
Oscar de Bruijn, Imperial College of Science, Technology & Medicine (GB)
Hans de Graaff, KPN Research (NL)
Morten Fjeld, IHA (CH)
Richard Harper, University of Surrey (GB)
Mark Hawley, Barnsley District General Hospital NHS Trust (GB)
Hans-Juergen Hoffmann, Darmstadt University of Technology (D)
Stefan Holmlid, University of Linköping (S)
Lars Erik Holmquist, Interactive Institute (S)
Phillip Jeffrey, GMD FIT (D)
Matt Jones, Middlesex University (GB)
Joaquim A. Jorge, INESC (P)|
Wendy A. Kellogg, IBM T.J. Watson Research Center (US)
Jonathan Kies, Qualcomm, Inc (US)
Shin'ichi Konomi, University of Colorado at Boulder (US)
Gerd Kortuem, University of Oregon (US)
Olivier Liechti, Hiroshima University (JP)
Peter Ljungstrand, Viktoria Institute (S)
Robert Macredie, Brunel University (GB)
Joseph F. McCarthy, Andersen Consulting (US)
Reinhard Oppermann, GMD FIT (D)
Fabio Paternò, CNUCE - C.N.R (I)
Mark Perry, Brunel University (GB)
Daniela Petrelli ITC-irst (I)
Dave Roberts, IBM (GB)
Marcus Specht, GMD FIT-MMK (D)
Kostas Stathis, City University (GB)
Leon Watts, CLIPS-IMAG (F)

Publication and Local Organisation

Peter Thomas	University of the West of England (GB)
Hans-W. Gellersen	TecO, University of Karlsruhe (D)
Jules Tuckett	University of the West of England (GB)
Sara Gwynn	University of the West of England (GB)
Jan Ward	HP Laboratories (GB)

Table of Contents

Intelligent Environments

Event-Driven, Personalizable, Mobile Interactive Spaces 1
Theo Kanter

EasyLiving: Technologies for Intelligent Environments 12
Barry Brumitt, Brian Meyers, John Krumm, Amanda Kern, and Steven Shafer

Beyond the Control Room: Mobile Devices for Spatially
Distributed Interaction on Industrial Process Plants 30
Jörn Nilsson, Tomas Sokoler, Thomas Binder, and Nina Wetcke

User Experience

POWERVIEW: Using Information Links and Information Views to
Navigate and Visualize Information on Small Displays 46
Staffan Björk, Johan Redström, Peter Ljungstrand, and Lars E. Holmquist

A Comparison of Free Interaction Modes for Mobile Layout System 63
Zhiwei Guan, Yang Li, Hongan Wang, and Guozhong Dai

Real-World Graphical User Interfaces 72
Toshiyuki Masui and Itiro Siio

Multimedia Augmentation

Lessons Learned from the Design of a Mobile Multimedia
System in the MOBY DICK Project 85
Gerard J.M. Smit and Paul J.M. Havinga

Notable: At the Intersection of Annotations and Handheld Technology 100
Michelle Baldonado, Steve Cousins, Jacek Gwizdka, and Andreas Paepcke

Location-Based Services

Creating Web Representations for Places 114
Deborah Caswell and Philippe Debaty

A Context-Sensitive Nomadic Exhibition Guide 127
Reinhard Oppermann and Marcus Specht

Exploiting Location-Based Composite Devices to
Support and Facilitate Situated Ubiquitous Computing 143
Thai-Lai Pham, Georg Schneider, and Stuart Goose

Context-Aware Messaging

Location-Aware Information Delivery with *ComMotion* 157
Natalia Marmasse and Chris Schmandt

CybreMinder: A Context-Aware System for Supporting Reminders 172
Anind K. Dey and Gregory D. Abowd

Intelligent Devices

Using Handheld Devices in Synchronous Collaborative Scenarios 187
Jörg Roth and Claus Unger

Smartcards: How to Put them to Use in a User-Centric System 200
Tage Stabell-Kulø

Infrastructure Engineering

Using Dynamic Mediation to Integrate COTS Entities in
a Ubiquitous Computing Environment 211
Emre Kıcıman and Armando Fox

EVENTMANAGER: Support for the Peripheral Awareness of Events 227
Joseph F. McCarthy and Theodore D. Anagnost

Wearable Computing

Safety and Comfort of Eyeglass Displays 236
Erik Geelhoed, Marie Falahee, and Kezzy Latham

Author Index 249

Event-Driven, Personalizable, Mobile Interactive Spaces

Theo Kanter

Ericsson Radio Systems AB, SE-16480 Stockholm, Sweden

theo.kanter@era.ericsson.se

Abstract Infrastructure is currently being deployed for delivering multimedia services IP end-to-end. Mobile devices and application resources, because of their computing capabilities, can be enabled with adaptive functionality to shape the services according to the communication conditions and the user's context. This raises the question of how events should be managed to create a common awareness of multimedia content and resources in mobile networks. These events can be generated either by the user's behavior, movement, availability of (new) mobile resources, or the application server content changes. In this paper, we propose XML-based protocols and agent functionality operating on a distributed tuple-space to accommodate common awareness of these events in applications for mobile users, without the necessity of these events being defined or announced in advance. This facilitates the creation of a new class of personalizable applications in interactive mobile spaces, as demonstrated in our urban wireless test bed.

1 Introduction

Presently, the telecom and datacom industries are converging in different ways. With respect to mobile telephony with GSM, new devices are appearing on the market that integrate data with the telephony voice service in new ways. So-called Smart Phones either include the functionality of an organizer, or can connect wirelessly to an external Personal Data Assistant (PDA) and integrate the functionality of the organizer for smart dialing and messaging with the application that is running in the handset. The Wireless Application Protocol (WAP) [1] is intended to move the point of integration of these services into the cellular access network. WAP-gateways can be used to adapt and convert Internet information, so that the mobile terminal can be used for interacting with a wider range of network-centric services (e.g. electronic payment, subscription to information services, unified messaging, etc.). However, WAP is neither intended nor well suited to transport multimedia content, but rather was targeted at simply extending GSM networks with low-bandwidth data services. Further, mobile devices can only be connected to services on the Internet through WAP-gateways. Therefore, WAP excludes mobile users from directly interacting with Internet content. On the other hand, simple low-bandwidth GPRS (General Packet Radio Service) is just being introduced in GSM-networks, which will provide direct Internet access to mobile users. GPRS enables the development of multimedia applications for the mobile device. These applications can directly integrate content that resides anywhere on the Internet. EDGE (Enhanced Data-rate for GSM Evolution), the successor of GPRS, will increase the bit-rate and thereby further relax the limits on the mobile applications and their use of Internet content, thus bringing even more multimedia applications to mobile devices. In addition, so-called 'hot spots' equipped with wireless LAN extensions to the Internet are becoming available, and today provide us with even higher bandwidths (e.g. 11 Mbps in IEEE 802.11b).

Mobile devices are now becoming available [2] that are able to perform significant computations based on events from various input devices and/or information sources. These events provide information about the user's context and the conditions, which the link is facing. Therefore, applications in mobile devices and nodes in the network that co-operate to deliver multimedia services to users can adapt their mode of communication dynamically based on such events. In such cases, the requirements for the delivery of multimedia IP-content over a link using wireless access networks are even further relaxed [3,4]. Even more importantly, the service multiplexing due to using IP over the wireless link, in combination with the capabilities of mobile devices to perform computations based on events from various input devices and/or information sources, enables entirely new classes of applications. Thus mobile users will now be able to experience applications that create a common awareness of events and resources. For instance, mobile users can be aware of each other's presence and locality, and share common resources, as would be the case in a shopping mall, where two users A and B can know each other's location. A and B can send each other notes about interesting items and prices, and even more importantly use voice over IP services on the local-area network. This local area network will be offered as a public resource for visitors, in order to facilitate communication within the store or perhaps to parties/devices outside the store.

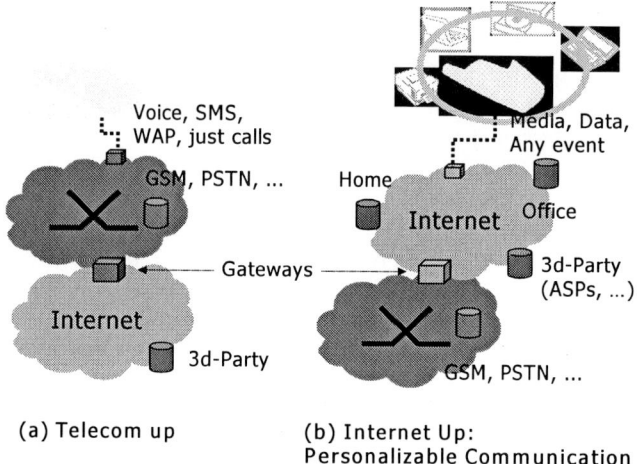

Fig. 1. Transition to Mobile Internet

2 Problem Statement

The same technologies that enable these new applications, in particular end-to-end IP connectivity (including over the wireless link), also enables third parties to deliver services directly to end users, and thus further accelerates the trend of services moving out of a network operator's network. This change to end-to-end IP based services is driving the transition from a Telecom centered network (as shown in figure 1a) to an Internet centered network (as shown in figure 1b). In this latter model, the mobile user will purchase access to the Internet from a network operator, buy a package of applications and services from an applications service provider (ASP), who in turn may have bundled these with applications and services coming from other parties. In [3], a strategy has been described for such an ASP regarding how to manage the delivery of multimedia content, so as to maximize the QoS and number of users that can use these services. In this paper, we address a different problem, namely how a third-party[1] can provide "aware" services for mobile collaborative applications, such that we can extend the notion of smart spaces [5] to the scale of cellular networks. This platform provides a vehicle for third-party application developers and providers, allowing them to be agnostic about the topology and design of the radio access networks. An important feature is that the services do not have to depend on a specific link-layer technology. The extension of the notion of smart spaces to the scale of cellular networks *and* the event-driven nature of this platform are the focus of this paper.

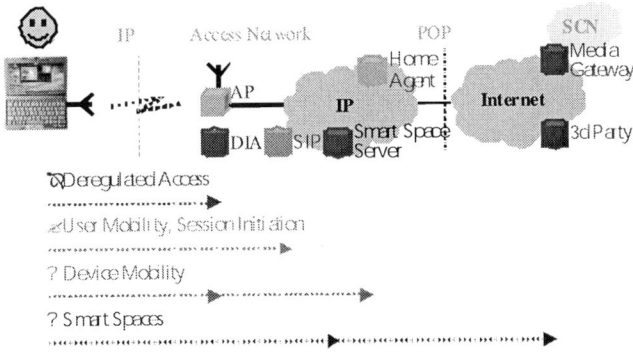

Fig. 2. Deregulated Wireless Internet

Irrespective of who is offering their services to the mobile user (either directly by a third-party or mediated by an ASP), the question remains of how events are managed to create *common awareness* of multimedia content and resources in mobile networks among groups of mobile users. These events can be generated either by the user's behavior, movement, the availability of (new) mobile resources, or because the application server's content changes. Clearly, mobile users and resources must be allowed to appear in the network without prior knowledge of either the network

---

[1] The end-user and the network operator are the other two parties.

operator or the operator of the service. This will be referred to as *ad-hoc application networking*.

Previous work in this area has been carried out within the scope of ubiquitous computing research, which assumes that resources and users have some sort of IP-connectivity, thus allowing these entities to share information. This previous research is less concerned with networking aspects, such as service-, personal-, and device mobility that have been matters of great concern in mobile networks. However, scaling the notion of smart-spaces to the level of cellular networks requires us to address these issues.

In this paper, I address these two challenges (providing events and scaling) by proposing XML-based [6] protocols and agent functionality operating on a distributed tuple-space to accommodate common awareness of these events in applications for mobile users, without the necessity of these events being defined or announced in advance. I will show that this facilitates the creation of a new class of personalizable applications in mobile interactive spaces.

3 Mobile Internet – The Smart Way

The term 'Mobile Internet' is commonly used to refer to applications in mobile handsets that include some information elements that are forwarded to and from Internet, perhaps by means of (WAP) gateways in the mobile operator's network. In contrast to this proxy or indirect approach, we have built an urban wireless Internet by extending the fixed infrastructure with wireless LAN access points in various locations in Stockholm, and plan to include GPRS access points for coverage of wider areas.

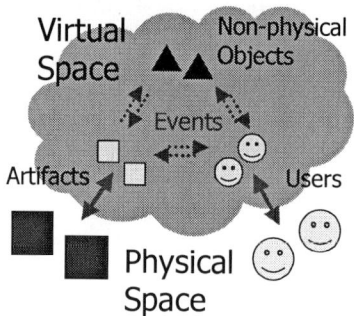

Fig. 3. Physical vs. Virtual Space

This network allows us to connect users anonymously and provide them with bandwidths ranging from 9.6 Kbps up to 11 Mbps, with end-to-end IP connectivity. This removes the necessity for gateways. Housing co-operations, even single households, can resell their fixed Internet connectivity to mobile users, thus offering a secure anonymous Internet access solution (❶ in Fig 2.). Thus, in urban areas, there will be an abundance of wireless, flat rate Internet connectivity with widely varying available bandwidth.

This of course calls for smart support for delivery of multimedia, as described in [3]. Even more importantly, removing the role of the network operator as the single provider (or negotiator) of services, allows us to create spontaneous communication that involves mobile users, mobile artifacts, resources, and even (potentially intelligent) objects [7,8] and build so-called 'Smart Spaces' (❹ in Fig.2.).

3.1 Smart Spaces

"Smart spaces" are ordinary environments equipped with sensing systems (e.g. location, movement, visual, audio, etc.) that can perceive and react to people. Conversely, by instrumenting the physical world, we enable people to influence the virtual world. The integration of the physical and virtual worlds is also referred to as mixed-reality [9].

In my licentiate thesis [8], I described a communication system for such a Smart Space, in which mobile users, mobile artifacts, and resources have corresponding representational entities in communicate space (the virtual world), see Fig. 3. Events sent between these entities enable them to respond intelligently using their internal logic. Thus, spontaneous communication between these entities can be triggered by events from any of these systems (e.g. location, movement, visual, audio, information change, etc.).

This architecture is further detailed in section 0. The propagation of these events may be network-wide without any intermediary (i.e. Smart Space Server, as it is referred to, later in this paper) between entities, but also scoped in the sense that a housing co-operation or a single household can install such an intermediary if they wish. The scope that this intermediary introduces can relate to the geographically bounded area (e.g. the range of the wireless access point), but could also relate to an abstract space (e.g. a cyber-mall, the aspects of which may physically be overlaid on top of a physical space in a mixed reality situation).

3.2 Mobility

One of the major concerns of cellular networks is supporting mobility. For the scenario that was envisaged in the problem statement and above, and to understand how our proposed solution works, it is important to clarify the mobility architecture that is available for services, devices, and users when these move to Internet. Mobility support can be divided into to three different cases: device mobility, service mobility, and user mobility.

Device Mobility. Device mobility (❸ in Fig.2.) is addressed by network level mobility protocols such as Mobile-IP.

Service Mobility. Service Mobility really is about session continuity, which falls into two categories: roaming (case similar to 'User Mobility' case below) and handoffs. In the case of handoffs, there are application level strategies (e.g. SIP inspired) [10,11], and network level (e.g. Mobile-IP inspired) strategies [12].

User Mobility. User mobility (❷ in Fig. 2.) concerns the issues of localization and the users' abilities to engage in communication sessions. The same strategy applies to mobile artifacts and resources (e.g., public displays, printers, web camera, software robots, etc.). Mobility support for users is implemented in our prototype by assigning a SIP URL [8] to users who then can be located and invited to (multimedia) sessions by means of SIP. Users must be able to announce their own capabilities and be aware of other's capabilities. Therefore a software object with an independent behavior (agent) is given this SIP-URL, such that with this SIP URL this agent can be located and invited to communication sessions. The agent can act on behalf of the user when the user is off-line. When the user goes on-line, the profiles are resynchronized, and the initiative is transferred to the mobile agent running in the user's device.

3.3 Smart Space Server

When (new) mobile resources become available and are to be used in the communication space, others must be able to locate them and interrogate them (or an intermediary) about their capabilities. In addition, there must be a naming and localization schema.

Corba [13], Jini [14], and UPnP [15] offer APIs and protocols for registration, localization, and invocation of resources; and thereby they dictate a specific predetermined format that not only requires a-priori knowledge of the mobile user, but also limits what can be discussed. It is worth emphasizing that part of the problem with Jini and UPnP is that while they support configuration and initialization of a new device, they don't support the necessary service dynamics required for a smart space. In particular, neither negotiation of services is within the scope of these technologies,

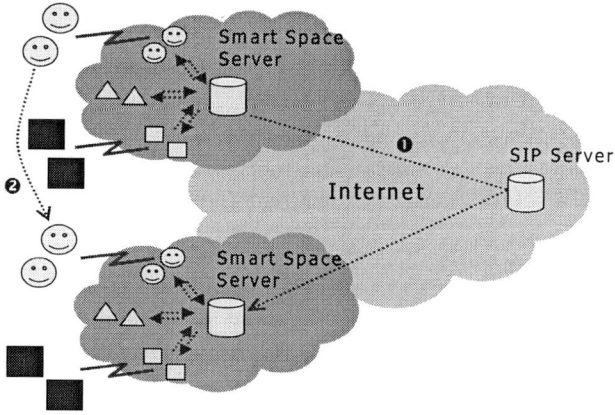

Fig. 4. Smart Spaces

nor do they address the dissemination of knowledge of what (new) resources are available. Jini systems provide mechanisms for discovery, joining and lookup of services in a distributed system. For instance, after first discovering a lookup service and then joining it, the printer is available for other devices. A digital camera first uses a lookup service to search for a matching print service and after configuring a matching print service, it can print the image and ask to be notified when the printer is done. UPnP also supports both peer-to-peer (where discovery is achieved by for instance SLP [16]) and server based systems, and uses XML to provide the description of services and capabilities of smart devices.

Therefore, a different strategy for the intermediary (the Smart Space Server, as mentioned earlier) is necessary. In my prototype, the Smart Space Server comprises a simple event communication mechanism based on a tuple space (blackboard) system [4], allowing for dynamic reconfiguration and loose coupling between entities. Events are text-based messages formatted as XML. In contrast to the remote method invocation which is used by Corba and Java/Jini, which demands object and their methods to be registered, using XML-descriptions of events in messages allow the structure and the content of messages to change dynamically in run-time, whereas UpnP uses XML merely as another format for describing similar information on device capabilities as in Jini. The events are stored on the Smart Space Server running an event-loop enabling it to handle subscriptions to events. Entities can register with the Smart Space Server using a SIP-URL and subscribe to events using a simple text-based protocol. The advantage of this approach it is open-ended in terms of what can be discussed. Besides the capabilities of a UPnP or JINI-based system, this system can store any type of events signifying knowledge, facts, as well actions pertaining to the entities participating in this mobile interactive space.

3.4 Ad-Hoc Introduction of Entities

Using this event store and propagation mechanism, (new) mobile resources can advertise themselves to whoever has subscribed to their presence. This allows an active entity to be introduced, such as a location agent, which can administer this event store thus creating a smart space. The location agent is a resource itself and thus must be addressable and locatable in the communication space. This is accomplished by assigning to it a SIP-URL [8].

Hence, a newly arriving SIP-enabled mobile device that is not equipped with these requisite capabilities to participate in this communication, can still find out about the Smart Space Server as it is SIP-enabled. Then they can download a basic client from the Smart Space Server with sufficient capabilities to bootstrap their participation with other entities that are already present in this space.

3.5 Scaling

The Smart Space Server may include SIP Server functionality. Thus entities can move between Smart Spaces in the same way that SIP terminals can move between SIP Servers. If a separate SIP Server is available, localization of entities is delegated to this server (❶ in Fig. 4). This approach scales excellent as the localization or invitation to sessions is based on SIP, which scales well itself. Sessions do not rely on the active mediation by means of a server, but are carried out peer-to-peer. Since SIP-redirect servers can be organized hierarchically, Smart Spaces can also be organized hierarchically. This is not to say they that they automatically are organized hierarchically from a conceptual point of view, but rather that they can be.

Smart Space Servers can be further developed to propagate facts to each other in order to disseminate knowledge of state changes with non-local relevance. Furthermore, when users move to other Smart Spaces (❷ in Fig. 4), events can be forwarded to their new location allowing them to participate in multiple spaces simultaneously.

4 Application Implications for Mobile Users

As new geographic areas with anonymous wireless connectivity to Internet become available, a Smart Space Server can serve mobile users in a mobile interactive space, having thus dramatic impact on the kind of applications that are possible in these locations. In this section I describe a few important scenarios that illustrate this.

4.1 Personalization of Multimedia

Personalization of multimedia requires maintaining a person's personal profile in an agent, which can move between mobile interactive spaces. A person can use the SIP URL that is assigned to this agent on his or her business card. Therefore this agent comprises a persons virtual representative (with capabilities to act if this person is off-line) but also a mobile profile. This profile reflects the preferences of the user, which it can acquire by studying the user's behavior. With this information it can start monitoring events in this mobile interactive space or others that the user has visited previously or learned about from others. Those who provide content (e.g., an Internet Radio Station) maintain electronic programs of this content, which they advertise on their sites. The mobile interactive spaces can act as redistribution centers for this content to mobile users. As mentioned earlier, in section 0, this is particularly interesting for content providers who can use this as a platform for distributing content to mobile users, and be agnostic about the topology and design of the radio access networks. Mobile users can move between interactive spaces and learn about the communication conditions and the distribution of media to the user is planned by the user's mobile agent according to these conditions. The user's agent can in certain situations ask the user for guidance, but in most cases it can look for relevant content and according the nature of this content plan where it should be delivered, and thus provide an unconscious service. For instance, visiting in one geographically area the user never views sports (probably work), but in other areas he or she might depending on the available bandwidth. For instance, during a train ride, the user might only have 9.6 kbps access to Internet permitting only reading mail, in which case the live content is available the user's home network and no attempt is made it download this. However, the personal agent recently learnt of a new high-bandwidth area that the user passes on the way home. The positioning system in the present area tells the user's mobile agent, that the user will pass this higher bandwidth area and that there is enough time for the content provider to send the required content there. The mobile agent soon receives a confirmation and the user is notified as soon as the content is available and is able to watch the desired sports event before coming home, where there are other matters to attend.

4.2 Coordinated Events

In mobile interactive spaces, multiple devices can be involved in ad-hoc applications. For instance, groups of mobile users (a good example would be teenagers) are aware of each other's presence and actions. This group can enter the same mobile interactive space, which is modeled as a mixed reality shopping mall, with multimedia content overlaid on top of a public space, either related to location or simply related to the items (e.g., by including a bar-code reader in the handset). The teenagers, as they move through the shops, receive offers related to specific items or areas and monitor each other's findings to know where to get the best deal. One in the group might find some interesting content; for instance a new multiplayer 3D-game and wants to share it with the others. He or she posts an event to the others with an action that downloads the demo and causes them to enter its virtual world and share a walkthrough. Another example might be, finding a new mobile device, and forward the 3D presentation and audio to those in the group who responded they were interested in this item.

4.3 Ad-Hoc Networking Situations

The usage of a Smart Space Server to manage resources and communication of events is also relevant in an ad-hoc networking situation, for example when no connectivity with the network is available. A member of a group of mobile users in an ad-hoc network can host such a Smart Space Server and thus represent a local space. For instance, when a family goes outdoors equipped with wireless communicators, they can clone the family Smart Space Server on one of their communicators and meet friends, store events, and corresponding electronic content that belongs to the household. Certain resources in the family home will be unavailable during this time, but upon reconnecting with the network the Smart Space Servers can be resynchronized and events propagated to the actual resources. Similarly, events, which are received by the Smart Space Server in their home, are passed to the users when they return home.

5 Conclusions

Future mobile networks will provide users with end-to-end IP connectivity. Existing mobile networks, such as GSM will be upgraded to provide packet data services (GPRS), and later at higher bit-rates (EDGE). At present, hot spots are being deployed offering wireless access to Internet at even higher speeds. As broadband

Internet access is becoming a commodity, this bandwidth can be resold wirelessly to provide mobile users with an increasing number of locations where anonymous access to Internet is available, with varying bandwidth. End-to-end IP connectivity allows users and providers to provide and users services that are multiplexed over a single (perhaps wireless) and at the same time be agnostic about the link layer technology. This puts us in the position to transfer the concept of smart spaces to the scale of mobile networks, where sensing systems (e.g. location, movement, visual, audio, etc.) that can perceive and react to people are networked and thus can change our mode of communication. Conversely, we enable people to influence the virtual world, resulting in mixed-reality applications.

In this paper I have described an architecture for building mobile interactive spaces based on smart spaces servers that relay events between entities in this space. The entities, except for (potentially intelligent) virtual object such as software robots, are modeled as agents and represent physical entities (i.e., mobile users, mobile artifacts and resources). These agents are able to respond intelligently to these events and invite other entities to sessions. An important contribution of this paper was that by basing the naming schema and localization of entities on SIP, this architecture scales well. Another important contribution of this paper is that it avoids some of the limitations in Jini or UPnP regarding the necessary service dynamics required for a building smart spaces by incorporating mechanisms for generating and parsing XML descriptions of events. Such a design is open-ended and allows for the dynamic change of structure and content of messages in run-time, and thereby achieving the necessary service dynamics. This was illustrated by a few key scenarios, which illustrate how these mechanisms result in flexible communication applications for mobile users.

We have deployed a test bed infrastructure in central Stockholm and suburbs, featuring a wireless packet data, agent servers, media servers and -gateways with anonymous wireless access to Internet over wireless LAN, and expect to add GPRS later this year [17,18]. We have started out to prototype the envisaged scenarios, which we expect to produce research results regarding the required minimal properties for service protocols in order to display the dynamic behavior and allowing bootstrapping of functionality.

References

1. WAP Forum (Wireless Application Protocol Forum Ltd.), Proposed 1.1 technical documents, http://www.wapforum.org/docs/technical.htm
2. Mark T. Smith, "SmartCards: Integrating for Portable Complexity", IEEE Computer, August 1998, pp. 110-112, and 115.
3. T. Kanter, P. Lindtorp, C. Olrog, G. Maguire, "Smart Delivery of Multimedia Content for Wireless Applications", to be presented during the 2nd International Workshop on Mobile and Wireless Communications Networks (MWCN'2000), May 2000.

4. Joseph Mitola III, "Cognitive Radio for Flexible Mobile Multimedia Communications", Proceedings of the Sixth IEEE International Workshop on Mobile Multimedia Communications (MoMuC'99), IEEE, ISBN 0-7803-5904-6, November 1999, pp. 3-20.
5. TSpaces: The Next Wave", published in the Hawaii International Conference on System Sciences (HICSS-32), January 99.
6. Extensible Markup Language (XML) 1.0, URL: http://www.w3.org/TR/1998/REC-xml-19980210
7. T. Kanter, C. Frisk, H. Gustafsson – "Context-Aware Personal Communication for Teleliving", Personal Technologies (vol. 2 issue 4, 1998: p. 255 - 261).
8. T. Kanter, "Adaptive Personal Mobile Communication", Licentiate Thesis, KTH, March 2000.
9. H. Tamura: "Mixed reality: Merging real and virtual world," Journal of the Robotics Society of Japan, vol.16, no.6, pp.759-762, 1998.
10. M. Handley, H. Schulzrinne, E. Schooler, J. Rosenberg - RFC 2543 on SIP: Session Initiation Protocol, IETF/Network Working Group – March 1999.
11. E. Wedlund, H. Schulzrinne, "Mobility Support using SIP", Proceedings of the 2nd ACM International Workshop on Wireless Mobile Multimedia (WoWMoM'99)
12. A. Campbell, J. Gomez, S. Kim, C. Wan, A. Valko, "A Cellular IP Testbed Demonstrator", Proceedings of the Sixth IEEE International Workshop on Mobile Multimedia Communications (MOMUC'99) (p. 145-148)
13. Object Management Group, Inc., CORBA/IIOP 2.2 Specification, 98-02-01
14. Sun Microsystems Inc., "Jini Architectural Overview", Technical White Paper, — January 1999.
15. Microsoft Corporation, "Universal Plug and Play Device Architecture", Version 0.91, March 2000.
16. J. Veizades, E. Guttman, C. Perkins, S. Kaplan, RFC 2165, "Service Location Protocol," IETF Networking Group, June 1997.
17. T. Kanter, "An Application Architecture for Mobile Interactive Spaces", Submitted to the third IEEE Workshop on Mobile Computing Systems and Applications (wmcsa2000), December 2000.
18. T. Kanter, T. Rindborg, D. Sahlin, Do-It-Yourself-4G and Enabled Adaptive Mobile Multimedia Communication, Submitted to the Twentieth Annual Joint Conference of the IEEE Computer and Communications Societies (Infocom 2001), April 2001.

EasyLiving: Technologies for Intelligent Environments

Barry Brumitt, Brian Meyers, John Krumm, Amanda Kern, and Steven Shafer

Microsoft Research, One Microsoft Way, Redmond, WA, 98052, USA
{barry, brianme, jckrumm, amandak, stevensh}@microsoft.com

Abstract. The EasyLiving project is concerned with development of an architecture and technologies for intelligent environments which allow the dynamic aggregation of diverse I/O devices into a single coherent user experience. Components of such a system include middleware (to facilitate distributed computing), world modelling (to provide location-based context), perception (to collect information about world state), and service description (to support decomposition of device control, internal logic, and user interface). This paper describes the current research in each of these areas, highlighting some common requirements for any intelligent environment.

1 Introduction

The EasyLiving project [17] at Microsoft Research is concerned with the development of an architecture and technologies for intelligent environments. An intelligent environment is a space that contains myriad devices that work together to provide users access to information and services. These devices may be stationary, as with acoustic speakers or ceiling lights, or they may be mobile, as with laptop computers or mobile telephones. While the traditional notion of a PC is a part of this vision, a broader goal is to allow typical PC-focused activities to move off of a fixed desktop and into the environment as a whole.

An intelligent environment is likely to contain many different types of devices. First, there are traditional input devices such as mice or keyboards and traditional output devices such as speakers or displays. To support richer interactions with the user, the system must have a deeper understanding of the physical space from both a sensory (input) and control (output) perspective. For example, it might be desirable for the system to provide light for the user as he moves around at night; to enable this, the system uses some form of perception to track the user, and must be able to control all of the different light sources. Input devices can include things such as active badge systems [20][21], cameras [3][17], wall switches, or even sensitive floor tiles [1]. Output devices can include home entertainment systems, wall-mounted displays, speakers, lighting, etc. Besides I/O devices, there will likely be devices dedicated to providing computational capacity to the system.

EasyLiving's goal is the development of an architecture that aggregates diverse devices into a coherent user experience. This requires research effort on a variety of fronts, including middleware, geometric world modelling, perception and service description. To motivate these areas of research, it is helpful to have a single concrete example scenario for reference.

2 Example Scenario

Tom is at home. He enters the living room sits down at a PC in the corner. He surfs through a selection of MP3's, and adds them to a playlist. He gets up and sits down on the couch. His session follows him to the large wall screen across from the couch. This screen is selected because it is available and in Tomís field of view. Tom picks up a remote control sitting on the coffee table and uses the trackball on it to request the room controls. They appear in a window on the wall screen, showing a small map of the room with the controllable lights. He uses this interface to dim the lights. Tom opens up his playlist and presses play. The music comes out of the room's large speaker system.

Sally enters the living room from the sliding doors to the outside and walks over to the PC. She has to manually log in, since she hasn't previously identified herself. She brings up a Word document that is an invitation to a shindig she and Tom are hosting. Wanting Tomís input, she asks him if she can use the large room display. He uses the remote to release control of the wall screen, and she uses the room's controls on her PC to move her session to that display.

Fig. 1. Tom & Sally discuss a document in their Living Room

3 EasyLiving Technology Overview

To support desegregated computing, many of the traditional activities of an operating system must be supported across a distributed heterogeneous set of networked devices. In this paper, this class of software is referred to as Middleware.

As the number of available networked devices for a given user interaction increases, the complexity of identifying and selecting the appropriate devices for that interaction increases greatly. Additionally, to enable user specification of devices desired for a given task, a mapping between network and physical identity is exceptionally helpful. Note that rather than requiring Tom to know the precise name (e.g.'Light 37') of the lights, he selects them based on their location. The EasyLiving Geometric Model, which represents the physical relationships between entities in the world, supports these needs.

The need for perceptual information about world state further differentiates intelligent environments from traditional computing. Sensing devices allow the system to have information about the state of the world, such as locations of people, places, things, and other devices in the space. Having this information makes the interaction with the user seem more natural. When moving beyond the isolated desktop model, failure to give the system information about world state is likely to produce a complex or intrusive user experience. For example, if the system can send you an audible message anywhere, unwanted intrusions could occur if the systems fails to perceive such things as an important meeting or a sleeping child. Perception introduces significant complications for an intelligent environment, including the need to model uncertainty, perform real time data analysis, and merge data from multiple, possibly disagreeing, sensors. Stereo computer vision is currently used in EasyLiving.

Multiple dynamic devices motivate the need for the separation of hardware device control, internal computational logic and user interface presentation. Rather than tightly coupling input/output devices to applications, it should be possible to flexibly change the interaction mechanism without requiring modification of the underlying application. EasyLiving enables this kind of decomposition by providing abstract descriptions of their capabilities.

This paper describes the middleware, geometric modelling, sensing capabilities, and service description that comprise the EasyLiving system. In addition, some integrated applications and the services that run on top of these facilities are described. All of these technologies are discussed in light of the example scenario.

4 Middleware

In the example scenario, two possible models of device integrations can be used: peripherals in communication to a central machine or standalone devices in direct communication. In other words, a device (e.g. a light switch) could be wired to a dedicated computer controller, or it could be capable of communicating on a network. If devices are peripherals, they will not have the extra expense of providing their own user interface, however, if the central machine stops working, the peripherals cannot be operated. So, while the cost of a central server is likely to be lower, the difference is not great enough to offset the increased reliability afforded by standalone devices. Many small devices in collaboration can provide more cost-effective computing power for tasks like computer vision and speech analysis. Therefore, although both models provide complete solutions, the networked standalone device is the current likely future of ubiquitous computing and has been used as the basis for EasyLiving. Many other intelligent environments projects [4][7][15] have chosen a similar approach.

Given a collection of networked devices, the need arises for a mechanism that supports inter-machine communication. By utilizing a middleware package the effort required to build individual components that can communicate in this distributed environment is reduced. Several packages are currently available for this task, such as DCOM [8], Java [10], and CORBA [5], others [4] have recognized that Intelligent Environments place unusual demands on a middleware system. The following is a brief evaluation of the demands for inter-machine communication and dynamic configuration changes, and a description of the InConcert Middleware platform.

4.1 Inter-machine Communication

Current middleware environments built on synchronous semantics, like DCOM [8], Java [10], and CORBA [5], suffer from several failings. First, they force programmers to employ a multi-threaded programming model if they wish to avoid the latencies inherent in synchronous communications. For example, a single-threaded program that needs to interact with multiple peers would have to serialize its interactions with them rather than engaging in multiple interactions simultaneously. A single-threaded program will also be unable to do other useful work while waiting for a reply from a remote server. Worse yet, should the server fail or become unreachable, the program or device will be locked-up until a delivery time-out is reached.

A second failing of synchronous communication techniques is that pipelining of messages between two endpoints is very inefficient, even in a multi-threaded environment. If both the sending and receiving programs are multi-threaded, then by having each program fork multiple threads that communicate in parallel, pipelining can be approximated. However, for messages to have a well-defined arrival order, both the sending and the receiving programs must individually implement message serialization code. Furthermore, it would still not be possible to have only a single reply message for an entire batch of pipelined messages.

4.2 Dynamic Configuration Changes

Another problem stems from the manner in which processes describe the target for a message. DCOM [8], Java [10] require machine names as part of the address for the message. CORBA [5] provides for an object reference, but does not allow that reference to be updated dynamically. This results in delivery problems when the target is moved to another machine. Although not previously viewed as a common occurrence, note that users frequently transition between laptops, desktops, and home machines. This implies that components that are linked to a user may need to transition between a variety of machines in order to retain network proximity. Mobile devices also often change both physical location and network connectivity as they move with the user. These devices are added and removed from the collection of available hardware in a particular environment. Finally, for load balancing, many services are hardware independent and may be stopped on one machine and restarted on a different machine. In each of these situations, the clients involved need to have updated target addresses.

Beyond the problems of delivering messages to processes is the issue of message encoding. All of the discussed systems rely on fully decorated method names for communication endpoint bindings. This forces the clients to be updated in lock step with the server. This means changes must be done *en masse* rather than incrementally and that offline devices, like an out-of-reach laptop, must be updated upon joining the network.

4.3 InConcert

In conjunction with other groups at Microsoft Research, EasyLiving has been involved in the development of InConcert, a middleware solution that address these issues. InConcert provides asynchronous message passing, machine independent addressing and XML-based message protocols.

By using asynchronous message passing, InConcert avoids blocking and inefficiency problems. This asynchronous approach also allows programs to handle offline and queued operation more naturally: clients are written to expect reply messages, if any, to arrive at some arbitrary later time rather than as a return from the original request.

Inter-machine communication is handled by integrating a naming and lookup service into the delivery mechanism. When started, a component requests a name (an'Instance ID') and while running provides the lookup service with a periodic keep-alive message. The name is unique to this instance of the component; it remains constant even if the instance is stopped and later runs on a different machine. Instance IDs are never reused. When sending messages, an instance includes its ID in the'From:' field of the message header. Receiving components can use that ID in the'To:' field of any response messages. When InConcert is asked to deliver the message it will resolve the ID by asking the Instance Lookup Service for the instance's current location.

Once the message is delivered to the correct process, its content is decoded from the XML description. XML provides the ability to version each field and add additional information that in other systems would cause the endpoint binding to fail. As new parameters become supported on servers, clients can either omit or include the information. If the server requires the new field, then the error message returned can describe the exact field required rather than reporting a simple binding failure.

By using the InConcert package, it is possible to develop new components for EasyLiving relatively quickly. This has made it possible to develop components that more accurately reflect the desired decomposition of interactions, as will be introduced in Section . It also allows components to be conveniently moved between hardware in order to tune the system performance. Finally, by designing the applications to handle asynchronous messages, the user experience is still responsive even when the device is isolated from all or part of the network.

5 Geometry

The desktop PC model assumes that the display, mouse, and keyboard are connected to a single machine and are all appropriately physically located. When working in a distributed environment, it is no longer viable to assume this static fixed device configuration, both in terms of device presence and physical configuration. Geometric knowledge, i.e. information about the physical relationships between people, devices, places and things, can be used to assemble sets of UI devices for particular interactions. In the example scenario, geometric world knowledge provides three capabilities to Tom:

Physical Parameters for UI's: When Tom moves to the couch, his display is able to follow appropriately because the geometric model provides information which enables the selection of a visible display.

Simplified Device Control: When Tom starts playing the music, it is not necessary for him to select particular speakers or other AV components for the task. He was able to focus purely on the task, starting music playback, allowing the system to select devices based upon their location.

Shared Metaphor: When Tom turns down the lights, the provided map of the room allows him to quickly identify and control the needed devices based on their physical location. Without this representation, he would need to know particular names of the lights, or have some other way of mapping between physical and network identity. The geometric model provides this shared metaphor between the system and the user, allowing a more natural interaction.

5.1 Prior Work

Previous systems for geometric modelling have typically tightly coupled the sensor modality with internal representation and the application (e.g. using GPS, storing latitude/ longitude, all for providing location-based reminders [13]). A more general system should decouple the sensor from the application, providing an internal representation which can support a wide variety of both. This section examines three classes of sensors and internal representations, highlighting the capabilities and disadvantages of each.

Outdoor Beacons: GPS and Cellular Phone-based location systems have been proposed for many scenarios, including determining driving directions and delivering reminders based on the user's location [13]. Both these sensors provide location data that can be translated into an internal representation of latitude, longitude, and elevation. Due to the physics of receiving beacon signals, these sensors are only useful in outdoor situations that are free of obstructions such as tall buildings. While it is possible to internally store the location of everything in lat./long./elev., the lack of an explicit uncertainty representation forces applications which query this model to assume some nominal uncertainty, typically the nominal GPS accuracy of 15m. This resolution is insufficient for most of the tasks in the example scenario.

Indoor Beacons: In general, these systems consist of RF, IR or ultrasonic transceivers which can determine the presence [20] and perhaps location [21] of small (usually powered) tags which are attached to objects of interest in the world such as people, phones, printers, computers, etc. These systems represent geometry as a location in a single coordinate frame, such as a map of the building. To perform the example scenario, all items of interest (display, remote control, speakers, user, etc.) must be individually tagged. Additionally, if other positioning technologies are available, they are difficult to integrate, as they may not express their measurements in the same coordinate frame or with the same uncertainty. Active badge systems are useful for providing positional information, much as is GPS, but current systems [9] lack a general mechanism for expressing arbitrary geometric information, particularly that which includes uncertainty.

Network Routing: To avoid the perils of perception altogether, one can assume that network or data connectivity is equivalent to co-location [6]. This implies that if two devices can communicate directly (by RF, IR or other 'local' transmission method), they are co-located. However, RF transmission (not to mention physical network protocols) can easily span rooms, floors or even buildings. Without some more precise model of geometry, this type of assumption will result in an excessively large set of potentially available devices, many of which may not actually be available or usable for any particular task due to the vagaries of the transmission method. Some systems base their notion of location on semantic tags applied to network or electricity connections, e.g. "Ethernet tap 324 is in Tom's living room". This is problematic both because it requires ongoing administration and because it can break the shared metaphor between system and user. For example, if Tom plugs a light into an outlet in the den, but places the light in the living room, this new light would not appear on his room controls due to the limited geometric representation.

5.2   EasyLiving Geometric Model

The EasyLiving Geometric Model (EZLGM) provides a general geometric service for ubiquitous computing, focusing on in-home or in-office tasks in which there are myriad I/O, perception, and computing devices supporting multiple users. The EZLGM is designed to work with multiple perception technologies and abstract the application (including its user interface) away from any particular sensing modality. It is aimed at geometry 'in the small', that is, for applications which may require sub-meter localization of entities in the environment. Integrating this model with localization services for larger scales remains an open issue.

The base item in the EZLGM is an entity, which represents the existence of an object in the physical world. Measurements are used to define geometric relationships between entities. In particular, a measurement describes the position and orientation of one entity's coordinate frame, expressed in another entityís coordinate frame. Since objects in the physical world (as well as virtual objects like service regions) have some physical expanse, this can also be expressed as an extent in the geometric model using a polygon described in the coordinate frame of the entity. Additionally, measurements can have an uncertainty associated with them, expressed as a covariance matrix on parameters of the transformation [16].

Once a set of measurements has been provided to the geometric model, the model can be queried for the relationships between entitiesí frames. The measurements describe an undirected graph, where each vertex is the coordinate frame of an entity, and each edge is a measurement, as described above. If at least one path exists between two frames, then the graph can be processed to produce a single geometric relationship between the frames. Since a particular queried relationship may not have been previously directly measured, the response typically involves the combination of multiple measurements; uncertainty information is used to properly merge multiple redundant measurements as needed. Region-intersection queries are also supported, allowing, for example, selection of all devices within a particular radius of a user.

In the example scenario, the person tracking software continuously updates the measurement which describes the geometric relationship between Tom/Sally and the coordinate frame of the sensor which is observing them. Whatever process is responsible for keeping Tom's session available on nearby devices can query EZLGM for all devices that have service areas that intersect with his location. The process first looks at types and availability to determine the set of devices which could provide the display, text input, pointing, etc. It then further prunes the list by considering the physical constraints (e.g. visibility) and electronic constraints (e.g. availability), in order to reach a set of usable, available, and physically-appropriate devices. Visibility can be checked by examining all entities along the line of sight between the user and the device and ensuring none have an extent present which represents something that physically blocks Tom's view. Then, once Tom's location is stable with respect to a set of devices, the session can be directed to automatically move.

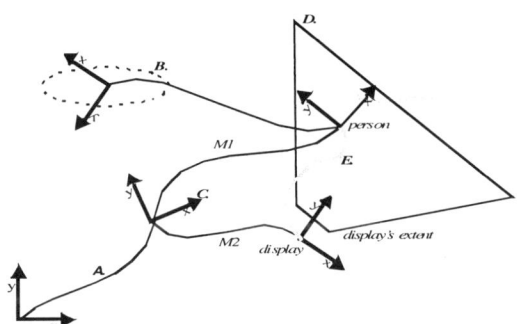

A. Measurements are comprised of three components, x,y,theta, plus,
B. An uncertainty estimate, represented here as an equiprobability contour ellipse.
C. Each entity has a coordinate frame, in which measurements to other entities and extents are expressed.
D. A polygonal extent can be used to describe physical attributes (like size) or virtual attributes (like a service area).
E. Queries, like "What is geometric relationship between the display and the person?", are resolved by combining measurements along a path, in this case, M1 and M2.

Fig. 2. The EasyLiving Geometric Model

5.3 Summary

EZLGM provides a mechanism for both determining the devices that can be used for a user interaction and aiding in the selection of appropriate devices. Note that no part of this example required any reference to the perception method which provided information about position: it could have been performed via some combination of cameras, badges, GPS, etc. with an appropriate uncertainty representation. Semantic location information can be powerful for many tasks, but it remains an open problem to gather and represent both semantic position tags and detailed geometric location in a single system.

6 Perception

Much of the information provided to the Geometric Model (and other attributed based directories) is data gained from the world through sensors. While much of this information could be entered into databases by hand, the more interesting case is when data is dynamically added and changed while the system is running. This data is gained from physical sensing devices that are attached to computers running perception components. These components support direct queries about information and keep data stores like the EZLGM updated as changes are detected.

6.1 Vision

Stereo computer vision is used as a way of tracking the location and identity in the example scenario. Vision is a natural sensing modality for this situation, because:

- Vision does not require that the room's occupants carry or wear special devices.
- Vision can resolve the location of people in the room well enough to infer a person's intent based on his or her position. For instance, it can tell the difference between Sally's position at the PC and Tom's position on a nearby couch. Vision can even tell when either person stands or sits.
- Vision can maintain the identity of people in the room, allowing the room's devices to react to a specific person's personal preferences.
- Vision can be used to find objects in the room. For instance, cameras are used to locate the wireless keyboard on the coffee table.
- Vision can be used to make a geometric model of the room. Images from the people-tracking cameras are used to make a floor plan of the room.

While vision has unique advantages over other sensors for tracking people, it also presents unique challenges. A person's appearance in an image varies significantly due to posture, facing direction, distance from the camera, and occlusions. It can be particularly difficult to keep track of multiple people in a room as they move around and occlude each other. Although a variety of algorithms can overcome these difficulties, the final solution must also work fast enough to make the system responsive to the room's occupants. The current vision system, using two sets of stereo cameras mounted high on the room's walls, successfully tracks the location and identity of people in the room with an update rate of about 3.5 Hz.

7 Person Tracking

There has been much research in computer vision for tracking people. The EasyLiving person tracking software is described in greater detail in [11], which also contains numerous references to similar work.

The components of the tracking system are laid out in Figure 3. This tracker uses two color Triclops stereo cameras [18], each connected to its own PC. Two cameras are used so each part of the room is seen by at least one camera. The combination of color and depth from these cameras makes it easier to track people than if color or depth were used alone. These two PCs run the Stereo Module program, which processes the registered color and depth images to produce reports about the likely locations of people in the room. The Stereo Module first performs background subtraction to locate 3D blobs in each camera's field of view. The background is modelled with a combination of depth and color pixels in an effort to avoid the potential confusion caused by the moving video of the room's displays and by people sinking into the soft cushions of the couch. The 3D blobs are normally broken up over the regions of peoples' bodies. The Stereo Module merges the blobs by comparing different, hypothesized clusters of blobs to a simple model of a generic person shape. The Stereo Module also maintains color histogram models of each person in the room to help distinguish them from each other. The 2D ground plane location of the blobs is reported from each of the two Stereo Modules to a single instance of the 'Person Tracker' which is used to integrate data from all the cameras.

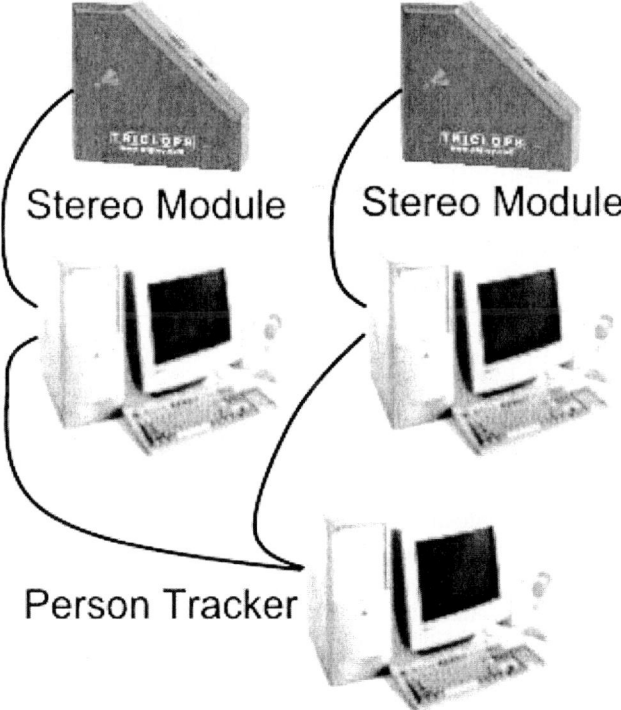

Fig. 3. Tracking SW Components

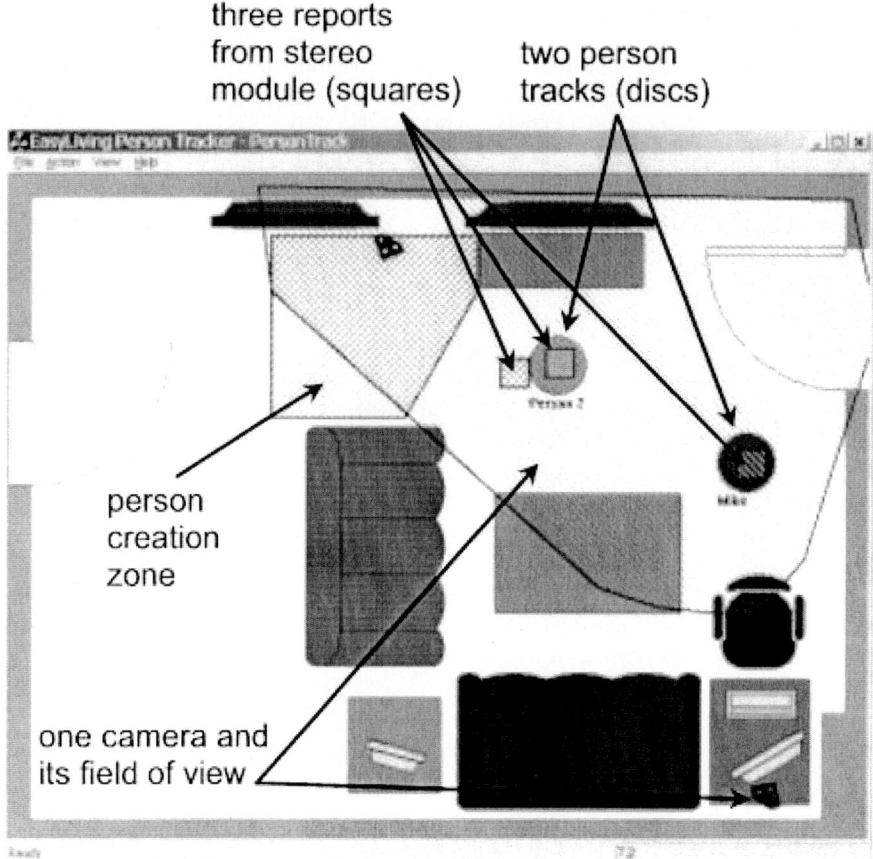

Fig. 4. Person Tracking Display

The Person Tracker (Figure 4) uses knowledge of the two cameras' relative locations, fields of view, and heuristics on the movements of people to produce a final report on the locations and identities of people in the room. The Person Tracker is able to smooth over missing or mistaken reports from the two Stereo Modules by keeping track of the recent locations of each person in the room. If the Person Tracker becomes confused about the identity of a person, it appeals to the color histogram models maintained by the Stereo Modules. The Person Tracker also manages a special area in the room called the "person creation zone". It is in this zone, normally established at the entrance to the room, that new instances of people are created and deleted as they enter and leave. The Person Tracker can also calibrate the locations of the cameras with respect to each other by watching a single person walk around in the room.

7.1 RADAR

Location information can also be gained from systems that track beacons instead of people. RADAR [2] is an in-building location-aware system being investigated at Microsoft Research. RADAR allows radio-frequency (RF) wireless-LAN-enabled mobile devices to compute their location based on the signal strength of known infrastructure access points. Knowing the location of the devices allows components that are running on that device to provide location aware interfaces. It also provides a means for inferring the user's location.

7.2 Identity (Fingerprint Reader)

One novel sensor that provides input to the system is a fingerprint reader manufactured by Digital Persona. This device is connected via USB to a machine with a database of fingerprints. When the user places a finger on the device, it automatically activates and sends messages that assert the identity of the person. This information can be used in combination with other components to assign a network identity to data that is currently being sensed. Knowing the measurement between the fingerprint sensor and the camera and the geometric extent in which a person can use the reader, allows the system to map the network identity to the reports from the vision system. This mapping can also be accomplished when the user logs in using a keyboard with a known location.

7.3 Device Tracking

The locations of moveable devices can be important for the behavior of the intelligent environment. For example, if a wireless keyboard is near a certain person, it can be assumed that keystrokes coming from that keyboard are being produced by that person. The keystrokes can then be properly routed to that person's active application. As shown in Figure 5, a camera mounted on the ceiling is used to locate the wireless keyboard on the coffee table in the room. The keyboard is detected in the image using a combination of color and shape cues.

7.4 Integrated Perception

In the scenario above, these perceptual systems interact. When Tom and Sally enter the living room, they each pass through the person creation zone, at which point one of the Stereo Modules reports person-shaped blobs to the Person Tracker. The Person Tracker notes that the blob reports are coming from the person creation zone, and thus makes a new instance of a person to be tracked. The Person tracker starts keeping a history of the person's location, and reports the locations to the geometric model. The Stereo Module stores a color histogram to help disambiguate Tom and Sally if the Person Tracker becomes confused about who is who.

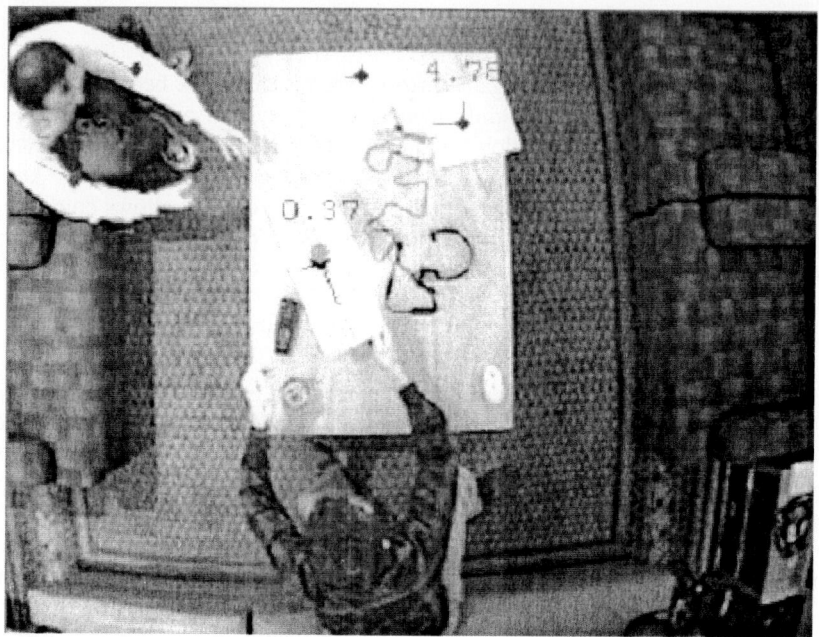

Fig. 5. Keyboard Tracking

Tom and Sally are regarded as unknown people until they actively identify themselves somehow. Tom is assumed to have previously identified himself somewhere else in the house, and Sally logs on to a PC. Once authenticated, the system attaches each person's identity to its internal representation of that person.

This vision system works well for live demonstrations, with about 20 minutes of continuous tracking. During the demonstration, people enter and leave the living room, with their tracks being created and deleted appropriately. Tracking works well with up to three people in the room, depending on how they behave. With more than three people moving around, the frequent occlusions cause enough poor clusterings in the Stereo Module that the Person Tracker cannot maintain coherent tracks. Demonstrators are not required to wear special clothes, although similarly colored outfits can cause tracks to be misassigned due to indistinguishable histograms. The demonstrators can walk around, stand still, sit, and brush against each other without the system losing track of them. There are also large areas of moving video in the cameras' fields of view that the tracking system tolerates easily.

8 Service Abstraction

Like many intelligent environment systems [3][14], EasyLiving incorporates a variety of sensing techniques, software components for reasoning, and controllable devices, such as lights, computer equipment, and audio/visual hardware. Each of these pieces is encapsulated in a unique service, which encourages the separation of hardware device control, internal logic, and user interface presentation. Furthermore, abstract service descriptions allow each service to expose a set of attributes or commands so that other services may interact with it automatically.

For example, if current resources support pointing via trackball, mouse or visual gesture and, for each of these methods, there is a service that generates a pointing output, a web browser can be driven by any of those services, dependent upon user preference, context, or other selection mechanism. In the example scenario, when Sally uses the room controls to move her display, the service descriptions for the available devices are used to dandiacal provide her with possible destinations.

8.1 Prior Work

The concept of abstracting and describing services arises naturally when developing a system that involves automatic interaction between program components or exposure of device attributes. Several commercial systems under development, such as Universal Plug and Play [19], provide for device descriptions. However, they fail to differentiate between the interface presentation and service description. Mozer [3] has proposed separating device control from decision logic but did not allow for configuration changes. JosÈ [12] encoded context information into the XML service descriptions, but did not separate the service semantics from the service description. Other intelligent environment systems [14] have not dealt with dynamic location-dependent services and automatically-generated UI.

8.2 Service Descriptions

Since an intelligent environment must support a changing collection of devices (and therefore services) it is necessary to handle service discovery. First, the system must discover the existence of newly available services. This is handled using InConcert's lookup capabilities. Next, it must determine the newly found service's capabilities.

Descriptions of services in the EasyLiving system are accomplished using a simple, open XML schema. In addition to ease of use, XML was chosen for two reasons. First, Extended Stylesheet Language (XSL) provides the ability to translate XML documents into multiple layouts. Second, it is straightforward to transform an XML-encoded description of a command into the XML-encoded command to be sent to the service.

The service description schema is designed to support queries about available commands and their legal values. Additionally, the commands are associated with human-readable tags. While not a complete solution, this is a first step toward the automatic generation of user interfaces for different modalities.

9 Demo Applications

The EasyLiving demo system utilizes the facilities described above to implement several applications within a one room intelligent space. This section describes some of these applications.

9.1 Room Controller

The Room Controller provides the user with direct access to the available services. The availability of a service is determined by intersecting the location of the user's current I/O hardware with the service's extent. The user interface is generated by examining each service description and displaying the appropriate XML documents. If there is no appropriate document, the Room Controller generates a document by merging the published commands with a standard XSL stylesheet. In the example scenario, Tom uses a version of the Room Controller to adjust the lights and to start the music playback and Sally uses a Room Controller to move her session to the wall display.

9.2 Remote Sessions

EasyLiving supports movable desktop sessions, similar to 'Bat Teleporting' [9]. This facility can be controlled either automatically or by direct user action. Both methods utilize a service that handles the mechanics of session movement. The service that provides automatic behavior redirects the session based on the geometric relationship between the user and the available screens.

9.3 Mouse Anywhere

The lab is equipped with an RF mouse. There is no tag-based or vision tracking of this mouse. However, when the room contains a single person, the Mouse Anywhere service redirects the mouse commands based on the display service region the user currently occupies as determined by EZLGM. So, when the user brings the RF mouse near any display, the mouse controls the cursor on that display. Querying for the relative position of a person and a particular device can also be used to play an electronic version of the children's game 'Warmer, Colder'. Audio cues are provided to the user based on his movement towards or away from a random spot in the room.

9.4 Media Control

When a user is authenticated to the system, custom preferences are loaded that direct automatic behaviors. In the example scenario, one of Tom's preferences was a standing MP3 playlist. Similarly, users can have behaviors that direct various media types, for example, a CD, MP3, DVD or Videotape, that plays based on their location context. Defining automatic behaviors and preferences for an intelligent environment in a consistent user-friendly manner remains an open challenge.

10 Future Work

The EasyLiving project is building an architecture for intelligent environment. The design and implementation of this architecture is an ongoing effort. While some progress has been made, there are still a number of major issues to address.

Events: As the number of connections between services increases, polling ceases to be a viable mechanism for detecting changing state. Currently, it is not possible to register event requests like 'Please inform me when entity 12 intersects the extent of entity 13' or 'Please inform me when CD player is finished playing.' Replacing polling with an asynchronous event system is a high priority for EasyLiving.

Lookup Services: Building robust lookup services that support discovery and scaling is still a major focus. While finding a service from a list of 20 is easy, building a system that can handle having thousands of services continuously updating their availability is a prerequisite to wide spread deployment of intelligent environments.

Extensibility: Moving from a single room to multiple rooms and hallways presents several new challenges. One geometric model may no longer suffice. Vision and other perception systems will need to cooperate and hand-off tracks of users between different disjoint spaces. Currently, it is unclear how services span boundaries between spaces or how these extents might be affected by network partitioning.

User Interface: As mentioned earlier, presenting the available services to the user in an understandable fashion and letting the user create and edit automatic behaviors are both on going work items.

The EasyLiving system can handle a single room and 10's of devices with dynamic changes to their configuration. One to three people can simultaneously use the facility. The system has evolved to the point that user interface issues can now be more rigorously examined. As EasyLiving evolves, it is expected that input and output devices will no longer be tied to a single machine or application but rather be able to flexibly support user interaction across a wide variety of tasks and modalities. Future work will build on this architecture, further exploring the migration of computing from the desktop and into everyday living.

11 Acknowledgements

Many thanks to Victor Bahl, Chad Ellman, Mary Czerwinski, Michael Hale, Steve Harris, Nebojsa Jojic, and Daniel Robbins for their invaluable contributions to the EasyLiving project.

References

1. M. D. Addlesee, et al,'ORL Active Floor', IEEE Personal Communications, Vol.4, No.5, October 1997, pp. 35-41.
2. P. Bahl and V. N. Padmanabhan,'RADAR: An In-Building RF based User Location and Tracking System', Proceedings of IEEE INFOCOM 2000, Israel, March 2000.
3. Michael Coen,'Design Principals for Intelligent Environments', Intelligent Environments, Papers from the AAAI Spring Symposium, March 23-25, 1998, Technical Report SS-98-02, AAAI Press.
4. M. Coen, et al,'Meeting the Computation Needs of Intelligent Environments: The Metaglue Environment', Managing Interactions in Smart Environments, Springer-Verlag, 1999, pp. 201-213.
5. CORBA,'Remote Invocation', http://sisyphus.omg.org/gettingstarted/corbafaq.htm#RemoteInvoke .
6. P. Couderc, A.-M. Kermarrec,'Enabling Context-Awareness from Network-Level Location Tracking', Handheld and Ubiquitous Computing, First International Symposium, Springer-Verlag, 1999, pp. 67-73.
7. A. Dey, et al,'A Context-based Infrastructure for Smart Environments', Managing Interactions in Smart Environments, Springer-Verlag, 1999, pp. 114-130.
8. G, Eddon, et al, Inside Distributed COM, Microsoft Press, 1998.
9. A. Harter, et al,'The Anatomy of a Context-Aware Application', Proceedings of the MOBICOMí99, August 1999.
10. Java, http://www.java.sun.com/ .
11. J. Krumm, et al'Multi-Camera Multi-Person Tracking for EasyLiving', Third IEEE International Workshop on Visual Surveillance, July 1, 2000, Dublin, Ireland.
12. R. JosÈ and N. Davies,'Scalable and Flexible Location-Based Services for Ubiquitous Information Access', Handheld and Ubiquitous Computing, First International Symposium, Springer-Verlag, 1999, pp. 52-66.
13. N. Marmasse, C. Schmandt,'comMotion: a context-aware communication system', http:// www.media.mit.edu/~nmarmas/comMotion.html .
14. M. Mozer,'The Neural Network House: An Environment that Adapts to its Inhabitants', Intelligent Environments, Papers from the AAAI Spring Symposium, March 23-25, 1998, Technical Report SS-98-02, AAAI Press.
15. N. Minar, et al,'Hive: Distributed Agents for Networking Things', Joint Proceedings of ASA/MA, 1999.

16. R. Smith, P. Cheeseman,'On the Representation and Estimation of Spatial Uncertainty', International Journal of Robotics Research, Vol. 5, No. 4, Winter 1986, pp. 56-67.
17. S. Shafer, et al,'The New EasyLiving Project at Microsoft Research', Proceedings of the 1998 DARPA / NIST Smart Spaces Workshop, July 1998, pp.127-130.
18. Triclops Stereo Cameras, Pt. Grey Research, http://www.ptgrey.com/ .
19. Universal Plug and Play, http://www.upnp.org/resources.htm .
20. R. Want., A. Hopper,'Active Badges and Personal Interactive Computing Objects', IEEE Transactions on Consumer Electronics. Vol 38. No.1, Feb. 1992, pp.10-20.
21. A. Ward, et al,'A New Location Technique for the Active Office', IEEE Personal Communications, Vol. 4, No. 5, Oct. 1997, pp. 42-47.

Beyond the Control Room: Mobile Devices for Spatially Distributed Interaction on Industrial Process Plants

Jörn Nilsson, Tomas Sokoler, Thomas Binder, and Nina Wetcke

Space & Virtuality Studio, Interactive Institute
Beijerskajen 8, 205 06 Malmoe, Sweden
{Tomas.Sokoler, Thomas.Binder, Jorn.Nilsson, Nina.Wetcke}interactiveinstitute.se

Abstract. The industrial control room has been a strong shaping image for design of information technology at process plants and even for information and control systems in other areas. Based on recent studies of the work of process operators and on ethnographically inspired fieldwork this paper question the relevance of control room type interfaces. The paper suggests new types of mobile interfaces, which enables the operators to configure and apply individual temporary views of the plant, originating in the problem focus of the operator. To explore the relevance of such new interfaces a number of design concepts are suggested. The design of a particular device: The Pucketizer (Personal Bucket Organizer) has been developed in close collaboration with process operators at a wastewater treatment plant. The paper concludes that mobile interfaces for spatially distributed interaction such as the Pucketizer seem to have generic qualities reaching beyond the immediate context at process plants.

1 Introduction

In the growing literature on handheld and ubiquitous computing, most application examples originates in use context with little and rather uniform technology such as office environments [6]. There is also a dominance of examples which have a clear imprint of the culture and artefactual environment of the research community. In a simple and not exhaustive search on the web with a combined search on 'coffee' and 'ubiquitous computing' quite a number of hits turn up. This is not in itself a problem, but perhaps an indication that we might find new inspiration from entering contexts of use which are more foreign to our own community. When we started the project on which this paper is based we were deliberately searching for contexts outside the office and also contexts where technologically mediated interactions have a long and varied history. We decided on process plants and control rooms, because these settings are very obviously constructed of a large palette of technological components. We also saw it as an interesting domain because it has early been lending guiding images to other areas where information technology is applied. We entered the world of process plants with a user-centred and action oriented approach to design that form part of the heritage for most of us [5]. We wanted to see to what extent such an approach could guide us into an unknown setting, and possibly also give us a grounding of our design work in the existing practice among process operators. In the project reported here we worked closely with a group of process operators and technicians at a waste water plant in Malmö.

The use of information technology on waste water plants, and in process control in general, has for many years been synonymous with the idea of having a centralised control room as the main gateway to information about, and control of, the plant. In the centralised control room architecture a server collects data from sensors distributed on the plant and presents the plant operators with mainly visual representations of the data. The operator's main role is to monitor the plant's state via these representations and the alarms initiated by the system. Operator intervention in most cases involves physical inspection of the components on the plant. This implies a shift in the interaction domain from interaction with digital representations of the plant to interaction with the physical components. A strictly centralised control room model inherently precludes a smooth transition between these two domains of interaction. Further on, observing waste water plant operators go through their daily routines it becomes clear that physical inspection goes beyond a simple 'get an alarm, find the error and fix it' scheme. While walking around on the plant the operator uses all his senses, his expertise, and his accumulated knowledge of the plant to get a feel for the plant's current state. Interaction with the plant during inspection is not only a matter of highly focused data collection and hands on adjustment of physical components (vents, pumps etc.), but involves a more subtle mode of interaction simply taking in impressions from the plant. Peripheral awareness expressed as the ability to make use of informational resources in the environment on and near to subconscious level of attention seems to be an invaluable part of the daily inspection. We have been looking for systems that supports the process of physical inspection and attempts to make the transition between physical interaction with the plant and interaction with digital representations of the plant smooth.

2 The World of Process Plants

In early studies, automation of process control was expected to reduce the role of the operator to a 'machine-minder' with no need for manual skills that only intervened when process information deviated from specified norms [1], [4]. Zuboff [16] have later argued that computerised process control systems force operators to leave their manual skills behind to develop the more intellectual skill of operating a process through symbolic representations on a computer display. However, in more recent studies it has been argued that knowledge of manual operation and machinery and knowledge of computerised process control are two inseparable components of operator skill. The process operator rely very much on the ability to understand the process through various representations, where process information on computer displays is just one form of representation. In particular operators need the ability to bridge the gap from symbolic representations on computer screens to a detailed understanding of the machinery on a physical level coupled with tacit knowledge of process dynamics [9]. With this in mind we designed the Pucketizer system with active participation from operators at a local waste water plant. We started out following three operators going through their daily routines and video taped two full days of work at the plant. These rounds of observation and informal interviews were followed by two workshops held at the plant. The workshops included brainstorming, enactment of scenarios, and discussions centred around paper mock-ups and foam models prepared by the research group illustrating several design ideas [3]. Through these workshops researchers and operators developed a common understanding of the problem area and the design process converged towards a design concept for, what later on was to be named, the Pucketizer.

2.1 The Importance of Physical Inspection

A central observation that emerged from our collaboration with the process operators was that physical inspection of the plant plays a crucial role. The round is not only establishing the individual 'mapping' between system representations and actual state of plant components. It is also helping the operators to maintain a shared understanding of the process. Every operator is making one or more non-alarm driven rounds of inspection everyday, following a more or less fixed route through the area of which he has responsibility. During this round he uses all his senses, and is equally attentive to the operation of components as to the quality of the processed sludge. During the round the process operators are also getting an overall picture of what is going on at the plant. They occasionally 'bump in' to one another and exchange information but they learn as much from interpreting traces of their colleagues' activities (could be tools left for later use or dismounted components).

Even though the operators typically follow a fixed path the 'points of interest' on the plant seem to be constantly shifting. A certain part of the plant may be out of operation, and this will cause the operator to pay particular attention to other parts that may be running 'heavy duty'. It could be that a component during the round has appeared to be 'ready for a breakdown', so the operator has to have an eye on that particular section of the plant. And it could also be that the sludge coming in has certain properties that put stress on certain parts of the plant.

Fig. 1. Fig. 1. The Operator takes several daily rounds. A process operator goes through 'his area' on the computer. He has his own logs to keep track of parameters that he knows are critical. Later he will walk through the plant to listen to and sense such things as pump vibrations, valve operation and sludge quality. If time permits, he does adjustments and optimizations.

2.2 Alarms Are Not Always Important

In the plant we worked with alarm messages are immediately sent to the operator responsible for the area. He receives the alarm on his pager if he is not at a monitoring station, and he has to sign off the alarm personally on the monitoring station. Despite this we found that alarm handling only plays a minor role in keeping the plant running. Very often sections of the plant are under repair or maintenance and this frequently causes alarms that do not call for action (see figure 2). In other situations the actions of the operators in themselves causes alarms e.g. because a level meter gives a false reading. On the other hand it is often so that operators try to foresee situations that may cause problems before an alarm or even a warning has been sent out. E.g. the cluttering of a pipe or a valve is best dealt with if the problem is detected by the operator before it is detected by the monitoring system. For the operators the focus on alarm handling in the conventional design of control and monitoring systems appear to distract attention from a more deliberate focus on upcoming problems.

Fig. 2. Alarms can often be ignored. Most SCADA systems are designed for operators to act on alarms only. Reality is however often quite different. A lot of alarms are caused by well-known and unproblematic events. When e.g. a process operator flushes a tank to avoid sediments he triggers the level meter and gets an alarm. Even though he is on the spot, he can only see the alarm at his pager. To cancel the alarm he has to go to one of the SCADA workstations and log in.

2.3 An Experimental Approach to Problem Solving

When process operators identify a potential problem in a particular area, they often engage in a series of experiments in order to find out what relevant measures have to be taken (see figure 3). If e.g. a pump vibrates excessively, an operator might choose to examine if a parallel pump will be able to handle the flow on its own. Such experimentation will often involve setting up a problem specific configuration of monitoring devices at different places in the plant. Monitoring is here rarely restricted to observing control room information. Typically the operator has to set up monitoring devices on different components as well as monitoring the resemblance of data obtained from different places in the chain from sensors to computer monitoring system. Frequently the sensuous perception of the operator of e.g. sound or smell on particular spots form an integral part of the diagnostic activity. Shifting between different domains of interaction introduces a discontinuity in the operators' workflow, because co-ordination of observations in the plant and information presented by the centralised control room system is poorly supported.

Fig. 3. Experimentation is part of every day work for the process operator. Operators never know quite how much can be demanded from the components and to avoid larger problems they do experiments. One process operator wants a pump shaft sealing to be replaced, but he is not sure if the remaining pump can handle the sludge flow on its own. As many other times during the day he happens to meet two colleagues, and asks for advice. He and another process operator decide to check how much current the pump is using when running alone. The test works out fine, because sludge is not that heavy today, so they decide to exchange the sealing.

2.4 Confronting the Control Room 'Panopticon'

What emerged in our collaboration with the process operators was the increasingly clear picture of a guiding image in SCADA systems design that begs to be challenged. Rather than designing control room installations with a claim for the perfect centralised information support of a 'panopticon', we wanted to dissolve the static user interface with its fixed views of the process. The aims were to make it possible for the operator to create and modify his own points of interaction on the locations and at the times of his own choosing. This would make it possible to get away from a situation, where the operator has to leave his current work context in order to obtain information or gain control. Further more we wanted to support a more continuous transition between interaction with focal points selected during physical inspection and interaction with the corresponding representations in the digital domain.

3 Instrumenting People and Places

Framing the design problem as one of transferring control from the centralised controlroom out into the production environment raises questions about the level of monitoring and control needed in the plant and how it should be distributed between the operator and the local machinery. At the water treatment plant steps had already been taken in the direction of decentralisation before our study. Access points had been positioned at a few strategic places in the plant with PC:s running the SCADA system. Even if this reduced the distance for the operators to the nearest point providing access to the system while being out in the plant, it still required the operator to move from his current work context to access information and control facilities. Also, the interface to the system in the centralised computers was simply duplicated at all access points, providing the same fixed view of the process as before. In some contexts this strategy can improve support for control work. For example, at a printing press in another of our case studies control instrumentation was duplicated at different stages of the printing process along the layout of the machine set-up, providing control access close to physical inspection points.

However, our goal to dissolve the static user interface, and provide both control possibilities across local work contexts and smoother transition between physical focal points and digital representations, called for more flexible solutions. A move towards small portable units that could be temporarily connected to machine components during problem solving seemed to be a better way of increasing flexibility. Also, in our work observations a problem solving activity typically revolves around a few focal points, and only a small subset of process information and control facilities is used. Providing possibilities for temporary instrumentation of machinery related to a problem context therefore evolved as one design goal in increasing control flexibility.

In addition to small portable units for temporarily instrumenting machinery, facilities for monitoring these temporary focal sets 'on the move' are needed. *Firstly*, one important aspect of the process control work in this case is the proactive strategy that operators exhibit. Since problems are sometimes addressed long before they generate alarms in the SCADA systems, the set of focal points in a potential problem context is typically maintained over a period of time. The operator therefore needs to keep track of one or more temporary focal sets as he moves through the plant during a working day. *Secondly*, the spatial extension of a temporary focal set in the work environment creates a need for remote monitoring of instrumentation. The issue of transferring control from centralised to distributed access is not simply a dichotomy between local and central. It is not a matter of *either* central control *or* local control facilities in the vicinity of physical inspection points at a particular place in the plant. In our perspective, a temporary focal set evolves out of the problem situation at hand, and reflects the particular perspective on the problem constructed by operators. It contains a number of focal points constituting a view of the production system where certain parts of machinery are temporarily connected through a set of casual relationships constructed in a problem framing activity by the operators. These focal points may be geographically dispersed throughout a large part of the plant. Also, the temporary perspective that the focal set represent may change as the operators collect more information about the problem, or set up experiments to test problem solving strategies, leading to focal points being removed or added to the set.

Finally, our observations show that many problems require operators to co-operate in problem solving, since typically a malfunction in one part of the plant results in other problems along the production chain. Communicating about problems and co-ordinating work activities is an important part of process control work. In summary, our analysis of process control work has pointed out four required functions in process control as input to the design process:

- Facilities for setting up temporary focal points and instrumentation of machinery in the plant based on a problem at hand;
- Facilities for a dynamic representation of temporary focal sets, where focal points can be added or removed as needed;

- Facilities for monitoring temporal focal sets while being 'on the move'; and
- Facilities for communicating information about problem situations to other operators in the plant.

With these requirements as a starting point we developed four design concepts that addressed different aspects of the design problem.

3.1 Smart Messages

The first concept (figure 4) combines three ideas: an intelligent notepad providing a personal log of focal points in the daily inspection round; a view organiser for individual configuration of focal points in the SCADA system, where the graphical representation changes according to activities in the daily inspection round; and possibilities for leaving 'post-it notes' at different points in the plant available for other operators.

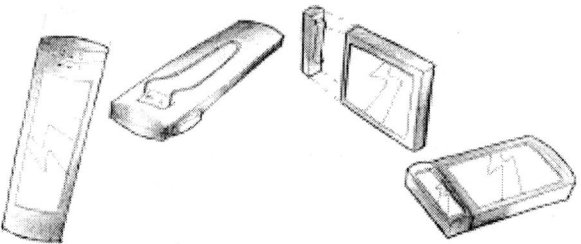

Fig. 4. Smart Messages (*left*) and Double-check (*right*).

3.2 Double-Check

A flexible display locally configured for monitoring and controlling a single component (figure 4). By separating the display from the control unit, a symbolic representation can be carried as a reminder of the problem.

3.3 Multi-check

As 'Double check' but a set of flexible displays that are configured for a temporary focal set.

3.4 Personal Organizer

A system with a personal assistant and a number of displays configured using the assistant for a temporary focal set. A symbolic graphical representation of each set function as a reminder of ongoing activities in the plant.

4 The Pucketizer Concept

The four different design concepts were evaluated together with process operators at the water treatment plant. As all of the concepts had one way or another their roots in the ethnographic field work they were not foreign to the operators. Never the less turning our understanding of work into design suggestions highlighted aspects of practice which we had not been aware of. The Smart Messages concept was our 'mirroring' of the careful observation we had seen the operators do as they toured the plant. When confronted with this design concept the operators were however reluctant to accept the idea of 'taking notes' on what they saw, as they had also been sceptical to the introduction of mobile phones, which seemed to threaten their established practice of associating certain action and certain consideration to certain places. The post-it notes on the other hand were well received as an enhancement of the possibilities of leaving clues for action. We got positive feedback on the idea of having a large number of displays at the operators disposal as in the double-check and multi-check concepts. The double-check idea of leaving one display at a particular component did not however grasp the composite nature of creating a temporary view at the process. As one of the operators said this idea would probably result in a lot of forgotten displays around in the plant. Our interpretation was that the problem with the double check concept was that it maintained a too simple notion of locality. The concept presupposes somehow a one-component focus and it reproduced a simple dual notion of globality (where the operator is) and locality (where the component is), which did not seem to match the view of the operators, The Personal Organiser concept captured the multiple views of the plant which even the individual operator is engaging in simultaneously, but it was conceived by the operators as going too far in the direction of equipping the operators with a whole array of tools they had to carry along.

Based on the reactions we got, we decided to combine elements of the four concepts into what we came to call the Pucketizer system. The main shift in orientation that guided us was a shift from focusing on locality to a slightly different focus on presence. We maintained the idea of creating interfaces that enable the operators to organise their environment according to their temporary focal set We also kept the idea of annotating the plant. But instead of bringing monitoring and control information to a particular spot, whatever this may be by the components or at the place where the operator is located, we decided to create a system where the operators can establish and keep links to a variety of spots and configure in principal any spot as an outpost for that particular view of the process.

We increasingly came to see the plant as one large mixed-media interface in which the operators should be able not only to annotate but also to bookmark and create links between objects, and the devices we could see a need for should basically allow for establishing places and points of view through extensive configurability. The idea of the Pucketizer letting the operator create a number of collections of associated objects, seemed in this light promising.

4.1 The Bucket Metaphor

In the Pucketizer design, the support for creating, maintaining and monitoring temporary focal sets, has been created around a Bucket metaphor for interaction with the plant. The underlying idea being that the operator while walking around on the plant can grab components of interest and group these components into one or more Buckets, where each bucket corresponds to a temporary focal set. Obviously it is not the actual physical components that are grabbed and kept in the Buckets but a representation establishing a link to the components. The grouping of components within a Bucket is left entirely open to the operator thereby enabling him to create his own problem specific view of a possible interdependency between components. The Buckets are carried along and represents the operators' personal collection of work activity focal points. The Buckets contains a minimal visual representation (icons) of the components collected and whenever the operator needs to take a closer look at a specific component the content of a Bucket can be 'poured' onto one of many displays distributed throughout the plant.

The Pucketizer system consists of:

Fig. 5. The Pucketizer System

A handheld unit containing the Buckets. The Pucketizer serves as the operators interface to the plant and is used by the operator for the grab and pour operation on components. More operations available to the operator are discussed later;
- The physical components already present on the plant including pumps, motors, vents, and numerous sensors; and
- A number of displays in different shapes and sizes distributed throughout the plant. Some of these displays are mobile and constantly travels the plant following the focal points of work activities. The displays serve several purposes as discussed later.

Fig. 6. Grabbing a component to a Bucket.

Grabbing components into a Bucket and pouring components onto a display are seen as the two basic functions provided by the Pucketizer. Any interaction with components via the Pucketizer starts with the grabbing of a component. Figure 6 shows Per, an operator at the waste water plant, using an early foam model of the Pucketizer to illustrate how he would grab a component. It is important to note that the selection of the component to grab is done simply by pointing at the physical component without entering any symbolic reference to the components ID. This frees the operator from the cumbersome task of mapping physical components to their symbolic names before grabbing them. Standing in front of a component the operator already knows that this is the component he wants and going through any further component identification seems like a waste of effort. The notion of a collapsed name space [2] facilitating information management through links attached to physical objects has an immediate use in the Pucketizer system. The physical objects are already present on the plant and the existing central server contains the digital information, hence, only a tagging mechanism sensitive to the Pucketizer pointing needs to be added. Displays are seen as a subset of the component domain and pouring a Bucket's content onto a display is done by selecting the Bucket on the Pucketizer and pointing at the display. The components pointed at thereby determine whether the Pucketizer grabs or pours.

4.2   The Pucketizer as Memoriser and Annotator

The process operator is not only using the Pucketizer to grab components for later use. It can be seen as a memory aid in the sense that it bookmarks and keeps a reminder of particular points of interest. In the prototype we have implemented we have also included the opportunity to monitor a core value of the memorised components. As the components memorised in the Pucketizer have no need for further indexing is has been easy to include the opportunity for the operator to annotate the grabbed components. After grabbing a component the operator can attach an audio post-it note to it. The audio can be accessed as long as the component is present in one of the Buckets carried by the operator. Audio notes serve two purposes: making comments for the operator's own later use; and telling other operators about activities relating to the component. Each component has a 'voice mail box' attached and operators automatically gain access to the mailbox when grabbing the component. In this way the Pucketizer enables the operators to extend the practice of leaving traces of their activities 'on location'.

In principle the Pucketizer system opens up for a more active configuration of process monitoring including temporary re-instrumentation. In one of the scenarios we developed together with the group of process operators, the Pucketizer was used together with a mobile display and a wireless fieldbus connection to set up local monitoring of electrical current and flow. Thus, the Pucketizer concept can take advantage of a communication infrastructure that is already in place. However, existing points for communication is not a prerequisite. In cases where the sensors and actuators needed for a particular temporary focal set are not installed, the operator can bring equipment for temporary instrumentation of the machinery. This also opens up for a more flexible approach to process control system design. Recurring problems involving the same focal set may lead to a permanent instrumentation of the machinery, letting the process control system expand continuously as needed.

5 Prototyping the Pucketizer

As a research group encompassing competencies both in embodiment design, interaction design, computer science and engineering one of our initial aims was to test what we could gain from working with a participatory approach while engaging in an iterative and concurrent design process simultaneously developing shape, interaction and system functionality. We wanted to keep our design work anchored in the collaboration with the process plant by continuing and expanding work on possible use scenarios. We wanted to evaluate our ideas in concrete form by actually designing a prototypical device which we could test in simulated use situations. And we wanted to dwell more deeply into questions of system design and compatibility with existing informational plant infrastructure, by actually building a functional prototype system. Part of the reason for engaging with such a rather ambitious prototyping strategy was to stress our own multi-disciplinary research and design team to tease out the essentials of the design when confronted with the design problems involved in producing viable demonstrators.

5.1 Envisioning the PUCKETIZER in Use

Already when we did our initial ethnographically inspired field work we had worked with video as a kind of design material in which we could capture prototypical work situation that prompted our design work [3]. When we moved into more detailed design of Pucketizer prototypes, we expanded this approach by inviting process operators to script possible use scenarios. The scripting was typically made out in the plant and in front of a video camera, in order to explore and maintain possible ways of using the new device. A number of basic scripts were made focusing on i.e. how to monitor a pump with declining performance. The scripts were 'attached' to particular parts of the plant which had recently shown that kind of behaviour and after a number of 'walkthroughs' where various associated components were identified, a full 'stage' for future use scenarios were established.

Process operators from other similar plants were invited for a full-day workshop, where they were confronted with these basic scripts. In mixed groups of in-house and visiting operators they were asked to detail and act out how they would use the Pucketizer in the setting. They produced a number of on the spot improvised video scenarios which were later presented and discussed in the full group.
Some of the scenarios were later picked out and further elaborated to examine if the design could withstand such 'simulated' real life situations. A final scenario documenting how we envision the Pucketizer in use was carefully staged and video-recorded with a group of process operators at the plant (see figure 7).

5.2 Interaction Design

Fig. 7. Rolf creates a 'story' on the Pucketizer in use. In one of the scenarios, Rolf, a process operator wants to inspect a motor valve which he believes is not operating properly. He goes to the valve and pick it up with the PUCKETIZER. He has brought a mobile display, and he now 'pours' the valve to the display in order to be able to manually close it and monitor how it 'shows up' on the screen. He realises that more has to be done so he dictates an audio note which he leaves 'on the valve'.

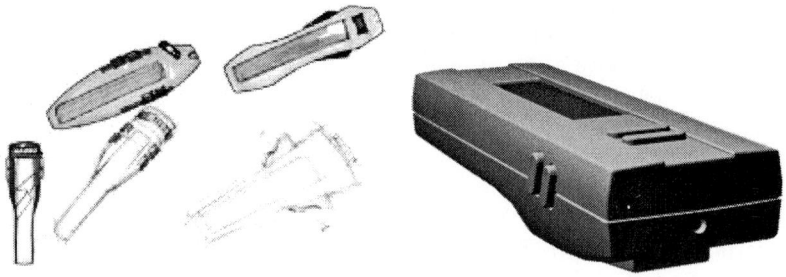

Fig. 8. Some proposed forms (*left*) and final form (*right*) for the Pucketizer.

We decided early on in the design process to build a customised Pucketizer unit as opposed to implementing the Pucketizer functionality on one of the commercially parts of the design (see figures 8 and 9). This decision also gave us the freedom to specifically support the Bucket metaphor without having to force our ideas on top of a pre-existing general purpose interaction scheme. We also decided to build a prototype under the constraints of using standard off-the-shelf components. This meant that the possibilities for designing the visual information content shown in the 122 x 32 pixel display was strongly limited. We chose to strive for a 'flat' and simple design trying to avoid software buttons and menu hierarchies. The Pucketizer is operated by the use of 6 buttons and a rectangular display shows the current state of Buckets and components in these Buckets. The 6 buttons have the following functions:

- *Bucket selection.* By pressing this button the Pucketizer advances to the next of the 4 Buckets available. Whenever a Bucket is selected its components are shown in the Bucket display area.
- *Selection of components already held in the current Bucket.* By pressing this button the Pucketizer advances to the next component in the current Bucket.

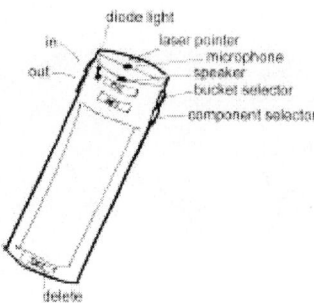

Fig. 9. The Pucketizer interface.

- *Grabbing a component.* Pressing this button activates the Pucketizer's laser pointer. Holding the button down and pointing the Pucketizer at a physical component in the environment makes an icon of that component appear in the Bucket display area. Still holding the button down while moving the Pucketizer as you would move a search light scanning the environment the Bucket display area continuously show the icon of the last physical component pointed at. When the button is released an icon of the last component pointed at is grabbed and kept in the current Bucket.
- *Removing a grabbed component.* Pressing this button removes the currently selected component from the current Bucket.
- *Leaving an audio note.* Pressing this button initialises the recording of an audio note to be left at the component currently selected. Recording ends when the button is released.
- *Listening to an audio note.* Pressing this button initialise the playback of an audio note found at the component currently selected. Playback ends when the button is released.

5.3 Prototyping Functionality

A functional laboratory prototype of the Pucketizer system was implemented with a custom built handheld Pucketizer unit controlled by an 8-bit micro controller, a standard PC running a JAVA application under Windows95, and hardware for wireless radio communication and identification of components. The current implementation does not include small displays distributed in the environment but uses a standard PC monitor for the time being.

6 Related Work

The work reported has been inspired by research in ubiquitous computing [13], augmented reality [14] and tangible bits [6]. There are currently numerous approaches to augmenting physical objects. The *Informative Things* approach is proposed by

Barrett & Maglio as a new approach to information management [2]. Links are created between physical objects and digitally stored information giving the impression that the information is stored on the object and eliminating the need for creating and managing symbolic references to the information. In the described implementation floppy disks are used as objects with the ID stored on the disk, requiring no extra hardware to read it.

The *Insight Lab* is an immersive environment supporting teams in creating design requirements documents [7]. The connection of physical design documents to digital information is one element of the concept. Whiteboard printouts and paper documents are linked to associated multimedia data stored in a computer using barcodes as identification.

Barcodes are also used for tagging in *WebStickers* which is a low-cost method for associating web pages with physical objects [8]. A sticker with pre-printed barcode is attached to the object, which is then linked to one or more URLs. The links are stored in a networked server and the URL can later be retrieved by scanning the barcode.

Want et al [12] argue that, while the low cost of using for instance barcodes for tagging allows larger numbers of augmented objects and support multi-location use, the visual obtrusiveness of the tags and the awkwardness of the readers limits their use. Instead they propose RF ID tags for augmenting objects already naturally occurring in the environment, providing a more seamless interaction by being unobtrusive, and still using inexpensive infrastructure.

In the context of process control the Pucketizer provides inherently unobtrusive tagging since the infrastructure for linking already is in place. Also, as mentioned above, the physical objects referred to are already in focus in the work activities of the process operator, providing a more seamless interaction with the environment. The Bucket metaphor also introduces the possibility for organising the established links with the same device as used for tagging and annotation.

Another related approach is Pick-and-Drop [10] which is a direct manipulation technique allowing a user to exchange information in multi-computer environments. By recognising Id's of pointing devices an object can be picked up from one computer screen and dropped on another, much like physical objects are moved without the need for symbolic references to locations. The notion of Pick-and-Drop relates to the Pucketizer concept on a more abstract level. The Pucketizer allows the user to 'pick up' physical objects in the work environment and then 'drop' them onto different displays (or rather symbolic references to them). The idea of having various displays available in the work environment that are not regarded as distinct computers also corresponds to the notion referred to by Rekimoto [10] as 'Anonymous Displays'.

Finally, the audio annotations of objects provided by the Pucketizer correspond to the notion of augmentable reality introduced by Rekimoto et al [11] where augmenting information can be created dynamically and attached to the user's surrounding physical environment. The information is then shared by users with wearable computers and networking facilities. However, the 'situated information' can also be accessed with other technology, e.g. from a desktop computing environment using a digital representation of the physical environment.

7 Conclusion and Future Work

We have described the Pucketizer system that was designed to smooth the transition between interacting with physical objects in process control and digital representations of the same objects. Main functions include establishing links to physical objects that are grouped in Buckets, remote monitoring of readings from linked objects, and the annotation of each link with audio post-it notes. The work has been carried out as a participatory design process involving process operators in a waste water treatment plant. In the process control context, the Pucketizer system opens up for a more dynamic and flexible configuration of process monitoring than provided in a traditional centralised control room context.

We have also come to the conclusion that the Pucketizer has generic qualities that could be further explored. The concept of using a handheld device for 'collecting' and grouping links to physical objects in order to later manipulate their digital representations in other contexts seems transferable to other application areas. The concept can also be extended to include linking to digital objects. In an interactive workspace, as described by Winograd & Guimbretiere [15], with shared digital objects visible on a wall-mounted display for group interaction, the Pucketizer could allow each participant to collect digital objects in their personal buckets for later use.

Future work involves implementing the display side of the Pucketizer system and evaluating the prototype system in process control contexts. We will also further explore the generic qualities of the Pucketizer concept in other use contexts.

Acknowledgements

The authors want to thank Henrik Janssen and Lars Malmborg from Nef Engineering for their work on the hardware design and CAD drawings for the Pucketizer handheld unit. Sincere thanks are also due to the process operators at Sjolunda waste water plant (Malmoe, Sweden) for their stimulating co-operation in the design process.

References

1. Bainbridge L. The Process Controller. In Singleton W T (ed.) *The Analysis of Practical Skills.* MPT Press Ltd, Edinburgh 1978.
2. Barrett, R., and Maglio P. P. Informative Things: How to attach information to the real world. *Proceedings of UIST'98, ACM Symposium on User Interface Software and Technology,* pp. 81-88, October 1998.
3. Binder, T. Setting the Stage for Improvised Video Scenarios. *Proceedings of CHI'99,* Pittsburgh, 1999.
4. Crossman E. R. F. W. Automation and Skill. In Edwards Elwyn & Lees Frank P (eds.) *The Human Operator in Process Control.* Taylor & Francis Ltd, London 1974.
5. Greenbaum. Joan and Morten Kyng (eds.) *Design; Design at work: co-operative design of computer systems,* Hillsdale, N.J.. Lawrence Erlbaum Associates Inc. Publishers.
6. Ishii, H. and Ullmer, B. Tangible Bits: Towards Seamless Interfaces between People, Bits and Atoms. *Proceedings of CHI'97,* pp. 234-241.

7. Lange, B. M., Jones, M. A. and Meyers, J. L. Insight Lab: An Immersive Team Environment Linking Paper, Displays and Data. *Proceedings of CHI'98*, pp. 550-557.
8. Ljungstrand P., and Holmquist L. E. WebStickers: Using Physical Objects as WWW Bookmarks. *Proceedings of CHI'99*.
9. Perby M. The Art of Mastering a Process – on the Management of Working Skills (in Swedish). Gidlunds forlag, Smedjebacken 1995.
10. Rekimoto, J. Pick-and-Drop: A Direct Manipulation Technique for Multiple Computer Environments. *Proceedings of UIST'97, ACM Symposium on User Interface Software and Technology*, pp. 31-39, October 1997.
11. Rekimoto, J., Ayatsuka, Y. and Hayashi, K. Augment-able Reality: Situated Communication through Physical and Digital Spaces. *Proceedings of ISWC'98, 2nd. International Symposium on Wearable Computers*, 19-20 October, 1998, Pittsburgh, Pennsylvania.
12. Want, R., Fishkin, K. P., Gujar, A., and Harrison B. L. Bridging Physical and Virtual Worlds with Electronic Tags. *Proceedings of CHI'99*, pp. 370-377.
13. Weiser, M. The Computer for the 21st Century. *Scientific American*, 265 (3), 1991, pp. 94-104.
14. Wellner, P., Mackay, W., and Gold, R. Computer Augmented Environments: Back to the Real World. *Commun. ACM*, Vol. 36, No. 7, July 1993.
15. Winograd, T. and Guimbretiere, F. Visual Instruments for an Interactive Mural. *Proceedings of CHI'99, Extended Abstracts*, pp. 378-385.
16. Zuboff S. In the Age of the Smart Machine - the Future of Work and Power. Heinemann Professional Publishing, Oxford 1988.

PowerView
Using Information Links and Information Views to Navigate and Visualize Information on Small Displays

Staffan Björk, Johan Redström, Peter Ljungstrand, and Lars Erik Holmquist

PLAY: Applied research on art and technology
The Interactive Institute, Box 620, SE-405 30 Göteborg, Sweden
http://www.playresearch.com
{staffan.bjork, johan.redstrom, peter.ljungstrand,
lars.erik.holmquist}@interactiveinstitute.se

Abstract. PowerView is a PDA application designed to support people with situational information, primarily during conversations and meetings with other people. PowerView was designed to address a number of issues in interface design concerning both information visualization and interaction on small, mobile devices. In terms of information visualization, the system was required to provide the user with a single integrated information system that enabled quick access to related information once an object of interest had been selected. In terms of interaction, the system was required to enable easy and efficient information retrieval, including single-handed use of the device. These problems were addressed by introducing *Information Links* and *Information Views*. An evaluation of the application against the standard application suite bundle of the PDA, a Casio Cassiopeia E-11, proved the interfaces equivalent in usability even though the PowerView application uses a novel interface paradigm and the test subjects were given no training time with the system.

1 Introduction

The popularity of Personal Digital Assistants (PDAs) has increased rapidly in the last few years. One area where PDAs have become especially widespread is among mobile workers, as such devices give users access to digital information while on the move. However, the environment in which PDAs are used is often quite different from a typical office environment, in which many environmental variables can be predicted. In contrast, when designing the user interface for PDAs not only must one assume that the environment may lack comfortable working positions, have bad lighting and be distracting, but also that it may change during a single use session. For instance, using a PDA on a subway means that the lighting changes as the subway car moves between stations. Further, a slight shaking can be expected during the whole ride, and if one hand is occupied with holding a handle in order for the user to keep his or her balance, the use situation becomes even further distanced to the traditional office environment.

In addition to the constraints posed by the physical environment, the small size and form factor of PDAs introduce several new constraints for human computer interaction design (cf. [19]). PDAs typically have much smaller screens, less computational power and memory, and perhaps most important, limited input facilities. Most PDAs rely primarily on stylus-based input using a touch-sensitive screen, something that demands the use of both hands. Further, the standard components of traditional graphical user interfaces, such as scrollbars, buttons and menus, which on desktop displays only take a small percentage of the available screen space, take up a considerable percentage of the screen space on PDAs, forcing a search for alternatives.

These new situations of computer use do not only create new interface problems regarding user interaction with applications, new requirements are also posed on how information should be visualized on the limited display area. With PowerView, we have explored the design issues of how information visualization techniques can be applied on PDAs, how information navigation can be facilitated in order to enable fast retrieval of information relevant to the situation at hand and how to allow single-handed use of PDA applications. In this paper we describe the PowerView application, the design issues and their respective solutions, as well as how the application works in practice.

2 PowerView

PowerView was designed to support the user with relevant information during activities such as conversations and meetings with other people. To do this, we designed an integrated interface to the most common kinds of information stored on PDAs, i.e., contact lists, emails, tasks and meetings. Even though PowerView technically is an application running under Windows CE, it was designed not to use any of the GUI components of Windows CE in its user interface in order to fully explore alternative interaction techniques. In doing so, we tried to avoid or minimize the use of widgets commonly used in large screen GUIs, e.g. buttons, menus, checkboxes and window managing operators (see **Fig. 1** for an typical screenshot of the application). A short description of the system has previously been published.

As different variants of PDAs provide different interaction possibilities in terms of display area, computational power, and input methods, the choice of device greatly influenced the design of the application. The PowerView application was implemented on a Casio Cassiopeia E-11 (see Fig. 2), being one of the more common PDAs on the market. It is relatively powerful, and it was used as it offered the possibilities of quick prototyping in the high-level object-oriented language Waba (a subset of Java). The device weighs slightly less than 200 grams and can be held by one hand. It is equipped with a touch-sensitive screen capable of displaying 240*320 pixels and 4 shades of gray, a 49 MHz NEC Vr4111 CPU, and 8 Mb RAM. Besides the use of a stylus for input, it has six buttons (excluding the on/off button) of which two can easily be accessed when programming the device in Waba. One of the two buttons is an exit button, similar to the escape key on a keyboard. The other one is an "Action Control" (see Fig. 2) that can be used in three ways: to rotate upward, to rotate downward, or to select by pressing it (inwards). These operations correspond to using the up and down arrow keys and the enter key on a traditional computer keyboard.

48   S. Björk et al.

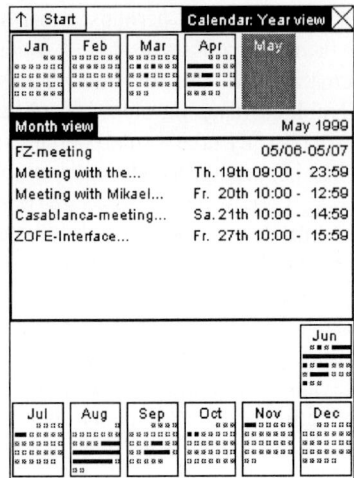

Fig. 1. Typical screenshot from the PowerView application.

2.1 Design Issues

PowerView was designed to address a number of issues in interface design concerning both information visualization and user interaction on PDAs.

Fig. 2. The Casio Cassiopeia E-11 with a close-up on the Action Control.

Information Visualization. Providing a user with as much information as he or she needs to perform a task is an almost ever-present problem when designing computer applications. Many information visualization techniques have been developed and claim to give users efficient views of information (e.g., [5,7,11,13,15]). This problem often becomes more difficult with PDAs, as users often need access to almost the same information as they do on their desktop computers despite having only a fraction of the space of an ordinary display available.

Several information visualization techniques have recently been applied to devices with small screens [4,18]. However, when techniques developed for desktop displays are to be used on PDAs, they often have to be modified to fit the new constraints posed by the small devices. This includes not only the limited display area (which may require designers to abandon ideals such as showing all available information), but also taking into account limited computational powers, memory space and changing networking capabilities.

Information Navigation. Regardless of how the information is visualized, PDAs need to use several separate views to present information that could be presented simultaneously on a device with a larger display. Increasing the resolution of PDA displays to show more information does not resolve this problem, since the limited size of the screen would make the presentation too small to be readable. Thus, users need to navigate between several different views on PDAs in order to access the same amount of information as displayed on a single view on a desktop or laptop. Each switch between two views requires the user to re-focus on the new information presented, and also requires the user to relate it to the previous information in order to make sense of it. These transitions add an overhead cost to the interaction as the user must explicitly choose what view to switch to, make the switch, observe the effects of the switch and make sense of the new information displayed. This added overhead takes time and concentration from the user's intended activities.

This overhead can partly be mitigated by closely mapping how the information is visualized with how the underlying information is structured. For example, if an address book can not show all entries at once, it is feasible to divide the presentation of contacts into groups where all names in a group starts with the same letter. In this way, if the user must navigate to find a contact, each change of view corresponds to moving from one letter to another.

When the number of items in a group becomes too large, or the number of groups becomes too large to be displayed simultaneously, further divisions are required, creating hierarchical structures of views. These structures require the user not only to switch between different views when moving between items, but also to move between different levels of views, as some views will be used to categorize other views. This creates further overhead, as the user is presented with the same information on several different levels of detail. This becomes most apparent when a user moves from viewing an individual piece of information to viewing another individual piece of information of another information type, as the user has to move from the bottom of a hierarchical structure to the top, switch to viewing another hierarchical structure and navigate to the bottom of that structure. A typical example of this problem is when switching between reading an email from a person to looking for that person's phone number in the contact list application.

While applications like Microsoft Outlook or the Active Desktop on Windows CE devices do integrate a few common types of information, they are still organized in a way that requires the user to explicitly switch between different views or modules in order to obtain the desired information. The PowerView application described in this paper aimed at taking this integration one step further to better support quick retrieval of related information once a certain interest, or focus, had been selected.

Interaction Constraints. One of the major differences between the use of desktop computers and PDAs is that many PDAs rely on stylus-based input. This has several implications for interaction design. First, input is slower than using a keyboard, which makes text-based operations, such as searching, less attractive. Second, when the user manipulates an object on the display with the stylus, the stylus and the hand holding the stylus covers parts of the screen. Third, if the user is walking, riding a bus, etc., the PDA is likely to be slightly in motion, which makes high-precision stylus-based manipulation on the screen more difficult to accomplish.

Ethnographical studies have shown that in many work situations, it is not feasible to require that users have both hands available for interacting with a device [10]. For instance, the user might be using a mobile phone with one hand while she is trying to retrieve information from the PDA. Various new input forms have been introduced that allow single-handed control, e.g. by using key cards [17], enhanced track point devices [9], or making a device tilt-sensitive [14]. However, all of these require new, or at least modified, hardware that have yet to become integrated in publicly available PDAs.

Interestingly, many commercially available PDAs already have buttons that can be used by the hand holding the device. Currently, such buttons are only employed to a limited extent, for instance to scroll in menus, as commercially available PDA user interfaces require point-and-click interaction with the stylus for nearly all operations (an interaction style seemingly inherited from mouse operations on desktop computers). Instead of designing new input devices, we wished to take advantage of these already present buttons to explore single-handed interaction. The use of such buttons for navigation avoids some of the problems associated with stylus-based interaction, but requires that the navigation can be achieved using only a few degrees of freedom.

In order to improve usability in situations where the user only has one hand available for interaction, PowerView was designed to be possible to control solely using the buttons available on the PDA (see Fig. 2). This constrained the interface to be possible to control using four degrees of freedom only, corresponding to forwards and backwards, select/enter and exit/up.

Context of Use. One difference between stationary and mobile IT support is that while users have to bring their task or problem to the stationary computer, they can bring their mobile devices with them for use when and where they need them (cf. [12]). Since mobile devices such as PDAs rarely have the capabilities of stationary computers, they are not likely to be the complete solution to the users' problems. Instead, they are more of a support in activities where, ideally, the users' main focus is on the activity taking place rather than the technology supporting it. One implication of this is that applications on PDAs should be able to support activities while requiring as little attention (in the form of interaction) as possible, since the user may have focus on an activity outside the device. PowerView is not actively context sensitive in the sense of *context-aware computing* (cf. [16]), but adding sensors providing such functionality is an interesting option for future development.

As an illustration of this difference between stationary and mobile computing, we can think of the how users typically work with text on a PDA in comparison to a stationary computer: on stationary computers users often work with word processors in order to write full texts like this paper; on a PDA short notes during a meeting or a phone call are more likely. Even though both tasks could be accomplished on both platforms, this typical usage illustrates a basic difference in the design objectives of PDAs compared to desktop computers.

3 Using PowerView

In order to illustrate how the PowerView interface works, a sequence showing a typical interaction with the system is given in figures **Fig. 3-8**. In this example, the user wishes to find out what meetings are booked with "Mikael Goldstein". To do this, the user locates and selects the name in the Contact list. This creates a *Context View* that provides information linked to the person, including past and future meetings booked with him, email sent to and received from him, and tasks that are related to him. Within this Context View, the user then chooses to obtain more information about meetings, getting a detailed list of all meetings with Mikael Goldstein.

Initially, the user is presented with the *Overview*, in which information from all domains are visible in four different tiles (see Fig. 3).

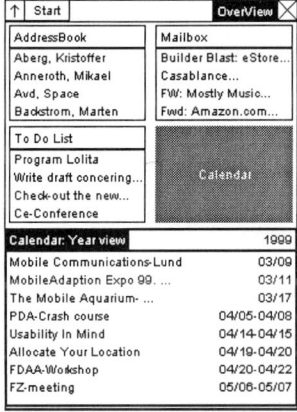

Fig. 3. The Overview, the initial view in the PowerView application.

By clicking on one of the tiles with the stylus, the system sets that tile as focus tile and changes the visualization accordingly. Clicking on the focus tile with the stylus activates one of the *navigational views*, from which the user can navigate to individual data entries. To find Mikael Goldstein, the user sets the meeting tile as the focus tile (see Fig. 4) and activates the navigational view for meetings by selecting it again.

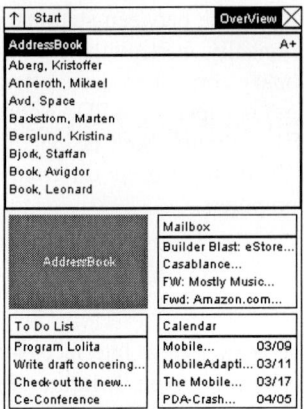

Fig. 4. The Overview with focus on the AddressBook.

As soon as the meeting tile of the Overview is selected, the system switches to the Address Book View. This navigational view divides all contacts into tiles based on the first letter of the surname, representing the number of contacts in the context tiles as black lines, and the full names in the focus tile (see Fig. 5).

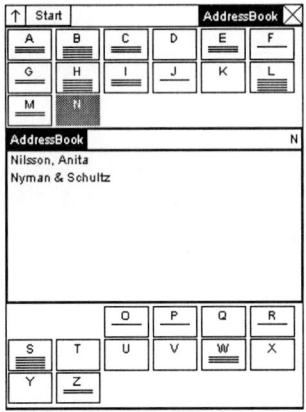

Fig. 5. Initial view in the Addressbook.

Similar to the Overview, the user can move the focus between tiles by clicking on them or by using the action control. By moving the focus to the tile containing contacts with surnames starting with G, the contact Mikael Goldstein is identified (see Fig. 6).

Fig. 6. The Addressbook with focus on the letter G.

As the individual piece of information is now shown, it can be selected in order to switch to the Context View information view.

Fig. 7. The Context view with the entry Mikael Goldstein selected.

The Context View (see Fig. 7) visually resembles the Overview as it depicts information from all information domains in four separate tiles. However, the information shown in the context tiles is selected because it is linked with the object in focus. This gives a limited context containing only the information that the user has previously deemed relevant. In this view, the user can decide to look at one of the information objects in detail by moving the focus between the tiles. To examine the meetings associated with Mikael Goldstein, the user simply moves the focus to the Calendar (Fig. 8).

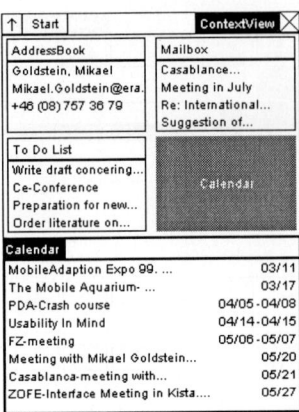

Fig. 8. The Context View with focus on the Calendar.

It should be noted that as all interaction in the example, and in the application as a whole, can be performed by exclusively using the Action Control (see Fig. 2). This ensures that every step can be performed using only the hand that is holding the device.

4 Interface Design

In order to create an integrated user interface for the PowerView application, all the design issues discussed previously had to be solved together. We addressed this by using *Information Links* and *Information Views*. By using the two concepts together, a unified presentation was created that at every point focused on supporting the user with information and allowed for a coherent way of navigation for all information types.

4.1 Information Links

In order to solve the problem of extensive information navigation to move between individual pieces of related information of different types, it was necessary to find a way of showing several different information types simultaneously. To do this, we needed a system to describe what information was related to a chosen piece of information. *Information links* was introduced to solve this problem.

Information links simply indicate a (semantic) connection between two pieces of information, where the two pieces of information can belong to different information domains. Information links enable the collection of various pieces of information that together form a heterogeneous context to an object (focus) the user selects, while still preserving a homogenous structure for every information domain. Thus, the information links form a semantic layer of relations between objects in the different data types on top of the storage of each data type. Information links differ from hyperlinks in that they are not used to traverse different presentations (e.g. web pages), but rather to define a context for any given piece of information. The strategy of using links or connections between objects to represent semantic properties is frequently used in other research field such as linguistics (e.g., WordNet [6] and other semantic networks).

The type of connection provided by an information link is consciously designed to be explicit, i.e. the user determines if two pieces of information should be linked together and can choose any criteria for doing so. This makes the system, and the visualization, flexible and enables the user to adapt the visualization in some respects to the environments in which the application is used. While this makes it necessary for the user to perform additional actions in order to establish these links, this effort can be made in advance at the user's leisure.

4.2 Information Views

An *information view* is a collection of correlated objects displayed together to help the user with some activity. The objects are active in that they can change their appearance depending on the user's actions and are used to activate changes in the application, including switching to other information views. However, an information view should always be identifiable independently of the current state of the objects in it. The information views can present several different types of information, distinguishing them from (most) 'standard' applications, and are designed to function together with each other to support the user in more complex tasks that traditionally would have required the use of several different applications.

The information presented in an encyclopedia about individual countries can be used as an example of an information view, with the exception that it is a static presentation. Such presentations often give a collection of several different types of information, e.g., a map showing geographical data, a box containing demographical data, and a text body describing history, religion etc. These provide an informative overview of the country in which several different types of information are presented together.

As the PowerView application was designed to support the user with information during meetings and conversations, three categories of tasks, and thus information views, could be identified: showing what information was available on the device, selecting the information of interest, and presenting the selected information. Further, these tasks have to be completed in this order, which made the design of how the information views should be used together easier.

Focus+Context Visualization. Based on our experiences of working with the Flip Zooming visualization technique [8], including applying it to small screens [4], we decided to base each information view on a Flip Zooming visualization. Flip Zooming belongs to a class of information visualizations techniques called focus+context visualization. These are characterized by having one central object, the focus, presenting more detailed information, while simultaneously presenting contextual information in the surrounding area. Flip Zooming does this by dividing the information into a number of rectangular tiles of which one is the denoted the focus tile and the remaining context tiles. When creating Information Views using the Flip Zooming technique, each object in the Information View is simply mapped to a tile in the Flip Zooming visualization. The tile selected as focus is given most of the display area and the user can change which tile is in focus using random access methods such as a stylus or mouse. As the tiles are ordered sequentially, it is also possible to "flip" an object into focus by navigating "forward" and "backward". Having a focus tile allows the user to have a more detailed presentation of information before changing to another information view by selecting it. This enables some exploration at every point without hiding tiles or immediately changing information view.

The Flip Zooming technique allows for hierarchical visualizations [1], i.e., the ability to use one information visualization within another. This allowed for a natural mapping of how the information in the application is structured to how it is visualized, with an information view at each node in the hierarchy. The tasks handled by the different information views had to be presented in a certain order. That order determined the order in the hierarchy, with the information view responsible for presenting the available information at the top and the information view presenting a chosen piece of information at the bottom. The hierarchical Flip Zooming technique is possible to navigate using only four operators, i.e., forwards, backwards, select and exit/up. Thus, it meets the requirement for single-handed use with the Cassiopeia device.

On ordinary desktop displays, it is possible to show all information visualizations used in a hierarchical Flip Zooming visualization simultaneously. For several reasons, this approach was not suitable for PDAs. Firstly, the limited display area of PDAs made it impossible to intelligibly show all information views simultaneously. Secondly, as each information view was designed to help the user with one particular activity, the information given in the surrounding information views would not add information vital for that activity, and thus distract the user and lower the usability of the application as a whole. By limiting the application to show only one information view at any one time, we gave up the idea of having a global context consisting of all information views, in order to have a local context for every view that helps solve the task associated with that view. It should be noted that this limitation differs from most applications, where the presentation of more information of one type is prioritized over the possibility of showing information of several different types throughout the application.

4.3 Description of the Information Views Used in PowerView

For each category of sub-tasks, one or more information views were created. First, The OverView information view shows a summary of the information available from all four information types. Second, to allow the user to select a piece of information, one or more Navigational views (depending on the number of objects and detail in the information structure) were created to navigate within each of the four information domains. Third, the Context View is used to present the information selected by the user. (See **Fig. 9** for a model of how the information views are related.)

OverView. The presentation of the top level of the hierarchy is named the Overview view, as it presents information of all four information types. Here, four objects representing four separate types of information are presented: contacts, email, tasks and meetings. When the user selects one of the objects, PowerView switches to the navigational view corresponding to the information type of the object.

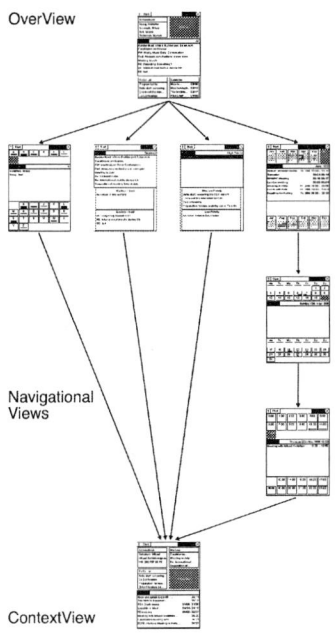

Fig. 9. Flow model of interaction with the PowerView application.

Navigational Views. After selecting information domain in the OverView, the user is presented with the corresponding navigational view. This view shows all available information in that domain in an abstract form, ordered into objects according to the nature of the information domain. By choosing one of these objects, the user can move to another navigational view that only presents the selected part of the information. Thus, each view helps the user with the task of choosing a region or an item of an information domain, and the navigational views as a whole provide the user with a structured navigation for selecting an individual piece of information.

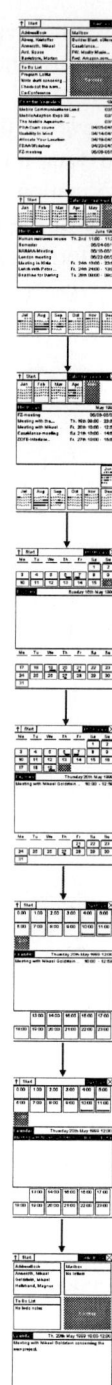

Fig. 10. Interaction flow scheme.

As PowerView handles four information domains, four groups of navigational views were created. The information domain in the previous usage example was navigated by using only one navigational view. In cases where the information domain is structured into hierarchical structures, the user would have to move to other navigational views before being able to select a piece of information, and then switch to the Context View. For a flow scheme of such an interaction example, without the changing of focus in either the OverView or the Context View, see Fig. 10.

Depending on the amount of information and the structure of the information, different numbers of navigational views were required for each domain. In the case of meetings, different navigational views was created for handling years, months, days and hours, while for email only one navigational view separating received, sent and draft email was required. For the purpose of exploring information visualization on PDAs, we did not deem it necessary to create numerous navigation views for each information domain. In use situations where the amount of information requires more navigational views, these can easily be incorporated into the application when needed.

Context View. When the user selects an individual piece of information at the bottom level in a navigational view, the system switches to the Context View. In this view, the selected piece is displayed together with all information linked to it with information links. For instance, if a meeting is selected, the Context View shows information about people associated with that meeting, as well as email received from or sent to them and tasks that have to be done before the meeting. By mixing the information domains in this fashion, the problem of having to navigate through all the information in the system to move between two related pieces of information of different types was reduced.

As the types of information displayed vary depending on which piece of information the user selects, the Context View was designed to be able to show individual pieces of information from all domains simultaneously. This had the added benefit that the same Context View (with different information) could be used from all navigational views.

5 User Evaluation

In order to evaluate the application, the PowerView interface was benchmarked against the standard application bundle in Windows CE. Sixteen paid university students (10 women and 6 men, aged 17-43) were given 7 tasks to be performed on both systems in two different user situations. The main difference between the two situations was that in one the users were told to hold a mobile phone while performing all tasks, thereby inclining the users to use single-handed navigation. None had any prior experience of a PDA but all were familiar with using the Windows operating systems on stationary computers. The experiment was conducted at the Usability Lab at Ericsson Research in Kista, Sweden.

Both systems passed the set usability criterion, completion of 70% of all tasks. In one of the two user situations, 100% of the tasks were solved using the PowerView interface, while only 75% of the tasks were solved using the Windows CE bundle. Although not statistically proven, this indicates that PowerView provides more efficient usability. Further, the evaluation showed that the users perceived that the arrangement of information was significantly better on the PowerView application ($F[1,15]=8.497$, $p=0.011$). Although users received no description of the PowerView interface, and were only allowed six minutes to freely familiarize with the interface before the experiment, no significant difference between task completion time could be found. The main problems identified with the PowerView interface was that users tried to double-tap (similar to double-clicking in standard graphical window systems), sometimes became confused over which information view they were viewing, and mistook "grayed-out" areas for buttons.

Surprisingly, none of the users utilized the single-handed navigation offered by the action control, despite situations where two-handed navigation led to physical discomfort (e.g., holding a mobile phone by the neck).

6 Concluding Remarks

PowerView allows mobile users to access information using an interface designed to work in a supportive rather than attention-demanding fashion. The use of information links and information views offers a new solution to the presentation and navigation of information on devices with small displays, breaking away from the traditional concept of using one application for each information type.

PowerView also supports single-handed navigation and retrieval of information in the entire application due to the restricted degrees of freedom in the interface. Although this was a feature that subjects in the evaluation did not employ, we have argued that single-handed navigation may be necessary in some use contexts since users may have the other hand occupied. Despite the restricted degrees of freedom in the interaction process, the usability evaluation showed that the PowerView application was equivalent in usability for completely novice users in comparison to the Windows CE application bundle.

The use of information views and information links in applications has only briefly been explored in the work described here. Future work is needed to fully validate the generality and usability of these concepts. Considering PowerView, the evaluation identified several possible improvements regarding both interaction and visualization, which will be addressed in future research. Further, PowerView has been identified as a possible basis for an application to organize communication and information together, which will also be explored in the future.

7 Acknowledgements

The authors thank Mikael Anneroth, Magnus Hellstrand and Mikael Goldstein at the usability lab at Ericsson Radio Systems AB, who performed the evaluation. This research was funded by SITI, the Swedish Institute for Information Technology, as part of the Effective Display Strategies for Small Screens project within the Mobile Informatics research program.

References

1. Björk, S. Hierarchical Flip Zooming: Enabling Parallel Exploration of Hierarchical Visualizations. In Proc. of AVI 2000, pp. 232-237, ACM Press, 2000.
2. Björk, S., Holmquist, L.E., Ljungstrand, P., and Redström, J. PowerView: Structured Access to Integrated Information on Small Screens. In Ext. Abstracts of CHI'2000, pp. 265-266, ACM Press, 2000.
3. Björk, S., Holmquist, L.E. and Redström, J. A Framework for Focus+Context Visualization. In Proc. of IEEE Information Visualization '99, pp. 53-57, IEEE Press, 1999.
4. Björk, S., Holmquist, L.E., Redström, J., Bretan, I., Danielsson, R., Karlgren, J., and Franzén, K. WEST: A Web Browser for Small Terminals. In Proc. of ACM UIST '99, pp. 187-196, ACM Press, 1999.
5. Card, S.K., Mackinlay, J.D., and Shneiderman, B. Information Visualization. In Card, S.K., Mackinlay, J.D., and Shneiderman, B. (Eds.) Readings in Information Visualization: Using Vision to Think, pp. 1-34, Morgan Kaufmann Publishers, San Francisco, California, 1999.
6. Fellbaum, C. (ed.). WordNet; An electronic lexical database. MIT Press, 1998.
7. Furnas, G.W. Generalized Fisheye Views. In Proc. of CHI '86, pp. 16-23, ACM Press, 1986.
8. Holmquist, L.E. Focus+Context Visualization with Flip Zooming and the Zoom Browser. In Ext. Abstracts of CHI '97, ACM Press, 1997.
9. Kawachiya, K., and Ishikawa, H. NaviPoint an input device for mobile information browsing. In Proc. of CHI 98, pp. 1-8, ACM Press, 1998.
10. Kristoffersen, S., and Ljungberg, F. "Making Place" to Make IT Work: Empirical Explorations of HCI for Mobile CSCW, In Proc. of Group'99, ACM Press, 1999.
11. Leung, Y.K., and Apperley, M.D. A Review and Taxonomy of Distortion-Oriented Presentation Techniques. In ACM Transactions on Computer-Human Interaction, Vol. 1, No. 2, pp. 126-160, ACM Press, 1994.
12. Norman, D.A., The Invisible Computer, The MIT Press, Cambridge, Mass., USA, 1998.
13. Rao, R., Pedersen, J.O., Hearst, M.A., Mackinlay, J.D, Card, S.K., Masinter, L., Halvorsen, P-K., and Robertson, G.G. Rich Interaction in the Digital Library. In Communications of the ACM, Vol. 38, No. 4, pp. 29-39, ACM Press, 1995.
14. Rekimoto, J. Tilting operations for small screen interfaces. In Proceedings of the ACM symposium on User interface software and technology (UIST) '96, page 167, ACM Press, 1996.

15. Sarkar, M., and Brown, M.H. Graphical Fisheye Views. In Communications of the ACM, Vol. 37, No. 12, pp. 73-84, ACM Press, 1994.
16. Schilit, B., Adams, N., Want, R. Context-Aware Computing Applications. In Proceedings of Workshop on Mobile Computing Systems and Applications, pp. 85-90, Santa Cruz, Ca, U.S, IEEE Computer Society, 1994.
17. Sugimoto, M., and Takahashi, K., SHK single hand key card for mobile devices. In Proc. of CHI '96, pp. 7-8, ACM Press, 1996.
18. Taivalsaari, A. The Event Horizon User Interface Model for Small Devices, Technical Report TR-99-74, Sun Microsystems Laboratories, 1999. Available at http://www.sunlabs.com/technical-reports/1999/
19. Want, R, Schilit, B, Adams, A, Gold, R, Petersen, K, Goldberg, D, Ellis, J. & Weiser, M. The ParcTab Ubiquitous Computing Experiment. Technical Report CSL-95-1, Xerox Palo Alto Research Center, March 1995.

A Comparison of Free Interaction Modes for Mobile Layout System[1]

Zhiwei Guan, Yang Li, Hongan Wang, and Guozhong Dai

Intelligent Engineering Laboratory
Institute of Software, Chinese Academy of Sciences
P.O. Box 8718, Beijing 100080, China
gzw@imd.cims.edu.cn

Abstract. The interaction mode in a mobile layout system was studied. An evaluation experiment was designed and conducted to compare five interaction modes: single pen-based, pen + voice, pen + keyboard, mouse + voice, mouse + keyboard. Subjects were instructed to fulfill the basic tasks of a layout plan design system, such as locating, shaping the property of, and modifying the coordinate setting of an object. In plan setting, modification time, accuracy rate and subjective preferences a pen-based system proved the best, pen + voice followed. This experiment confirmed that different availability of interaction modes resulted in different interaction efficiency in the mobile layout environment. The experiment also provided information on the possible efficient combination of interaction modes. This paper gives statistical support to indicate that use of pen is preferable to voice in setting and modification procedures in mobile technology.

1 Introduction

In order to improve communication efficiency between users and computers, many new interactive tools have been developed. These interaction tools allow users to use different input modalities simultaneously. Multimodal User Interfaces (MMUIs) are designed to make full use of the user's sense and motion channels or modalities, e.g. gesture, speech, eye gaze, handwriting etc. [1].

1.1 Background on the Study of Interaction

According to studies in psychology and ergonomics, these different modalities are mutually supplemental [2]. However, some studies indicate that the supplement and redundancy would hinder the use of multimodal interaction modes. Since the late 1980s, research has paid attention to the user-centered interface. One important aspect considered was how a computer could be used as an intuitive aid to perform particular

---

[1] The research is supported by the key project of China 863 Advanced Technology Plan (No. 863-306-03-501).

tasks. In the computer domain, pen-based technology is currently emerging as an important new access technology. The pen is a suitable artifact for mobile computing. Together with a voice-recognition engine, the pen can be an efficient command input tool. Many former studies of multimodal user interfaces have been done in other fields where the research focus was not fixed solely on the pen-related interaction mode, such as text processing, package sorting and Computer Aided Drafting [3] and in the communication environment. Studies on speech and keyboard input [4] [5], mouse and speech input [6], speech and gesture input have also been conducted [7] [8]. Research and experimentation has shown pen and voice-based interfaces to be efficient and intuitive [9] [10]. However, there remains large gaps both in the literature and in practice regarding multimodal interface studies. Little has been studied in the way of experimental evaluation on practical systems, for example, a mobile layout plan design system.

1.2 Organization of Paper

In this paper, the intention is to display some useful results for the design of mobile architecture layout systems. A multimodal user interface environment was set up, where users could use pen, keyboard, voice, and mouse to create and modify the architecture layout plan. Based on this environment, an evaluation experiment was designed to investigate the differences in five interaction modes: pen-based mode, pen+voice mode, pen+keyboard mode, mouse+voice mode, and mouse+keyboard mode.

Section 2 gives a brief description of the multimodal environment developed, and the interaction style of the layout system; section 3 gives a description of the experiment; section 4 shows the discussion and results based on the analysis of the experimental data.

2 Mobile Layout System

The computer-based city layout is used to represent the layout of a city. Also, the city layout system is a complex interactive system, within which users can freely manipulate the map information, modify graphics objects and arrange and locate the object at a proper site, and designing an overall layout plan. Based on the current research environment, a Beijing LayOut System (BLOS) was developed. The motive of the system was to combine the computer-human interaction technology with the application of layout, making the city building design more reasonable and easy. Consideration was given to typical manipulations, namely; a layout task including location, drawing, modification and property (name, dimension etc.) setting.

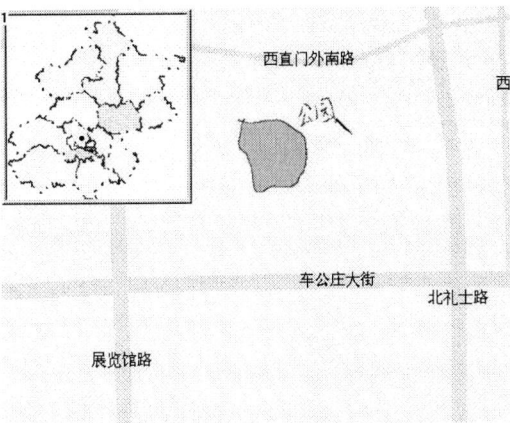

Fig. 1. The interface of BLOS was developed based on PenBuilder. By employing pen and gesture usability, the user can improve planning efficiency. A pen-based system was employed using a C++ programme (PenBuilder). The core of PenBuilder is based on a set of independent classes, which are independent of the development environment. Based on the PenBuilder, BLOS occupied a multi-agent structure [11]. The multi-agent structure is helpful in attempting to reduce the complexity of the dialogue procedure and extend the system's functions.

3 Method

3.1 Subjects

Forty-eight subjects (24 male, 24 female, all right handed; 24 students, 24 workers) were tested for the experiment. The main purpose was to evaluate the relationship between different devices and the usability of the interaction mode. 12 workers and 12 students were selected who were familiar working with computers. The blueprint had to be drawn using only mouse and keyboard. The rest of subjects had previously only worked using the traditional paper-based mode and had never used a computer before. Amongst the 24 workers, 12 of them were professional layout plan stylist. Their ages ranged from 20 to 35. None of them had previous experience using this kind of layout system.

3.2 Equipment

The hardware used was a mobile tablet (WACOM), a stylus pen, a microphone and a mobile laptop computer (PII450, IBM Corp.). All experiments were run on Windows 98. The software used in the experiment included a layout system which was developed based on MapX (provided by MapInfo Corp.), a gesture recognition system (developed by us), a handwriting recognition system (provided by Han Wang Corp.) and a voice recognition system (ViaVoice developed by IBM Corporation).

3.3 Design

Before we performed the experiment, professional designers were consulted concerning common working tasks. Based on their advice, two sets of basic tasks in the real layout system were studied.
- Creating a new architecture layout plan included Orientation Location (setting the location of a new object), Shape Drawing (setting the rough shape of the object), and Property Setting (setting the acreage and the relationship of other objects).
- Modification of old architecture layout drawing included Object Selection, Object Redrawing, and Property Resetting.

The ability to quickly set out the architecture and change the feature of the object was equally important. To suit the professional requirements, the focus of the experiments was set on practicality, usability, validity and efficiency. A range of possible interaction modes were considered in the context of previous research. Among the possible interactions were mouse, pen, voice, and keyboard:
- Mouse, voice, keyboard + voice and keyboard could not accomplish the planning task individually as they couldn't be used simultaneously. Users needed to move frequently between mouse and pen. Alternating between items encumbered the communication between user and system.
- Pen and mouse are conflicting devices. Similarly, pen + mouse, pen + mouse + voice and "pen + mouse + keyboard" conflict.

Based on the initial analysis of interaction combination mode, five further interaction modes were set up. In order to investigate the efficiency of different interaction modes and the degree of feasibility, each subject tested five further possible modes: Pen-based, Pen+Voice, Pen+keyboard, Mouse+Voice and Mouse+keyboard mode.

3.4 Procedure

First, the subject was given a formal layout template. The task was to draw and set a new layout plan, which should be similar to a given formal layout plan. The experiment system was then explained to each of the subjects. A 20 minute demonstration of The Beijing Layout system was played to the subjects, including a brief introduction of the five interaction modes, the usage of the four interaction devices, pen, mouse, keyboard, and voice. Those familiar with computers and already skilled using mouse and keyboard were able to skip the coordinate introduction section.

The tests began after a 20 minute familiarisation period. The first test was to set up an interface which included the five interaction modes. Subjects then selected coordinate lists to begin the test. Once the test mode had been selected, the other devices not included in the test session were frozen. After finished the tasks, subjects could use coordinate tools to end the test. Performance times were recorded by the system. In addition, the system would measure to what degree the drawing feature and property items were used.

In the second session, subjects used the same devices to modify their draft. They were instructed to modify their design until the error was no more than 5%. During the modification, the system would display the remaining error. Once all of the errors had been modified, the system informed the subject to end the session. The system recorded the modification time.

After each subject finished the task, they were questioned about their preferences to each mode of interaction. They were asked to rank (on a scale of 1-10) each mode according to their satisfaction and ease of use.

4 Results and Discussion

An Analysis of Variance (ANOVA) with repeated measures on the subject factors on the interface modes subjects was used. The variables were; setting time, modification time, total time (setting time + modification time), accuracy and subjective performance.

4.1 Difference of the Plan Setting Time and Plan Modification Time

Table 1. Mean and standard deviation of plan setting time and plan modification time

		Pen-based	Pen+ Voice	Pen+key board	Mouse+ voice	Mouse+key board
Plan Setting time	Mean	17.6292	18.4	24.2167	25.2167	26.9042
	Stand. Dev.	0.34196	0.41703	1.1875	0.63429	0.99016
Plan modification time	Mean	4.8328	5.6	6.76	8.112	8.468
	Stand. Dev.	0.36203	0.25495	0.51559	0.45122	0.50804

Table 1 displays the means and standard deviations of plan setting time and plan modification time of different interaction modes. The mean plan setting time across all experimental trials was 22.4733; the mean plan modification time across all experimental trials was 6.75456.

The data was analysed by fitting an ANOVA. The ANOVA model tested each of the five interaction modes (Pen-based, pen + voice, pen + keyboard, mouse + voice, mouse + keyboard) on the plan setting time and plan modification time dependent variable. There were significant differences in the mean value of the dependent variable (plan setting time and plan modification time) as a function of five main effects ($F(4,115)=22.17277$, $p<0.05$; $F(4,115)=3.591845$, $p<0.05$). Different interaction modes had an effect on plan setting time and plan modification time. The pen-based mode resulted in the highest score, followed by pen+voice, mouse+voice, pen+keyboard and mouse+keyboard modes.

In plan setting time aspect, a significant difference was found when a comparison of means was conducted. There was significant difference between the modes (pen-based and pen+voice mode, $F(1,46)= 48.22807$, $p<0.05$; pen-based and pen+keyboard mode, $F(1,46)= 32.4941$, $p<0.05$; mouse+voice mode and mouse+keyboard mode,

F(1,46)= 49.4265, p<0.05). pen+voice mode and mouse+voice mode, F(1,46)= 84.56788, p<0.05. The results revealed that a pen-based mode is the fastest way to perform tasks, with the pen+voice second.

In plan modification time aspect, there was also a significant difference between similar interaction modes, pen-based and pen+voice mode, F(1,46)=9.518136, p<0.05; pen-based and pen+keyboard mode, F(1,46)= 6.247054, p<0.05; mouse+voice mode and mouse+keyboard mode, F(1,46)= 1.999417, p<0.05; pen+voice mode and mouse+voice mode, F(1,46)=1.89546, p<0.05.

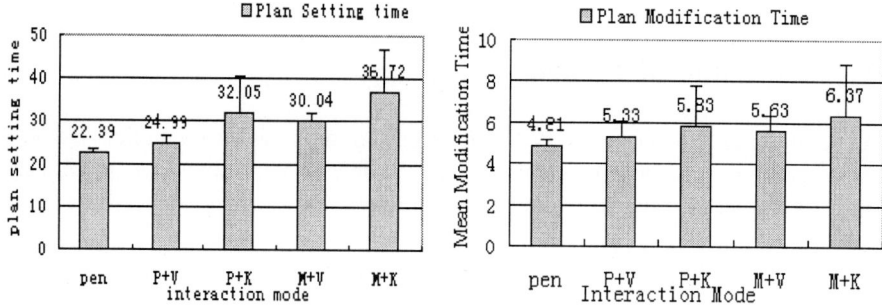

Fig. 2. The mean Plan Setting Time and the mean Plan Modification Time in terms of the interaction mode. The short lines indicate the standard deviation of Plan Setting Time and Plan Modification Time.

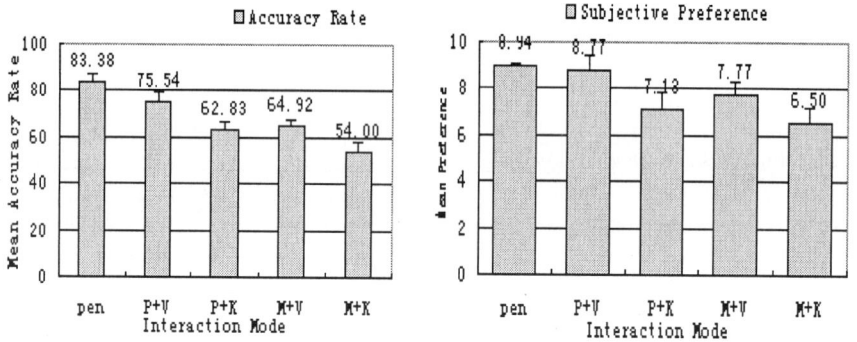

Fig. 3. The mean Accuracy Rate and the mean Subjective Preference in terms of the interaction mode. The short lines indicate the standard deviation of the Accuracy Rate and Subjective Preference.

Further analysis revealed that the total time of trial activity varied between each of the five interaction modes. In the total test time of 36 minutes (the longest time), the mouse + keyboard mode was slowest in the layout plan test task. In contrast, it was discovered that subjects in pen-based interaction had maximum free time after they had performed their tasks, the experiment averaged 27 minutes. The average time for pen+voice was 30 minutes. The comparison of pen-based mode with pen+voice mode showed that the combination of pen and voice may not improve performance. Conversely, there was a significant difference between mouse+voice and mouse+keyboard mode. These results refute previous results, which claim that voice is the most useful mode in interacting with computers. The result of using voice may vary with the interaction mode with which it would be combined.

4.2 Mean Accuracy of the Five Interaction Modes

A comparison of means indicated that different interaction modes affect the mean accuracy of the task significantly. The ANOVA of pen+voice and pen+keyboard mode showed that there was significant difference between them, $F(1,46)=110.9796$, $p<0.05$. The ANOVA of mouse+voice and mouse+keyboard mode showed that there was also a significant difference between them, $F(1,46)= 120.52$, $p<0.05$. The three comparisons revealed that in the accuracy of task aspect, voice appeared significantly to assist function when used instead of a keyboard. However, voice is not the perfect mode. The ANOVA of pen-based and pen+voice mode showed that there was significant difference between them, $F(1,46)=44.828$, $p<0.05$. When voice and pen were combined, the accuracy of the completed task was lower than when using pen only. The ANOVA of pen+voice and mouse+voice mode showed that there was a significant difference, $F(1,46)= 108.603$, $p<0.05$. The ANOVA of pen+keyboard and mouse+keyboard mode showed that there was also a significant difference between them, $F(1,46)= 55.5520$, $p<0.05$. Comparison revealed that pen interaction improved accuracy.

4.3 Subjective Preference

There were significant differences among the five interaction modes for the subjective evaluation, $F(4,115)=48.75581$, $p<0.05$. The mouse+keyboard mode was the least preferable. After eliminating the mouse+keyboard mode, there was also a difference between the remaining four interaction modes, $F(3,92)=64.30857$, $p<0.05$. The data demonstrated that there were two main modes suitable for the requirement of the subjects, i.e. the pen-based mode, whose mean preference rate was 8.94 and the pen+voice mode, whose mean preference rate was 8.77. After analysing the pen-based and pen+voice modes, we found significant difference, $F(1,46)= 1.510096$, $p<0.05$. The results showed that the pen-based mode is the most satisfactory, followed by the pen+voice mode. However, the error rate for pen+voice mode was 0.67 and the error rate for pen-based mode was just 0.13. The comparison of the error rates revealed that pen+voice was also a promising interaction mode. Although the mean preference rate of pen+voice was lower than the mean preference rate of the pen only mode, a few subjects still preferred pen+voice, nine of them reporting even higher preference than pen only. Some subjects remarked that if voice recognition had been better, they would have preferred to use pen and voice together.

Among the five experimental interaction modes, two interaction modes scored very low; the pen+keyboard mode, whose mean preference rate was 7.13 and the mouse+keyboard mode, whose mean preference rate was 6.75. By performing ANOVA, we found that there was a significant difference between them, $F(1,46)=1.97292, p<0.05$. The result implies that when combined with a keyboard, the use of a pen shows better functionality than a mouse.

5 Discussion

Five interaction modes were discussed concerning their effects on the plan setting time, plan modification time, accuracy of task fulfilled and subjective preference. From the collected data and analysis result, we can conclude that:

Pen-based interaction mode is a feasible, usable and efficient way to interact in an architectural field whilst performing the particular layout plan task. This supported out hypothesis. As a common technology the pen is the only widely distributed tool for its mobility, facility and appropriateness for tasks such as drawing and writing, relevant to the experimental tasks.

Voiced based interactions provoked conflicting perceptions. This may be due to the adaptability of voice activated software. As voice recognition is an imperfect system, the result of recognition may vary with person's pronunciation and speech habits. The majority of subjects who attained high scores were those whose voice was easily recognised. Accordingly, their plan setting and plan modification times were shorter than the mean time for their group. Other subjects whose voice recognition results were poor could correct the results by repeating commands. This proved boring to the subjects. However, some did claim that they would repeat the tests and proposed that the results would be different if the voice recognition was better.

Mouse and keyboard would definitely be abandoned. In all of four aspects of the experiment, mouse+keyboard proved the least preferable mode. The mean task perform time was the longest, the mean fulfilled accuracy the poorest and the mean preference rate the lowest. This result matched former research [2][3]. Four subjects reported that mouse+keyboard performed well as they were used to using this medium to enter information quickly. All of them belonged to the professional half of the group, who were familiar with using a computer. All were proficient keyboard users. Their claims coincided with the high error rate of plan setting time, plan modification time and accuracy rate.

6 Conclusion

The results imply that pen evolved interaction can outperform more efficient designs in certain cases and the pen-based interaction mode can be very suitable for geography style systems. The pen device performed well when manipulating objects, and proved very suitable for writing the property setting directly. With voice assistance, if the recognition rate is high enough for the subject to use it fluently repetition be kept to a minimum, pen+voice proved to be the most useful interactive combination mode. However, the degree of usability of the voice assistant needs to be studied further.

The experiment provided clear evidence that the proper use of modality can improve the efficiency and intuition of design system. We recommend that more attention be paid to location and modification technology based on the pen for geography mapping systems. These results suggest that we may need to design a system that employs the pen as the major modality device, allowing the user to freely perform tasks with a pen.

References

1. Guan Z., Wang H., Dai G., (1999), Agent_Based Multimodal Scheduling and integrating, International conference on CAD/CG 99
2. Ren X., Moriya S., The Effect of Target Size, Pen-Movement-Distance and Pen-Movement-Direction on Target-Selection Strategies for a Pen-based system, Workshop on Computer in Beijing, pp247-254
3. Haru Ando, Hideaki Kikuchi, and Nobuo Hataoka, (1995), Agent-typed Multimodal Interface Using Speech, Pointing Gestures and CG, Symbiosis of Human and Artifact, pp.29-34.
4. Gale L.Martin, (1989) The utility of speech input in user-computer interfaces, International Journal of Man-Machine Studies, 1989, no. 30 , pp.355-375.
5. LucJULIA and Adam CHEYER, A Multimodal Computer-augmented Interface for Distributed Applications, Symbiosis of Human and Artifact,1995, Elsevier Science B.V., pp.237-240.
6. Steve, Whittaker. Patrick, Hyland. & Myrtle , Wiley .Flochat: Handwritten Notes Provide Access to Recorded Conversations, Human Factors in Computing Systems , 1994, April 24-28
7. Zhang Gao, Li Maozhen, Dai Guozhong, Study & Application of Distributed Multimodal User Interface, cscwid'97, pp255-262
8. Zhang Gao, Guan Zhiwei, Dai Guozhong, A comparison of Four Interaction Modes for CAD system, APCHI'99, July 15-17, 1998
9. J.J.Mariani, Speech in the Context of Human-machine communication,ISSN-93, 1993.Nov , pp 91-94
10. Damper, R. I. &Wood, S. D., Speech versus keying in command and control applications, International Journal of Human-Computer Studies, 1995, No.42, pp.289-305.
11. Oviatt Sharon, Ten Myths of Multimodal Interaction, Communications of the ACM, 1999, Vol.42, No.11, pp74-81

Real-World Graphical User Interfaces

Toshiyuki Masui[1] and Itiro Siio[2]

[1] Sony Computer Science Laboratories, Inc.
3-14-13 Higashi-Gotanda, Shinagawa, Tokyo 141-0022, Japan
masui@acm.org
http://www.csl.sony.co.jp/person/masui.html
[2] Faculty of Engineering, Tamagawa University
6-1-1 Tamagawa-gakuen, Machida, Tokyo 194-8610, Japan
siio@acm.org
http://www.edp.eng.tamagawa.ac.jp/~siio/indexe.html

Abstract. Although the age of information appliances is getting close, current remote control devices are too awkward, and we cannot control sophisticated equipments without using graphical computer terminals. We propose a new interaction technique called the *Real-world GUI*, where users can control real-world appliances just like performing GUI operations on graphical computer terminals, using a new input device called the *FieldMouse*. FieldMouse is a device which consists of an ID recognizer and a motion sensing device. Using a FieldMouse, various GUI tools like buttons, menus, sliders, and others can be used on any surface and objects, just like using a mouse on a desktop computer. Users can control or program various information appliances as easily as performing GUI operations on graphical computer terminals.

1 Introduction

People expect that more and more computers and information appliances are going to be used hidden in the background of our households [8]. In such an environment, all the audio devices, VCRs and computers will disappear from our living rooms, leaving more space for our life. This sounds like a promising future, but current limitations of remote controllers and input devices seem to prevent us from achieving this goal. Many of the control panels of current appliances are difficult to use, and most of the wireless remote controllers are filled with many obscure buttons, hard to find, and easily lost. People these days usually have to use many remote controllers, and it is hard to remember the mappings between buttons and their functions.

As appliances become invisible, controlling them may become more difficult. If wires are not visible, people may not be able to know easily how to send a video signal from a VCR to a screen. If all the VCRs are connected to a single network cable, people may have to give a name to each of them to distinguish them, just like we are giving names to network-connected computers and printers. If all the music CDs are stored in a hidden server, people may have problems remembering the name of a music and cannot retrieve it from the server. Without appropriate control devices, sophisticated information appliances and computers would be almost useless.

Although current personal computers are still not very easy to use, the interaction environment is much better on computer desktops than doing jobs with remote controllers, owing to the improvements of various sophisticated graphical user interface (GUI) techniques. Icons are useful for remembering data and functions, and they can be copied and put to anywhere we need. Menus are useful for structuring hierarchical data and hiding unnecessary elements. Drag-and-drop is useful for specifying the flow of data without using symbols. Scroll bars and zooming interfaces are useful for handling large data. We cannot use these GUI techniques with remote controllers, and using many remote controllers is like using a computer with all its menu opened and spread on the desktop.

If techniques used in graphical user interface were available for handling VCRs and information appliances, and if GUI tools were available anywhere, people could control them much more easily. People can use a menu to specify the direction of a signal, use a scroll bar to select a CD, etc. We believe that various interface techniques invented for computer desktops are also useful for controlling appliances in the real world, so we are investigating hardware/software techniques to enable Real-World Graphical User Interfaces (RWGUI).

2 Real-World GUI

To realize RWGUI, we have developed a simple inexpensive control device called the *FieldMouse* that enables us to perform RWGUI without using computer screens or special sensing devices, which are often required for interaction in the real world. Using a FieldMouse for RWGUI, many of the problems of remote control devices are solved.

2.1 FieldMouse

A FieldMouse is a combination of an ID detection device and a motion detection device. The first device can be a barcode reader, RFID tag reader, etc., and the second device can be a mouse, a gyroscope, an accelerometer, etc. With the combination of these devices, various real-world interactions become possible [11].

We have been developing various combinations of the devices. Figure 1 (FieldMouse#1) is a pen-type FieldMouse which consists of a barcode scanner and a pen-mouse. Figure 2 (FieldMouse#2) is a combination of a pen-type barcode scanner and a mouse with a gyroscope.

Figure 3 (FieldMouse#3) is a combination of a PDA, a laser scanner, and a tilt sensor. FieldMouse#3 is constructed based on Symbol Technology's PDA SPT1500[1], which is a combination of a small laser barcode module and 3Com's PalmIII PDA. At the back of the print board of SPT1500, we put a tilt sensor chip ADXL202 by Analog Devices[2] and connected it to one of the unused pins

---
[1] http://www.symbol.com/palm/
[2] http://products.analog.com/products/info.asp?product=ADXL202

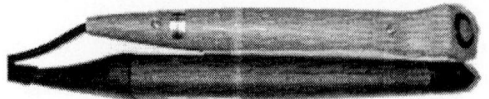

Fig. 1. FieldMouse#1: Combination of a barcode reader and a pen-mouse.

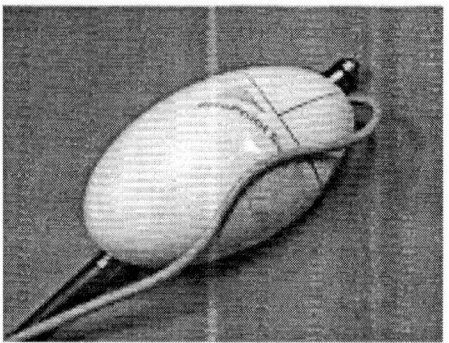

Fig. 2. FieldMouse#2: Combination of a barcode reader and a gyro-mouse.

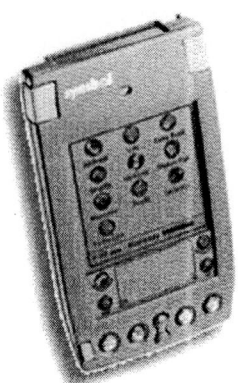

Fig. 3. FieldMouse#3: PalmIII PDA including a laser scanner and a tilt sensor inside.

of the CPU[3], so that SPT1500 can detect its angle relative to the horizon. ADXL202 can detect 2 tilt directions, so the CPU on FieldMouse#3 can tell how much it is tilted from its horizontal position.

---

[3] This technique and schematics are described in this page:
http://www.ibr.cs.tu-bs.de/~harbaum/pilot/adxl202.html

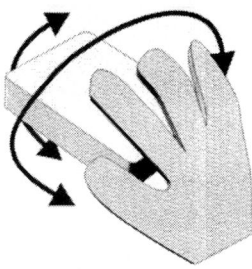

Fig. 4. Tilt detection using FieldMouse#3.

Table 1. Comparison of using a mouse and using a FieldMouse for selecting a menu item.

Using a FieldMouse in the real world	Using a mouse in a computer display
Move the FieldMouse to a barcode	Move the mouse cursor to the menu title
Click a button to initiate recognition	Click the mouse button
Wait until the barcode is recognized	
Move the FieldMouse from the barcode	Drag the mouse cursor
Release the button	Release the mouse button

2.2 Using FieldMouse for RWGUI

A FieldMouse can use the barcode reader to tell what and where it is pointing at, and measure the relative movement of the device after detecting the barcode. Fortunately, many of the GUI widgets are based on point-and-drag operations and require only these information for interaction, and they can easily be simulated by the FieldMouse. For example, a barcode symbol can be used like a pulldown menu, by using the amount of the movement for selecting items. If the system interprets the amount of the relative movement as an analog value, it works just like a slider or a scroll bar.

RWGUI operations with a FieldMouse can be very close to the GUI operations using a mouse. Table 1 shows the correspondence between using a mouse and using a FieldMouse when manipulating a menu. To use a menu or a slider, a user first moves the FieldMouse to a barcode, clicks a button to initiate the scanner, waits until the barcode is recognized, moves the FieldMouse and releases the button. Since barcodes are usually recognized instantly, there is almost no time lag in the recognition step, and users feels little differences between using a mouse in a computer display and using a FieldMouse for using a menu or a slider in the real world.

Barcodes have been used for many years in industries, and small, reliable, and inexpensive barcode readers are widely available. Mouse and motion sensing devices are also widely available, so FieldMouse can be very easily constructed.

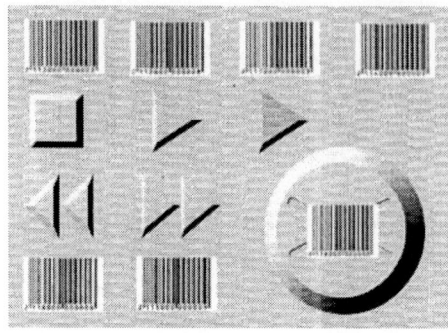

Fig. 5. A VCR control panel.

3 Examples

With the technique shown in the previous section, we can use a variety of GUI widgets everywhere, just by putting barcodes on objects. We can put volume control widgets on TVs, speakers, and telephones. We can print barcodes on a paper card for selecting music and controlling the sound volume. All the remote controllers can be replaced by papers with barcodes, and we no longer have to worry about managing remote controllers as long as a FieldMouse is available. In this section, we show various examples of using a FieldMouse for RWGUI.

Buttons Any barcode symbol can be used as a GUI button, just by mapping the codes to different functions. Figure 5 shows an example of mapping VCR control buttons to barcode symbols printed on paper.

Although this is one of the most conventional usage of barcodes and this does not seem to be much different from using a control panel of a VCR, this method has an advantage, because the buttons can be printed or copied and pasted on anywhere, and users do not have to worry about the correspondence between remote controllers and appliances. Using papers like Figure 5, users don't have to suffer from the problems of having many remote controllers and worry about losing them. Users can lay out buttons as they like, or put them on anywhere the function is needed. The controlled device does not have to be a real VCR; it can be a home video server, streaming video from the network, etc., but the interface can be the same.

Sliders and Rotators Using the FieldMouse, any barcode can be used as a scrollbar or a slider. By scanning a barcode and twisting the FieldMouse#3, the system can use the tilted angle for controlling the volume of an audio amplifier.

Figure 6 is an example of a RWGUI symbol for controlling the sound volume. The shape of the knob does not mean anything to the system, but like graphical symbols used in GUI, it helps the user understand that the barcode represents a RWGUI widgets for rotation.

Just like the RWGUI buttons, users can put the symbol anywhere they want. It can be pasted on a telephone, or it can be pasted on speakers to enable "direct

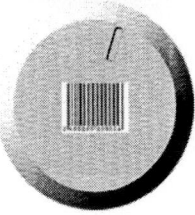

Fig. 6. A RWGUI symbol for controlling the volume.

Fig. 7. Controlling the volume at the speaker.

Fig. 8. A CD-Card.

manipulation". Even when there are multiple speakers, users can control each of them without confusion. Using conventional control panels and remote controllers, it is often hard to remember which button corresponds to each speaker.

Menus Menus can be implemented in the same manner. Since FieldMouse#3 can detect the rotation of the device after detecting the barcode, pie-menu like shown in the lower-right corner of Figure 8 can be used.

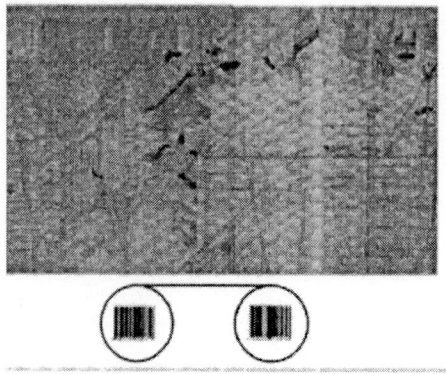

Fig. 9. A scroller panel.

Fig. 10. Using the scroll panel to browse a long scroll.

Using the volume control widget and the music selection widget, a paper card like Figure 8 can be used to select music instead of using many barcodes for all the songs.

Scrollers Figure 9 shows an example of a scroller widget icon for FieldMouse. With the drawing around the icon, users can easily tell in which direction they should tilt the FieldMouse. In Figure 10, a user is using the card and browsing a very long scroll, by tilting the FieldMouse left and right.

Drag-and-Drop Drag-and-Drop can be performed if barcodes are printed both on the source and on the destination. In most drag-and-drop operations used in the GUI systems, users have to select the data object first and drag it to the destination. Using the FieldMouse, users can tell the system which is the destination and which is the source, by tilting gestures or by the moving direction. For example, using a symbol like Figure 11, users can tell VCR1 that data should be sent to it by tilting the FieldMouse#3 downwards, or tell VCR1 that it is the source of the data by tilting the FieldMouse#3 upwards.

Fig. 11. An icon for specifying the signal direction.

Fig. 12. A zooming icon.

Fig. 13. Searching music with zooming interface.

Zooming Using a FieldMouse for zooming user interface is also possible. Zooming user interface (ZUI) is a new set of GUI paradigm suitable for handling huge amount of data [3]. Rotation of FieldMouse#3 after detecting a barcode like shown in Figure 12 can be used for controlling the zooming factor.

Figure 13 shows how a user can use the FieldMouse#3 to find a song from a huge MP3 database. The user can scroll the long list by tilting FieldMouse#3 up an down, and control the zooming factor by twisting it left and right, using the zooming mechanism described in [6].

Fig. 14. A programming panel.

Fig. 15. Time panel.

Authoring Using a FieldMouse, users can pick up data from any barcode symbol in the world. They can go to grocery stores and pick up UPC/EAN data or go to book stores and pick up ISBN data of interesting books. By interpreting an ordinary ISBN code as a menu, users can give additional information to the data. Using the FieldMouse, users can intuitively pick up data from any barcode symbol and give it to other barcode symbols. This means that programming or authoring can also be performed intuitively.

Programming a VCR has long been believed to be a complicated task for ordinary people. On the other hand, everybody can easily set the wakeup time on a clock. The difference between these systems is that setting the wakeup time is much more concrete and direct than programming a VCR. Using a FieldMouse and appropriate barcode symbols, programming a VCR and other information appliances can become much more direct and easier. Figure 14 shows an example panel for programming VCRs and other appliances. Users can pick up the condition part directly from other barcode symbols and drop it to the programming panel. For example, a user can pick up a time from the time panel shown in Figure 15 using the pick-up gesture, and give it to the "if" part. And the user can pick up the execution part from the VCR control panel shown in Figure 5 and give it to the "then" part.

Fig. 16. Examples of the ID card.

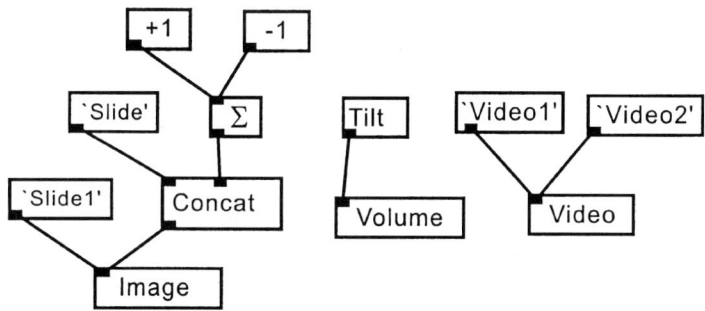

Fig. 17. A real-world program for slide presentation.

4 Real-World Programming

Just like visual languages and 2D drawing tools are suitable for creating GUI programs, using RWGUI is suitable for creating RWGUI programs. Using the FieldMouse and RWGUI tools described in the previous section, simple RWGUI programs can be created without using computer terminals. Conventional techniques used in various visual programming languages can be used for general programming activities in the real world, which we call *Real-World Programming*(RWP) [7].

Figure 16 shows the "ID cards" which represent programming elements used in our example RWP system. By drawing virtual lines between elements like drawing lines in data-flow visual languages, RWGUI programs can easily be created only by using the FieldMouse.

Figure 17 shows an example real-world program for slide presentation. In this program, when a user scans the barcode printed on the "+1" card, the value is accumulated and serial slide number is generated. The number is then concatenated with a string "slide", and the actual name of the slide file (e.g. "slide5") is generated and sent to the display module. The whole program cam be programmed only using the FieldMouse and ID cards.

5 Related Work

Many researchers have been trying to integrate the environment in the computer and the environment in the real world, and use real-world objects as GUI elements. Wellner's DigitalDesk [14] is an early example of this direction, and many systems based on similar ideas have been proposed [2][10]. In these systems, projectors are used to display computer-generated images on the desk or on the wall, and position sensing devices and cameras are used to get users' actions. Although this approach works well in a stable environment like a meeting room, the system can be used only in the fully-equipped room, and it is doubtful whether using many equipments just for mixing the environment is justified.

Some people are taking different approaches and trying to embed many small computers in the real world. This approach, called Ubiquitous Computing [13], is also promising, but it must still take long until everywhere is equipped with small computers.

Printed barcodes have long been widely used to identify objects, and various approaches have been investigated to use barcodes for augmented-reality applications. For example, Johnson proposed using a special 2D barcode for exchanging data between computers and printed papers [5]. Recently, RFID tags are becoming cheaper and popular, and methods for using them for linking real-world objects and computer is also proposed [12]. Using Arai's PaperLink system [1], any printed text can be used as a link or a command, by using a small camera for OCR. These approaches are promising because only small and inexpensive devices are required to realize real-world interactions, although there are more limitations than using equipped rooms or environments. Our approach is unique in that users can control real-world objects using gestures that are almost identical to GUI operations in computer display terminals.

Pick-and-Drop [9] is a system for exchanging data between different computers or between paper and computer, by a pick-up operation on a screen or on paper followed by a dropping operation on a computer screen. In this system, both the source and the destination computer should recognize the position of the electromagnetic pen, and the pick-up operation is not intuitive enough. Using a FieldMouse, special input devices are not required and intuitive paper icons for picking up and dropping data can be used for the same task.

6 Discussions

6.1 Evaluation

We have been using various versions of the FieldMouse only in the laboratories and we have not tested them in real households yet. However, one of the authors has hundreds of MP3 music data in his computer and using the FieldMouse for selecting it and controlling the volume in his office.

The impression of using it is quite promising. When a user want to control the volume using a conventional MP3 player program on a desktop computer, it usually takes several steps until being able to control the volume. Using the FieldMouse, controlling volume is as easy as having an amplifier next to the computer and control the volume manually. Based on this experience, one of the authors is planning to set up a MP3 server in his home and put all the CDs and audio cassettes hidden in a closet.

6.2 Interaction Feedbacks

Unlike GUI operations on computer displays, printed barcodes do not change when users move the FieldMouse after recognizing the barcodes, and visual feedback is not shown to users. This is clearly an disadvantage, but this is not a serious problem, since the system can give various feedbacks to the user in different ways. For example, when controlling the sound volume, audio feedback is given back to the users and visual feedback is not necessary. Giving audio feedbacks to other operations like selecting a pie menu is also usually sufficient as feedbacks to users.

6.3 Using Invisible Tags

We are currently using printed barcodes for RWGUI, and printing barcodes everywhere would be not aesthetically pleasant for most users. However, various other invisible ID tags like RFID tags and invisible printed barcodes (with special ink) can be used for other types of FieldMouse, and we are planning to investigate on using other types of ID tags than printed barcodes.

6.4 Idioms for RWGUI

Some of the symbols and gestures introduced in this paper are new to conventional GUI users, since RWGUI is a new interface paradigm. Before people got used to graphical user interface, many of the symbols currently popular on computers meant nothing to them. However, people these days are having no trouble clicking the "X" icon to close a window and using menus to select an item from an item list. These symbols and interaction methods are like "idioms", and good idioms are easy to remember and hard to forget [4]. Most of the current GUI elements like buttons and menu titles represent good idioms, since they have survived the selection step in the history of evolution. Currently there is no idiom for RWGUI yet, but there surely exist better idioms suitable for FieldMouse, and we hope we could design good idioms for RWGUI, as well as designing good hardware and software.

7 Conclusions

We have introduced a new interaction paradigm called the Real-World GUI (RWGUI), where users can use popular GUI widgets like menus and sliders in the real-world environment, only by using barcode symbols and a simple input device called the FieldMouse. Using our system, most of the appliances can be controlled by popular GUI operations, and all the awkward remote controllers can be thrown away. We are planning to use the system intensively both in the office and in the home, and get more evaluation results.

References

1. ARAI, T., AUST, D., AND HUSON, S. E. PaperLink: A technique for hyperlinking from real paper to electronic content. In *Proceedings of the ACM Conference on Human Factors in Computing Systems (CHI'97)* (April 1997), Addison-Wesley, pp. 327–334.
2. ARAI, T., MACHII, K., KUZUNUKI, S., AND SHOJIMA, H. Interactive desk: a computer-augmented desk which responds to operations on real objects. In *CHI'95 Conference Companion* (May 1995), Addison-Wesley, pp. 141–142.
3. BEDERSON, B. B., HOLLAN, J. D., PERLIN, K., MEYER, J., BACON, D., AND FURNAS, G. Pad++: A zoomable graphical sketchpad for exploring alternate interface physics. *Journal of Visual Languages and Computing 7*, 1 (March 1996), 3–31.
4. COOPER, A. *About Face – The Essentials of User Interface Design.* IDG Books, August 1995. ISBN4-88135-368-3.
5. JOHNSON, W., JELLINEK, H., JR., L. K., RAO, R., AND CARD, S. Bridging the paper and electronic worlds: The paper user interface. In *Proceedings of ACM INTERCHI'93 Conference on Human Factors in Computing Systems (CHI'93)* (April 1993), Addison-Wesley, pp. 507–512.
6. MASUI, T. LensBar - visualization for browsing and filtering large lists of data. In *Proceedings of IEEE Symposium on Information Visualization (InfoVis'98)* (October 1998), pp. 113–120.
7. MASUI, T. Real-world programming. In *Designing Augmented Reality Environments (DARE2000) Proceedings* (April 200), pp. 115–120.
8. NORMAN, D. A. *The Invisible Computer: Why Good Products Can Fail, the Personal Computer Is So Complex, and Information Appliances Are the Solution.* The MIT Press, 1998.
9. REKIMOTO, J. Pick-and-Drop: A direct manipulation technique for multiple computer environments. In *Proceedings of the ACM Symposium on User Interface Software and Technology (UIST'97)* (November 1997), ACM Press, pp. 31–39.
10. REKIMOTO, J., AND SAITOH, M. Augmented surfaces: a spatially continuous work space for hybrid computing environments. In *Proceedings of the ACM Conference on Human Factors in Computing Systems (CHI'99)* (May 1999), Addison-Wesley, pp. 378–385.
11. SIIO, I., MASUI, T., AND FUKUCHI, K. Real-world interaction using the FieldMouse. In *Proceedings of the ACM Symposium on User Interface Software and Technology (UIST'99)* (November 1999), ACM Press, p. to appear.
12. WANT, R., FISHKIN, K. P., GUJAR, A., AND HARRISON, B. L. Bridging physical and virtual worlds with electronic tags. In *Proceedings of the ACM Conference on Human Factors in Computing Systems (CHI'99)* (May 1999), Addison-Wesley, pp. 370–377.
13. WEISER, M. Some computer science issues in ubiquitous computing. *Communications of the ACM 36*, 7 (July 1993), 75–84.
14. WELLNER, P. Interacting with paper on the DigitalDesk. *Communications of the ACM 36*, 7 (July 1993), 87–96.

Lessons Learned from the Design of a Mobile Multimedia System in the MOBY DICK Project

Gerard J.M. Smit and Paul J.M. Havinga

University of Twente, department of Computer Science, Enschede, the Netherlands {smit, havinga}@cs.utwente.nl

Abstract Recent advances in wireless networking technology and the exponential development of semiconductor technology have engendered a new paradigm of computing, called *personal mobile computing*. This offers a vision of the future with a much richer and more exciting set of architecture research challenges than extrapolations of the current desktop architectures. In particular, these devices will have limited battery resources, will handle diverse data types, and will operate in environments that are insecure, dynamic and which vary significantly in time and location. The research performed in the MOBY DICK project is about designing such a mobile multimedia system. This paper discusses the approach made in the MOBY DICK project to solve some of these problems, discusses its contributions, and accesses what was learned from the project.

1 Personal Mobile Computing

Advances in technology enable portable computers to be equipped with wireless interfaces, allowing networked communication even while on the move. Whereas today's notebook computers and personal digital assistants (PDAs) are self contained, tomorrow's networked mobile computers are part of a greater computing infrastructure.

Two trends – multimedia applications and mobile computing – will lead to a new application domain and market in the near future. *Personal mobile computing* (often also referred to as *ubiquitous computing* [16]) will play a significant role in driving technology in the next decade. In this paradigm, the basic personal computing and communication device will be an integrated, battery-operated device, small enough to carry along all the time. This device will be used as a replacement of many items the modern human-being carries around. It will incorporate various functions like a pager, cellular phone, laptop computer, diary, digital camera, video game, calculator and remote control. An important issue will be the user interface: the interaction with its owner. The device will support multimedia tasks like speech recognition, video and audio.

Wireless networking greatly enhances the usability of a personal computing device. It provides mobile users with versatile communication, and permits continuous access to services and resources of the land-based network. A wireless infrastructure capable of supporting packet data and multimedia services in addition to voice will bootstrap on the success of the Internet, and in turn drive novel networked applications and services.

However, the technological challenges to establishing this paradigm of personal mobile computing are non-trivial. In particular, these devices have limited battery resources, will handle diverse data types, and will operate in environments that are insecure, unplanned, and show different characteristics in time.

Five years ago, in 1995, we started the MOBY DICK project, whose main focus was on the design of such a novel and versatile machine [12]. The MOBY DICK project started as a joint European project (Esprit Long Term Research 20422) to develop and define the architecture of a new generation of mobile handheld computers. The design challenges have been primarily in the creation of a single architecture that allows the integration of security functions (e.g. payment), externally offered services (e.g. airline ticket reservation), personality (i.e. these devices know what their owners want), and communication (mobile internet terminal). After one year, the research themes focussed on: systems architecture of mobile computers, reconfigurable computing, energy efficient multimedia communication, and QoS over wireless access networks.

In the next section we will describe the problems to be solved when designing an architecture for such a *mobile multimedia system*. In Section 3 we describe our contribution and approach to solve some of these problems, followed by a brief introduction to current systems and research on mobile multimedia devices in Section 4. Then in Section 5 we present the main lessons that we have leaned. We conclude in Section 6 and present our vision of future research.

2 Problem Statement

The main focus of the MOBY DICK project has been on those issues pertinent to the system design level, i.e. the area of the hardware system-designer and systems programming-designer. We did not delve into the lower level details of the VLSI realisation of the mobile system itself, nor into the higher levels of the operating system and applications.

2.1 System Architecture

Today, the choice of wireless devices is largely limited to simple wireless phones on the one hand, to complex and bulky laptops with wireless communication capability on the other. While these devices serve their purposes, they are neither the most integrated nor the most general: their functionality is often limited, they can operate for just a short time, and they are incapable of fully exploiting the emerging integrated wireless networks. Even while current devices have the ability to communicate and process data, they are and by large primarily either data processing devices *or* communication devices. Simply shrinking the processing devices and communication devices, and packaging them together does not alleviate the architectural bottlenecks of integrated mobile multimedia devices. The real challenge is to design a device where data processing and communication share equal importance.

Multimedia functionality is a driving force for many research challenges. For example, due to the size constraints on a portable computer, the user interface must be small. This is a main reason that pens have become the standard input devices for PDAs. The shortage of area on a mobile device can cause us to trade buttons in favour of recognising the user's intention from analog input devices such as handwriting, gesture [2] and voice. Speech generation and recognition seem an ideal user interface since they require no surface area and allow hands-free and eye-free operation. However, general-purpose speech input and output places substantial storage and processing demands on a mobile device. Other research investigates the use of head-mounted virtual reality displays Main problems to be solved are the required processing power or communication bandwidth and the required weight and size (i.e. a small and light headgear).

A key challenge of mobile computing is that many attributes of the environment vary dynamically. Mobile devices face many different types of variability in their environment. Therefore, they need to be able to operate in environments that can change drastically in short term as well as long term in available resources and available services. Some short-term variations can be handled by adaptive communication protocols that vary their parameters according to the current condition. Other, more long-term variations generally require a much larger degree of adaptation. Merely algorithmic adaptations are not sufficient, but rather an entirely new set of protocols and/or algorithms may be required. For example, mobile users may encounter a complete different wireless communication infrastructure when walking from their office to the street. They might require another air interface, other network protocols, and so forth. A possible solution is to have a mobile device with a reconfigurable architecture so that it can adapt its operation to the current environment and operating condition.

Reconfigurability also has another more economic motivation: it will be important to have a fast track from sparkling ideas to the final design. If the design process takes too long, the return on investment will be less. It would further be desirable for a wireless terminal to have architectural reconfigurability whereby its capabilities may be modified by downloading new functions from network servers. Such reconfigurability would also help in field upgrading as new communication protocols or standards are deployed, and in implementing bug fixes [9]. One of the key issues in the design of portable multimedia systems is to find a good balance between flexibility and high-processing power on one side, and area and energy-efficiency of the implementation on the other side.

2.2 Wireless Communication

Mobile computers require wireless network access, although sometimes they may physically attach to the network for a better or cheaper connection. Wireless communication is much more difficult to achieve than wired communication because the surrounding environment interacts with the signal, blocking signal paths and introducing noise and echoes. As a result wireless connections have a lower quality than wired connections: lower bandwidth, less connection stability, higher error rates, and, moreover, with a highly varying quality. These factors can in turn increase communication latency due to retransmissions, can give largely varying throughput, and incur a high energy consumption. Three key problems in networked wireless multimedia systems are 1) the need to maintain a minimum quality of service (throughput, delay, bit error rate, etc) over time-varying channels, 2) to operate with limited energy resources, and 3) to operate in a heterogeneous environment.

2.3 Energy Efficiency

Although the subject of low-power consumption of integrated circuits (ICs) is drawing considerable attention ("cool chips are hot"), this interest is only of recent date. There are several motivations for energy-efficient design. Perhaps the most visible driving source is the success and growth of the portable consumer electronic market. Today's desktop computers are not intended to be carried, so their design is liberal in their use of space, weight, energy consumption, noise, cabling, and heat dissipation. In contrast, the designer of a hand-held mobile computer should strive for the properties of a wristwatch: light, small, durable and long battery life.

Batteries are the largest single source of weight in a portable computer. Minimising energy consumption can improve portability by reducing battery weight and lengthening the life of a charge. Moreover, the functionality of the mobile computer is limited by the required energy consumption for communication and computation. Unfortunately, the rate at which battery performance improves (in terms of available energy per unit size or weight) is fairly slow, despite the great interest generated by the booming wireless business. Aside from major breakthroughs it is doubtful that significant reduction of battery size and weight can be expected in the near future. It has been generally expected that the battery technology alone will not solve the low-power problem. It therefore makes sense to look for alternative strategies for energy savings and energy management. The emerge of various applications and the need to support them in a wireless setting may open new possibilities for energy-saving strategies.

The way out is *energy efficiency:* doing more work with the same amount of energy. Traditionally, energy efficiency has been focussed on low-power techniques for VLSI design. However, the key to energy efficiency in future mobile multimedia devices will be at the higher levels: energy-efficient system architectures, energy-efficient communication protocols, energy-cognisant operating system and applications, and a well designed partitioning of functions between wireless device and services on the network.

A major challenge in achieving this will be that many attributes of the system environment can vary drastically by several orders of magnitude over the short and long term. Key to these issues will be *adaptability*. Research has shown that continually adapting the system and protocols can significantly improve the energy efficiency while maintaining a satisfactory level of performance [11]. Adapting to the variability is the shared responsibility of many layers in the system design of the mobile device, including the applications.

3   Contributions of the MOBY DICK Project

The research performed in the MOBY DICK project addressed the design of an architecture for a mobile multimedia handheld computer that can cope with the requirements and difficulties mentioned above. The main focus has been on the specification of a system architecture supporting the required functions for future handheld devices.

The approach made in our research was to study *practical* solutions to the inherent problems of handheld multimedia terminals. In this field too often, system architectures, protocols, and applications are developed with a theoretical background only and with a limited scope covering one horizontal layer in a system. In contrast, this research is characterised by a strategy that traverses *vertically* through various layers of the system architecture of a multimedia hand-held system and is driven by energy-efficient design considerations.

While low-level circuit and logic techniques have been well established for improving energy efficiency, they do not hold promise for much additional gain. As the issue of energy efficiency becomes even more pervasive, the battle to use the bare minimum of energy will be fought on multiple fronts: semiconductor technology, circuit design, design automation tools, system architecture, operating system, and application design. The key to energy efficiency in future mobile systems will be the higher layers of the mobile system, its system architecture, its operating system, and indeed the entire network, with energy efficiency in mind.

In its most abstract form, a networked computer system has two sources of energy drain required for operation:

- *Communication*, due to energy spent by the wireless interface and due to the internal traffic between various parts of the system, and
- *Computation*, due to processing for applications, the operating system, and tasks required during communication.

Minimising energy consumption is a task that will require minimising the contributions of communication *and* computation, making the appropriate trade-offs between the two [9]. For example, reducing the amount of transmitted data may be beneficial. On the other hand, the computation cost (e.g. to compress the data being sent) might be high, and in the extreme it might be better to just send the raw data.

Because communication has the foremost influence on both Quality of Service and energy consumption, we concentrated in the MOBY DICK project on the *communication channels* rather than the computational elements. The communication channels contribute a significant amount of the total energy consumption of a typical mobile system. As semiconductor technology improves, computation gets cheaper, whereas communication has much less advantage of the smaller feature size. Therefore, communication relatively will get even more expensive. This property also holds for multimedia applications, even though these applications typically require a significant computational effort as well. For a significant part this is due to the limitations of most current hardware and operating systems that are unable to differentiate between various traffic streams.

Specific contributions of our research are the design of an energy-efficient architecture for mobile multimedia systems and a reconfigurable connection switch, as well as the design of crucial wireless network functions (i.e. MAC protocol, adaptable network interface, and a model for adaptable error-correction) that are energy efficient and can support multimedia traffic [3,4,5,6].

3.1 System Architecture

The traditional architecture of a mobile is centered around a general-purpose processor with local memory and a shared-bus that connects peripherals to the CPU. However, in such an architecture several problem areas can be identified. Main problem areas are energy consumption, performance, and Quality of Service guarantees.

A large fraction of system time and power budget in a shared bus architecture is devoted to bus transactions. Busses are significant sources of power dissipation due to high switching activities and large capacitance. This architecture requires frequent traversal of multimedia streams over the bus and through the layers of the operating system software, and possibly also through to a network protocol stack which is composed of transport, network, link and medium access (MAC), and physical layer protocols [14].

Current systems based on a shared bus architecture are able to deliver the required performance for various multimedia applications not only by using the rapid advance in technology, but also by careful design and use of the interface modules. The process to achieve this requires a huge amount of effort of both the hardware designer of the I/O interfaces and the system designer. There are many subtle device issues that can influence the overall I/O performance of a system. Minor changes in the hardware or software configuration can have severe consequences for the performance of the system. The reason for these problems is often the interconnect and the interconnection protocols. Since a shared bus cannot give QoS guarantees, a single device or application can reduce the throughput that is available for all devices.

By designing a *connection-centric* architecture that moves processing power closer to the data stream, it is possible to solve these problems. The whole system is based on connections between modules. Each connection is associated with a certain QoS. This approach is especially well suited for continuous media data (e.g. audio, video, etc.), where the processing is actually of a very specialised nature (e.g. signal processing, compression, encryption, etc.) and needs to be carried out in real-time. In contrast to memory-centric (or CPU-centric) systems, a connection-centric system is decomposed out of application-specific modules. In such a system the data traffic is reduced, mainly because unnecessary data copies are removed. For example, in a system where a stream of video data is to be displayed on a screen, the data can be copied directly to the screen memory, without going through the main processor. The CPU is thus moved out of the data flow datapath, although it still participates in the control flow. The role of the CPU is reduced to a controller that initialises the system and handles complex protocol processing that are most easily implemented in software.

The approach used in our research [3] to achieve a system as described above is to have autonomous, reconfigurable modules such as network, video and audio devices, interconnected by a switch rather than by a bus, and to offload as much as work as possible from the CPU to modules placed in the data streams. Thus, communication between components is not broadcast over a bus but delivered exactly where it is needed, work is carried out where the data passes through, bypassing the memory. To limit the communication overhead and the required buffering, the granularity of the tasks on the devices is rather coarse, and the application is partitioned in large blocks.

The programmability of each module is more fine-grained and is controlled by the individual autonomous module.

The interconnect of the architecture is based on a reconfigurable communication network switch, called *Octopus*, which interconnects a general-purpose processor, (multimedia) devices, and a wireless network interface. Conceptually, the architecture is analogous to a self-routing packet switch. The connection-oriented approach using fixed sized cells and the asynchronous multiplexing are key factors. This not only eliminates the need to transfer a large number of address bits per access, it also gives the system the possibility to control the QoS of a task down to the communication infrastructure. All connections are identified with a connection identifier, which is used to identify the type of data, and the module destination address. This identifier provides the mechanism to support lightweight protocols that provide data-specific transport services that are associated with a certain QoS. This is an important requirement since in a QoS architecture all system components, hardware as well as software, have to be covered end-to-end along the way from the source to the destination.

3.2 Wireless Communication

Another important aspect in mobile multimedia systems is wireless communication protocols that provide multimedia services to mobile users.

We have shown that energy-awareness must be applied in almost all layers of the network protocol stack. To achieve maximal performance and energy efficiency, *adaptability* is important, as wireless networks are dynamic in nature. Furthermore, if the application layer is provided with feedback on the communication, advantage can be taken from the differences in data streams over the wireless link. To allow this, feedback is needed from many layers: the physical layer provides information on link quality, the medium access layer on effectiveness of its error correction, and the data link layer on buffer usage and error control.

Multimedia applications are characterised by their various media streams. Each stream can have different quality of service requirements. Depending on the service class and QoS of a connection a different policy can be applied by the communication protocol in order to minimise energy consumption. For example, by avoiding error-control overhead for connections that do not need it and by never transmitting stale data, efficiency is improved. This combination of limited bandwidth, high error rates, and delay-sensitive data requires tight integration of all subsystems in the device, including aggressive optimisation of the protocols that suits the intended application. The protocols must be robust in the presence of errors and they must be able to differentiate between classes of data, giving each class the exact service it requires.

The access to the wireless channel is controlled by data link protocols. Many protocols for wireless networks are basically adaptations of protocols used in wired networks, and ignore energy issues. A first step in improving the energy efficiency of the wireless network protocols is to *eliminate useless activity* of the wireless interface. There are various reasons for this useless activity. It has been shown that for typical applications like a web-browser or e-mail, the energy consumed while the interface is 'on' and idle is more than the cost of actually receiving packets. That is because these applications have little demanding traffic needs, and hence the transceiver is *idling* most of the time. Furthermore, in a typical wireless broadcast environment, the receiver has to be powered 'on' at all times to be able to receive messages from the base station, resulting in significant energy consumption. The receiver subsystem typically receives all packets and forwards only the packets destined for this mobile. Another cause is due to the *inactivity threshold*, which is the time before a transceiver will go in the 'off' or 'standby' state after a period of inactivity, which causes the receiver to be in an energy consuming mode needlessly for a significant time. Significant time and energy is further spent by the mobile in switching from transmit to receive modes, and vice-versa.

The next step is to *reduce the amount of data*, which must be pushed through the channel. This goal can be reached in a number of ways. One is to reduce the *overhead of a protocol* which influences the energy requirements due to the amount of 'useless' control data and the required computation for protocol handling. Another step is to avoid *collisions* that typically may occur in broadcast networks. This causes the data to become useless and the energy needed to transport that data to be lost. The high *error rate* that is typical for wireless links is another source of energy consumption for several reasons. First, when the data is not correctly received the energy that was needed to transport and process that data is spoiled. Second, energy is used for error control mechanisms. This includes energy spent in the physical radio transmission process, as well as energy spent in computation, such as signal processing and error control at the transmitter and the receiver. Finally, because in wireless communication the error rate varies dynamically over time and space, a fixed-point error control mechanism that is designed to be able to correct errors that hardly occur, spoils energy and bandwidth. If the application is error-resilient, trying to withstand all possible errors spoils even more energy for needless error control. Reducing the amount of data is also an application-layer issue. For example, the application might change the compression rate or possibly reduce the data resolution. Instead of sending an entire large full-colour image, one can send black-and-white half-size images with lossy compression.

The goals of low energy consumption and the required support for multiple traffic types lead to our communication system that is based on reservation and scheduling strategies [6]. For each connection a different set of parameters concerning scheduling, flow control and error control is applied [5]. The wireless network is composed of several base-stations that each handle a single radio cell possibly covering several mobile stations. The base-station controls access over the wireless channel based on communication requests for connections of the mobiles by dividing bandwidth into transmission slots. The key to providing QoS for these connections and the energy efficiency of the mobiles will be the scheduling algorithm that assigns the bandwidth. The premise is that the base-station has virtually no processing and energy limitations, and will perform actions in courtesy of the mobile. The main principles are: avoid unsuccessful actions by avoiding collisions and by providing provisions for adaptive error control, minimise the number of transitions by scheduling traffic in larger packets, synchronise the mobile and the base-station which allows the mobile to power-on precisely when needed, and migrate as much as possible work to the base-station.

We have implemented a test-bed of the network interface that we can use to experiment with the various techniques and mechanisms for e.g. error control and MAC protocol. It is build with off-the-shelf components (a Xilinx FPGA, a microcontroller, and memory) to allow a short design cycle. Fig. 1 shows a photograph of the network interface implementation.

Fig. 1. Network interface implementation.

We use a WaveLAN modem as the physical layer. Migration of some functionality from the mobile, for example to the base-station, allows reduction of the complexity of mobiles. Added complexity in the base-station or other parts of the fixed network is justified because they can be better equipped and are not battery powered.

4 Related Work

The growing popularity of mobile systems has spawned much interest and research by industry and universities in both computer science and electrical engineering. Most of the current research, however, often tackles just one horizontal layer of the design. Although this research is valuable, and must be applied whenever suitable, we will provide here merely a brief overview of those systems and current research that look into the problem of designing a mobile multimedia device in an integrated fashion.

Currently, there is a broad consensus that the existing mobile devices are by far not capable of supporting the required multimedia functionality. Some reasons are: processing power, energy consumption, communication bandwidth requirements, etc. About the solution to solve this problem there is much less consensus, however. Within the notion of mobile computing, there is considerable latitude regarding the role of the portable device. Is it a terminal or an independent, stand-alone computer? How many purposes shall the device serve? Many different architectural choices are possible, each with a different partitioning of functions between the wireless device and remote servers. These design choices greatly affect the issues mentioned in this paper.

Several architectures have been proposed that address mobile multimedia computing. Only few systems address energy reduction. Systems like the *InfoPad* [15] and

ParcTab [7] are designed to take advantage of high-speed wireless networking to reduce the amount of computation required on the portable. These systems are portable terminals and take advantage of the processing power of remote compute servers. No local computation, except for appropriate coding/decoding of the I/O data, is done at the pad. Such devices are known as *thin clients*, since the client itself does little work. This approach simplifies the design and reduces power consumption for the processing components, but significantly increases the network usage and thus potentially increases energy consumption because the network interface is energy expensive. These systems also rely on the availability of a high bandwidth network connectivity and cannot be used when not connected.

The *Merlin* project of the University of California at Los Angeles (UCLA) [11] is developing mobile computing and wireless communication technologies with the focus on creating a wireless I/O-network subsystem that can be used to create many different types of wireless connected multimedia nodes: handheld computes, wireless cameras, wireless IP phones, etc. The subsystem is composed of a wireless network processor, codecs, and radio to provide all the necessary wireless networking and multimedia processing capabilities. In the architecture of *WAND*, a low-power embeddable module built at UCLA for creating multimedia wireless terminals, the general-purpose processor is moved out of the packet flow data path, and the data streams flow directly between the radio and the speech and image codecs. A full-fledged PC or PDA may be adjunct to WAND, but its presence is optional and, in many wireless terminals unnecessary.

Other research mainly concentrated on specific topics, and did not cover the system architecture of a mobile computer as a whole. There is much research on multimedia processors, hardware accelerators, and heterogeneous multiprocessor architectures mainly targeted for DSP algorithms [e.g. 18,10]. In recent years much research has been done in providing QoS over a wireless link. Access protocols for these systems typically only address network performance metrics such as throughput, bit efficiency, and packet delay. However, thus far, little attention is given to energy conserving protocols, and researchers mainly focuses their effort on energy reduction by circuit design. Very recently there is a growing interest in energy-efficient design, although mainly concentrating on medium access and link-layer energy reduction techniques.

5 Lessons Learned

In the MOBY DICK project the following lessons have been learned:
- *Energy-efficiency is crucial in the architecture of a mobile multimedia system.* The increasing demands for performance and integration of computer systems will be accompanied by increasing levels of energy consumption. The requirement of portability of hand-held multimedia computers and portable devices places severe restrictions on size and energy consumption. Without a significant energy reduction techniques and energy saving architectures, battery life constraints will limit the capabilities of these machines. More extensive and continu-

ous use of network services will only aggravate this problem since communication consumes relatively much energy.
- *Apply a system-wide layer integration/co-operation.* The key to energy efficiency will be achieved in the integrated design of all layers of the system, its system architecture, its operating system, and the entire network. Co-operation or integration of the various layers significantly improves energy efficiency of the system because it reduces wasteful operations and data streams retain a high locality of reference. The art of low-power design used to be a narrow speciality in analog-circuit design. As the issue of energy efficiency becomes even more pervasive, the battle to use the bare minimum of energy will be fought on multiple fronts: semiconductor technology, circuit design, design automation tools, system architecture, operating system, and application design. We have shown that there is a vital relationship between hardware architecture, operating system architecture and applications architecture, where each benefits from the others. In our architecture we have applied several supplementary energy-reduction techniques on all levels of the system. In particular we have looked at the integration of the wireless network in the system. The combination of limited bandwidth, high error rates, and delay-sensitive data requires tight integration of all subsystems in the device, including aggressive optimisation of the protocols to suit the intended application.
- *Use a Quality of Service framework.* We have demonstrated in our research and in particular in the design of the system architecture, the switching network, and the wireless network design, that Quality of Service is not only important to provide an adequate level of service for a user, but can also be used as a tool to achieve an energy-efficient system. Users and applications request a certain QoS level. The system then operates in such a way that it will try to satisfy these requirements, but never gives more quality than required and necessary. As the mobiles must remain usable in a wide variety of environments, they must be flexible enough to accommodate a variety of multimedia services and communication capabilities and adapt to various operating conditions in an (energy) efficient way.
- *Communication is more important and has more influence than computation.* In the MOBY DICK project we concentrated on the communication channels (both internal in the system and the wireless network) rather than the computational elements, since the contribution of communication channels to the costs of the total system is increasing rapidly, and communication has a significant influence on both the energy-efficiency and the Quality of Service. A general theme in our approach was to reduce the amount of communication and avoid 'useless' and inefficient computation, which consequently reduces energy dissipation and increases performance of the system.
- *Focus on the core issues.* Early in the project we had a wide view of problems that we thought were important to solve. Therefore, we started with many topics (like data consistency and security). After one year, we focussed on those items that seemed to be the most compelling and in which we had the most expertise. Therefore, we concentrated on the key issues of energy-efficiency and Quality of Service and took a vertical, system wide, approach with the main emphasis on those issues pertinent to the system design level, i.e. the area of the hardware designer and systems-programming designer. We were not dealing with the lower

level details of VLSI realisation, nor the higher levels of the operating system and applications. We were not concerned in building a low-power system, but merely an *energy-efficient* system. Therefore, the test-bed we have made is designed to evaluate the *energy efficiency* of designs, and is *not* designed to be low power! The actual implementation of the test-bed is therefore primarily designed to be *flexible*, and suitable for doing experiments with various design alternatives. Because of this, the implementation test-bed used various flexible, but certainly not low-power components (i.e. we have used Xilinx FPGAs).

- Build experimental computer systems. Already early in the project we started building parts of the system, not just as a proof of concept, but also because it focussed us to the real problems of a systems design. We have found that this approach was very valuable since this pointed us to some practical problems that we would not have seen when we stopped just after simulation. Also, at the same time, we noticed that some potential problems were not as difficult to solve as expected. While it is certainly easier to quit after the simulation stage, we found that the results at that stage lack reality and are often wrong. This is in particular true for a system wide approach, in which the interaction between different layers plays a significant role. Although our testbed currently consists of various small printed circuit boards containing Field Programmable Gate Arrays (FPGAs), microcontrollers, and memory, the complexity of these designs is low. This low complexity will make it possible to transfer the architecture to a (large) custom IC.

6 Conclusion

Our vision of a personal computing device is even more compelling today than it was in 1995. The trend in wireless terminals has been to shrink a general-purpose desktop PC into a package that can be conveniently carried. Even PDAs have not ventured far from the general-purpose model, neither architectural nor in terms of usage model. Both the notebook and the personal computer generally use the same standard PC operating system such as Windows or Unix, same applications, use the same communication protocols and use the same hardware architecture. The only difference is that portable computers are smaller, have a battery, a wireless interface, and often use low power components.

A key challenge of mobile computing is that many attributes of the environment vary dynamically. Mobile devices face many different types of variability in their environment. Therefore, they need to be able to operate in environments that can change drastically in short term as well as long term in available resources and available services. Merely algorithmic adaptations are not sufficient, but rather an entirely new set of protocols and/or algorithms may be required. For example, mobile users may encounter a complete different wireless communication infrastructure when walking from their office to the street. A possible solution is to have a mobile device with a reconfigurable architecture so that it can adapt its operation to the current environment and operating condition. Adaptability and programmability should be major requirements in the design of the architecture of a mobile computer.

We are entering an era in which each microchip will have billions of transistors. One way to use this opportunity would be to continue advancing our chip architectures and technologies as just more of the same: building microprocessors that are simply complicated versions of the kind built today. However, simply shrinking the data processing terminal and radio modem, attaching them via a bus, and packaging them together does not alleviate the architectural bottlenecks. The real design challenge is to engineer an integrated mobile system where data processing and communication share equal importance and are designed with each other in mind. Integrating current PC or PDA architecture with a communication subsystem, is not the solution. One of the main drawbacks of merely packaging the two is that the energy-inefficient general-purpose CPU, with its heavyweight operating system and shared bus, becomes not only the center of control, but also the center of data flow in the system and a main cause of high energy consumption.

Clearly, there is a need to revise the system architecture of a portable computer if we want to have a machine that can be used conveniently in a wireless environment. A system level integration of the mobile's architecture, operating system, and applications is required. The system should provide a solution with a proper balance between flexibility and efficiency by the use of a hybrid mix of general-purpose and the application-specific approaches.

We, in the academic world, have the luxury of building a machine that demonstrates a vision of a computer system without concern for compatibility. The MOBY DICK project demonstrates the importance of building experimental computer systems. Simulation results do not reduce the perceived risk of new technologies sufficiently for industry to adopt them.

7 Future Work

Although we have come up with solutions to a number of problems in the field of mobile multimedia computing, many others have remained unsolved or received only minor attention. We attempt to give a few suggestions for future research.

Having an energy efficient architecture that is capable to handle adaptability and flexibility in a mobile multimedia environment requires more than just a suitable hardware platform. First of all we need to have an operating system architecture that can deal with the hardware platform and the adaptability and flexibility of its devices. Optimisations across diverse layers and functions, not only at the operating systems level, is crucial. Managing and exploiting this diversity is the key system design problem. A model that encompasses different levels of granularity of the system is essential in the design of an energy management system and in assisting the system designer in making the right decisions in the many trade-offs that can be made in the system design. Finally, to fully exploit the possibilities offered by the reconfigurable hardware, we need to have proper operating system support for reconfigurable computing, so that these components can be reprogrammed adequate when the system or the application can benefit from it.

The lessons learned from the design of the MOBY DICK architecture serve as a first step towards a system-level design of an energy-efficient mobile multimedia computer. Research in these items will be continued in *Chameleon* project [0] that will in particular perform research in reconfigurable computing for these systems.

8 Acknowledgements

We thank all of the many people who contributed to the success of the Moby Dick project. Special thanks go to Gunnar Hartvigsen, Terje Fallmyr, and Tage Stabell-Kulø from the University of Tromsø, Norway; Alberto Bartoli, Gianluca Dini, Luigi Rizzo, and Marco Avvenuti from the University of Pisa, Italy; Sape Mullender, Arne Helme and Ties Bos from the University of Twente.

References

1. Abnous A., Seno K., Ichikawa Y., Wan M., Rabaey J.: "Evaluation of a low-power reconfigurable DSP architecture", *proceedings 5th Reconfigurable Architectures workshop (RAW'98)*, March 30, 1998, Orlando, USA. (URL: http://xputers.informatik.uni-kl.de/RAW/RAW98/adv_prg_RAW98.html)
2. "Rock 'n' Scroll – Button-free Tilt and Gesture Input for Itsy", http://www.research.digital.com/wrl/projects/RocknScroll/RocknScrollOverview.htm.
3. P.J.M. Havinga, "Mobile Multimedia Systems", *Ph.D. thesis University of Twente*, February 2000, ISBN 90-365-1406-1, www.cs.utwente.nl/~havinga/thesis.
4. Havinga P.J.M., Smit G.J.M.: "Octopus: embracing the energy efficiency of handheld multimedia computers", *proceedings fifth annual ACM/IEEE international conference on mobile computing and networking (Mobicom'99)*, pp.77-87, August 1999.
5. Havinga P.J.M.: "Energy efficiency of error correction on wireless systems", *proceedings IEEE Wireless Communications and Networking Conference (WCNC'99)*, September 1999.
6. Havinga P.J.M., Smit G.J.M., Bos M.: "Energy efficient wireless ATM design", *ACM/Baltzer Journal on Mobile Networks and Applications (MONET), Special issue on Wireless Mobile ATM technologies,* Vol. 5, No 2., 2000.
7. Kantarjiev C. et al.: "Experiences with X in a wireless environment", *Mobile and location-independent computing symposium*, Cambridge MA, August 1993.
8. Leijten J.A.J.: "Real-time constrained reconfigurable communication between embedded processors", *Ph.D. thesis, Eindhoven University of Technology*, November 1998.
9. Lettieri P., Srivastava M.B.: "Advances in wireless terminals", *IEEE Personal Communications*, pp. 6-19, February 1999.
10. Mangione-Smith W.H., et al.: "Seeking solutions in configurable computing", *IEEE Computer*, pp. 38-43, December 1997.
11. Sheng S., Chandrakasan A., Brodersen R.W.: "A Portable Multimedia Terminal", *IEEE Communications Magazine*, pp. 64-75, vol. 30, no. 12, Dec., 1992.
12. Smit G.J.M., Havinga P.J.M., et al.: "An overview of the Moby Dick project", *1st Euromicro summer school on mobile computing*, pp. 159-168, Oulu, August 1998; Moby Dick homepage: www.cs.utwente.nl/~havinga/mobydick.html.

13. Smit G.J.M., Martinus Bos, Paul J.M. Havinga, Sape J. Mullender, Jaap Smit: "Chameleon - reconfigurability in hand-held multimedia computers", *proceedings First International Symposium on Handheld and Ubiquitous Computing*, HUC'99, September 1999.
14. Srivastava M.: "Design and optimization of networked wireless information systems", *IEEE VLSI workshop*, April 1998.
15. Truman T.E., Pering T., Doering R., Brodersen R.W.: The InfoPad multimedia terminal: a portable device for wireless information access", *IEEE transactions on computers*, Vol. 47, No. 10, pp. 1073-1087, October 1998.
16. Weiser M.: "Some computer science issues in ubiquitous computing", *Communications of the ACM*, 36(7):75-84, July 1993.

Notable: At the Intersection of Annotations and Handheld Technology

Michelle Baldonado[1], Steve Cousins[1], Jacek Gwizdka[2], and Andreas Paepcke[3]

[1] Xerox PARC, 3333 Coyote Hill Road
Palo Alto, CA 94304 USA
{michelle, cousins}@parc.xerox.com
[2] University of Toronto, 5 King's College Road
Toronto, Ontario M5S 3G8 Canada
jgwizdka@acm.org
[3] Digital Libraries Lab (InfoLab), Stanford University
Stanford, CA 94305 USA
paepcke@db.stanford.edu

Abstract. The Notable annotation system enables users to annotate paper documents using handheld devices in a mobile environment. This paper describes the design issues and solutions that arose in creating Notable, with a particular focus on design challenges at the intersection of annotations and handheld technology. Novel design strategies include separating the annotation writing platform from the document viewing platform, providing search as the method for document selection, offering context-sensitive phrase completion and icon-based graphical pinning for fine-granularity annotation anchoring, and including some support for coordinating group annotation activity.

1 Introduction

The Post-It™ note celebrates its twentieth birthday this year. The ubiquitous yellow sticky squares of paper can be found attached to a variety of objects, from paper documents to computer monitors. Among other reasons, people find that Post-Its™ are useful because they can be attached easily to physical objects (and subsequently removed), because they are small, and because they are highly visible. Yet the notes are not perfect—they can be hard to share with multiple people (photocopies are often problematic because the notes may obscure underlying text), they are difficult to attach to specific locations within documents, and the notes are easy to lose.

Using a Post-It™ note to attach a comment to another object is one example of annotation, an activity that takes many forms [1]. Examples range from highlighting words in a text to writing comments in the margins of a paper to assigning metadata to a literary work. More formally, we define an annotation as follows:

Definition of annotation: An annotation is a commentary on an object that:
- the annotator intends to be perceptually distinguishable from the object itself; and
- the reader interprets as perceptually distinguishable from the object itself.

Our observation that the screen size of the widely available Palm™ handheld device is about the same size as a Post-It™ note was one of the inspirations for creating Notable, a handheld-based system for annotation. We hypothesized that a handheld-based analog to the Post-It™ note would be valuable because it would afford sharing and finding annotations after their initial creation, while keeping intact the desirable size and portability features of the Post-It™. Currently, one of the most popular techniques for sharing handwritten annotations is to rewrite them in another medium (e.g., write comments in the margins of a paper, then summarize those comments in an e-mail message). Our goal was to eliminate the need for this intermediate step. While rewriting can often be of value during a writer's sensemaking process, it requires additional time and effort. Copiers make sharing without rewriting plausible, but few office workers have a personal copier; copiers are typically available in a shared common space rather than in an individual office or cubicle. Furthermore, copiers produce paper documents that must be distributed physically. Scanners and digital cameras offer more streamlined approaches to sharing handwritten comments, but the state-of-the-art of optical character recognition is still not advanced enough to make searching for handwritten comments reliable.

Digital annotation systems (see Sect. 5 for a brief review of annotation systems) have already proven useful for sharing annotations, but they typically require that the user sit at a desktop computer or use a laptop. Although desktop computers and laptops offer increased screen real estate, network capabilities, and processing power in comparison to handheld devices, they fall short of handhelds in portability and startup time. We believe that a small device that is easy to carry and "ready to hand" is likely to be a good fit for mobile work practices.

In this paper, we focus on the design issues and solutions encountered in designing a handheld-based annotation system. We begin with a usage scenario in Sect. 2, which shows how our myriad design decisions come together in a working system. Sect. 3 examines several specific design issues that arise in creating annotations, linking annotations and documents, and viewing and sharing annotations. Sect. 4 gives a brief overview of the Notable system architecture. Sect. 5 relates Notable to previous work. Finally, Sect. 6 summarizes the features of Notable and outlines some possibilities for future work.

2 Scenario

This section describes a scenario that shows how the Notable system might be used in practice. Historically, this scenario was a key element in the Notable design process. The scenario centers around a researcher who needs to review a journal submission. She has the document in paper form, and has also scanned the document into a searchable repository to create a digital identity for the document. Alternatively, she might have the document in digital form already, in which case she is likely to print it out for later reading.

In either case, before the reviewer leaves her office for the day, she uses a desktop application called NoteDesk (Fig. 1) to locate the article's digital handle via a search that specifies salient keywords for the article. Once the handle has been located,

NoteDesk creates a digital surrogate of the document, which contains sufficient information about the document to allow annotations to be attached to specific locations within the article. The surrogate is transferred to the reviewer's handheld device when she synchronizes it with her desktop computer as her last step before heading home.

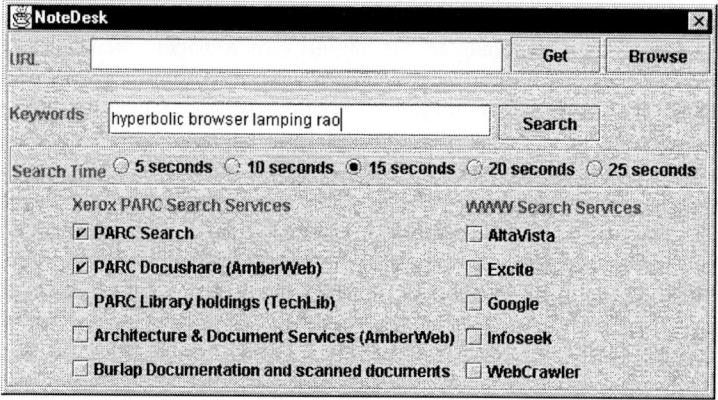

Fig. 1. Using NoteDesk (a desktop application) to search for an object's digital surrogate, which will be downloaded to the user's handheld device at synchronization time—thus enabling annotation

In the evening, she reads the paper copy of the document and makes corresponding digital annotations on her handheld (Fig. 2). For each annotation, she can specify whether it applies to the entire document (Option 1), to a particular region on a page (Option 2), or to a specific phrase in the document (Option 3). For region-level anchoring, she needs only to specify the page number and indicate on a graphical icon where the annotation belongs. For phrase-level anchoring, she uses context-sensitive phrase completion to identify the specific phrase with minimal text entry. Back at the office the next day, the annotations she has made are transmitted to a shared document repository (at synchronization time), and linked to the document. From her desktop computer, she can now access her annotations for inclusion in her final review of the article. For example, she can cut-and-paste annotations into her word processor.

In the design process for Notable, we have explored several variants on this scenario, including annotating for personal sensemaking and note taking on specific document types (e.g. calendars, agendas, etc.). We have also explored the possibility of annotating objects other than paper-based documents, such as museum objects and devices that require regular maintenance (e.g. office machines). More abstractly, our approach generalizes to almost any scenario in which a user needs to assign metadata to a physical object (with a digital surrogate) in a mobile context. Assigning grades to school essays, ratings to movies, and captions for pictures are all possible scenarios that Notable could support.

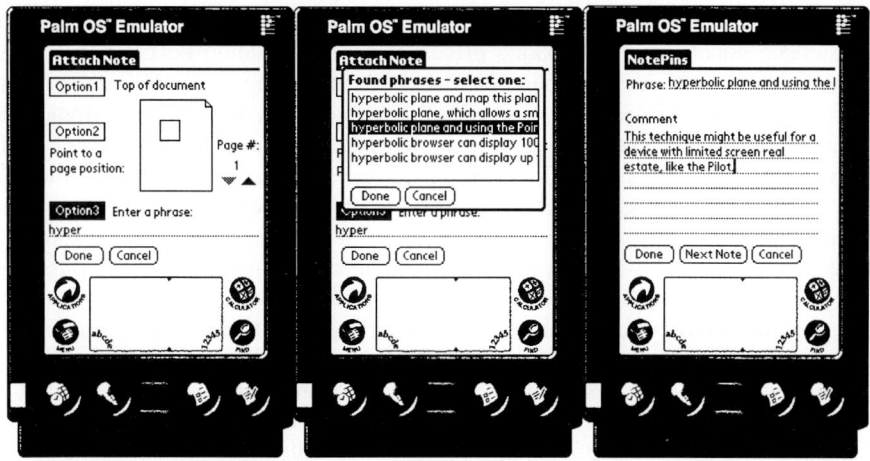

Fig. 2. Annotating a document with Notable: (a) choosing the level of granularity for the annotation; (b) attaching the annotation to a particular phrase; and (c) composing the annotation

3 Design Issues

Historically, many design challenges have lurked at the intersection of a task and a technology. Examples of fruitful intersections include financial modeling and personal computers, personal information management and handheld devices, and person-to-person communication and networked computers. In this section, we outline the design problems and solutions that arise in creating annotations, linking annotations and documents, and viewing and sharing annotations on the interactive platforms that comprise Notable—paper, handheld device, and desktop computer (the latter is optional if the handheld device has a wireless modem).

Throughout this section, we appeal to a framework that represents annotation systems as five interrelated components [2]: annotation writing platform (the platform on which annotations are created), annotations (the commentary), annotation target (the object to which the annotation applies), annotation correspondence (the link between the annotation and the annotated object), and annotation reading platform (the platform on which the annotation is read).

3.1 Creating Annotations

A Post-It™ note is authored on a piece of paper that is separate from the object to which it becomes attached. Our decision in Notable to separate the document reading platform (paper) from the annotation writing platform (the handheld device) owes much to our observations of how Post-It™ notes are used. Given the complementary nature of paper and handhelds, decoupling reading and writing is of particular value for a handheld-based annotation system. On the one hand, paper is a good medium for reading because it supports quick navigation, flexible spatial layout, and inline annotation (though as we have already observed, readers of paper documents often also create annotations on separate pieces of paper, including Post-It™ notes) [3]. Furthermore, most authors prepare their work for the familiar 8.5"x11" or A4 format, and make graphical decisions based on this assumption. For example, figures are often designed to make maximal use of the paper's width. A paper version of a document is thus perhaps more likely to reflect the author's intended presentation. On the other hand, handheld devices promise to form a good medium for annotation creation because of their connectivity (either via modems or via synchronization with a desktop computer), which facilitates annotation sharing and retrieval. Furthermore, this situation is likely to improve as advances are made in wireless connectivity.

However, connectivity alone does not ensure that users will be able to find the right annotation at the right time. The original Post-It™ model suggests that an annotation can only be found when its parent document is found. In Notable, we require that annotations be entered using Graffiti™, which means that the individual characters and words comprising an annotation are fully recognizable by the system. The consequence of this decision is that annotations can be located by keyword searches that refer either to the annotation text or to the parent document text. If annotations were instead entered in digital ink, finding annotations on their own would be more difficult (given the current state of handwriting recognition). On the other hand, digital ink affords easier annotation entry (text entry on handheld devices can be awkward) and allows for the possibility of annotation drawings. Digital ink also suggests the possibility of a gesture-driven annotation interface. Accordingly, a next generation version of Notable might allow users to combine these two methods of annotation entry.

Although Notable is designed under the assumption that users will prefer to read documents on paper, we expect that there will be some occasions when it is satisfactory to read a document on the handheld device itself. Accordingly, in cases where the text of the document is available in digital form, we allow the user to read the document directly on the handheld device if desired. We accomplish this for a variety of document formats by invoking a text conversion service (available via an online service developed in another research project in our lab) at the time the user selects a document for annotation. The plain text version of the selected document is downloaded to the handheld for viewing.

3.2 Linking Annotations and Documents

Given that the document reading and annotation writing platforms are separated in Notable, a digital equivalent for "stickiness" is critical to the design. Notable enables the user to link an annotation and an object by storing together in an annotation repository the text of the annotation and the digital identifier of the object—thus virtually attaching the annotation and object to each other. The indirect nature of this annotation correspondence can be exploited in cases where an annotation refers to multiple targets. For example, a reader might want to create an annotation that briefly compares the main thrusts of two related documents. Annotation systems that require inline, in situ annotations make this style of annotation difficult. In contrast, although cross-target annotation is not a supported feature in our current implementation of

Notable, our choice of annotation correspondence mechanism allows for this feature in the future.

Before annotation, Notable users perform searches for the digital surrogates of the objects to be annotated. Associated with each surrogate is a digital identifier—the piece of information that the system uses to associate annotations and their targets. In our first iteration on the Notable design [4], search took place directly on the handheld device, which was supplemented with a wireless data modem. After finishing the initial implementation, we reviewed this choice and concluded that it was important to support handheld owners without wireless modems as well. Accordingly, we developed a second version, in which search took place on the desktop and document identifiers were propagated to the handheld via synchronization. In both versions, search is by keywords, though a later version could support fielded search, in which a user can specify additional bibliographic metadata constraints, e.g., author's name.

More specifically, we use URLs (uniform resource locators) as our document identifiers. URLs are also used to link annotations and documents in Web annotation systems, e.g. ComMentor [5] and ThirdVoice™. URLs can be located easily by interacting with search facilities available from numerous sources (Web search engines, digital libraries, intranet searching tools, etc.). In addition, URLs are type-independent; Notable users can annotate any document with a URL, regardless of its format or its access restrictions. In addition, URLs can refer to the digital surrogate of a coffeepot just as well as to the digital surrogate of a document. Accordingly, we can envision future versions of Notable that allow users to annotate sculptures, office machines, or places.

One drawback of URLs is that they impose a new constraint on our system: each target needs to have an established URL before it can be annotated. Thus, if a user wishes to annotate an object that is not locatable by our search engines, a URL for the object must be established and it must be registered in a known document repository. For paper documents, we have established an additional requirement: they must be scanned so that fine-grained annotations can be supported. In many of our scenarios, we expect that the documents will already be available online, have URLs, and be easy to find with a simple search. Nevertheless, this strategy of asking users to scan in documents and register them in a repository allows us to realize the scenario of Sect. 2. A further potential problem with URLs is that they may change or become obsolete. We address this problem to some extent by copying the target data into a local repository. Widespread use of URNs would allow us to solve this problem more satisfactorily.

Of course, URLs alone allow only for target-level annotation. In the first iteration of the Notable design, we felt that target-level annotation was sufficient. We were inspired by the analogy to Post-Its™ and influenced by a study [6] showing that independent annotations, such as comments on a paper left on voice mail, tend to be higher-level comments than those written directly on a paper. However, all of the potential users who saw the system asked for finer granularity anchoring. We responded by deciding to support both phrase-level and region-level annotation anchoring. We quickly found that the separation of annotation writing platform from document viewing platform, the lack of screen real estate on the handheld device, the limited computational power (speed and memory) on the handheld, the time required for text entry on the handheld, and the high latency of the network link coincided to make the addition of fine-grain annotation a serious design challenge.

For digital documents, the supported level of granularity for annotations is usually intertwined with the governing document model. Structurally, annotations might be at a chapter level, section level, or paragraph level. Graphically, annotations might be at a page level or region level. Textually, annotations might be at a sentence level, phrase level, or word level. Variations abound. Given that our users were creating their annotations in a medium separate from the one in which they were viewing the documents, we needed techniques for the users to specify in more detail where the annotation should be attached regardless of the underlying digital document model. For inspiration, we looked at how users typically respond to this challenge in non-handheld environments. The most influential example we found was in e-mail—in particular, e-mail conventions for providing comments on articles. Typically, these comments include textual meta-information about where the annotation belongs. Fig. 3 is an excerpt from an e-mail message employing this approach.

> ** page 3, col 2, "By architecting our constructor tool...": Maybe this sentence (or paragraph) should be moved earlier; this makes it clear that we are talking about our approach...
>
> ** page 4, Figure 4 would not print on my printer, but I assume it prints elsewhere. In any case, Fig 4 seems to have too much "stuff" and I am not even sure it will print OK in black and white. If we keep it we need to add explanation about what the different patterns mean.

Fig. 3. An example of e-mail conventions in article reviewing

Note that the author of these comments is using two different techniques to "anchor" the annotation. He anchors the first comment by pinpointing the phrase to which it applies. He helps the reader to locate that phrase more quickly by identifying the page and region in which the phrase occurs. He anchors the second comment solely by identifying the page and region to which the annotation applies.

A direct translation of these techniques to the handheld is possible, but suffers from two problems. First, the user needs to employ a standard vocabulary for the anchoring meta-information (e.g., "** page 3, col 2") in order for the system to anchor the annotations accurately (the references must undergo computer interpretation rather than human interpretation). In a handheld environment, it is tricky to convey such a vocabulary to the user. Second, the user needs to enter a fair amount of text in order to specify the location fully, which is a high cost for a short annotation. On a handheld device with awkward text input, the technique is error prone and unacceptably demanding of the user. Accordingly, we have developed two specialized techniques for anchoring annotations to fine granularity locations in documents: context-sensitive phrase completion and icon-based graphical pinning. These two techniques can be combined to further decrease the input burden on the user.

Employing the first technique, a user anchors an annotation by beginning to write the phrase to which the annotation applies. After several characters have been entered, the system displays a pop-up menu with a list of the phrases in the document that begin with those characters. The user can choose the appropriate phrase for anchoring and proceed to create the annotation. The phrase list is of a manageable size due to our dual-pronged strategy of: 1) requiring the user to enter several characters before presenting matching phrases in the document, and 2) presenting only phrases that appear in the document (rather than phrases that are drawn from a dictionary or from the user's input history). A variant of this approach would be to compute a new matching phrase list after each keystroke by the user. In either case, an anchor phrase can be selected with minimal text entry.

Our context-sensitive phrase-completion technique requires that the full text of the document be available to the annotation system. This need coincides with our design decision (outlined in Sect. 3.1) to convert selected documents to plain text and download the text to the handheld. Space savings could be obtained by eliminating stop words from the downloaded text, although we do not do so at this time (given that the text is also available for viewing). This technique could also be of use at annotation creation time. Very often, an annotation includes some of the same words as the existing phrases. Thus, we hypothesize that context-sensitive phrase completion could potentially save users time both during annotation linking and during annotation creation.

The second technique allows the user to anchor an annotation by indicating a region on a page icon for the annotation. Moving a small rectangle over the icon specifies the region. The exact page is indicated by clicking on a scroll button until the desired page number appears (for long documents, an alternative direct page number entry area is clearly necessary). This low-cost graphical page icon is generic; it has the same appearance for every document the user annotates. An alternative would be to use full thumbnails of the page, thus allowing the user to point to a specific figure, etc. We deemed the computational cost of generating such thumbnails to be too high on our handheld devices; similarly, we deemed the required bandwidth too high to transmit such thumbnails to the device. The critical insight behind our regional anchoring solution is that a Notable user has the paper document at hand (our regional anchoring strategy is not applicable in the case where the annotator is viewing the plain text version of the document directly on the handheld device); thus, a perfect thumbnail is not necessary. For more precise anchoring, however, future work could include compromise strategies, such as "icon stationery," in which the visual appearance of the icon would be tailored to the known genre of the document. For example, two-column documents or letters might have associated specialized icons.

Our current implementation allows users to choose between context-sensitive phrase completion and icon-based graphical pinning as anchoring strategies (if finer granularity annotations are desired). We envision that the two techniques could be coupled to produce an even more efficient approach to annotation anchoring. The region and page selected by the user could constrain the list of possible phrase matches that is generated in response to user text input. This combined technique would require that the handheld device have a mapping from text to page position, but would allow for a handheld-specific counterpart to the first example in Fig. 3.

3.3 Viewing and Sharing Annotations

In addition to specifying the platform on which annotations are created and the platform on which the annotation target is viewed, the design of an annotation system must also specify where the annotations themselves can be read. In Notable, annotations can be read on the handheld device and can also be viewed on the desktop machine. An important design question concerning the annotation reading platform is: what is the technique used to display annotations? Are annotations displayed inline in the target document; are they overlaid on the document; are they independent of the document? The handheld view of annotations in Notable necessarily must show annotations independently from the document, since our assumption is that the document is viewed on paper. Users can navigate from one annotation to the next using on-screen arrow symbols. Each annotation displays its own meta-information, including its author and the specific location to which it applies. On the desktop, however, Notable need not be constrained in this way. Although currently annotations can only be read on the desktop by using the viewer built for the document repository in which the annotations are stored (anchoring information is available only as a declarative property of an annotation), future work could use the anchoring information associated with annotations to display annotations inline. The MultiValent Document (MVD) architecture [7] might provide a good substrate for creating such a view for Notable annotations, as has proven true for NotePals notes [8]. One of the challenges in displaying regionally anchored annotations at the correct place is to ensure that the digital version and paper version of the document both utilize the same graphical layout. For example, the annotation system might need the user to provide extra information to align the two versions (e.g., what is the last word on page 1 in the paper version?). Animated techniques for revealing annotations via progressive disclosure are also an interesting avenue to explore [9].

Decisions about annotation features play an important role in determining the work practices that evolve around an annotation system. For example, willingness to publish annotations is highly sensitive to the degree of access control that is associated with annotations. The ability to make simple distinctions among personal, group, and public annotations can have a large impact on the usability of the system in organizational settings. Notable records for each annotation who its author is so that access control will be possible in future versions. The ability to annotate an annotation is also significant in determining the degree of conversation that revolves around annotation. In Notable, we have built in the ability to annotate an annotation from the start. Our approach is to model annotations as documents in their own right, thus allowing for cascading annotations to emerge.

The scenario depicted in Sect. 2 was motivated by a common occurrence for researchers—a need to participate in the group review of an article. In our original version of Notable, coordination of groups was handled out-of-band from the annotation application. Individual users each had to search for the appropriate document handle, then proceed to annotate the document. In our second design iteration, we recognized that there was an opportunity for amortizing the cost of searching across a group, thus reducing the amount of interaction required of most users. The current design allows for an individual user to specify at document selection time that the document is destined for group annotation. The consequence of this declaration is that all members of the selected group automatically receive the document (and any associated annotations) the next time they synchronize their handheld devices. In the current implementation, group information is statically defined, but we see clearly how to extend this concept to arbitrarily defined groups. Future versions might allow users to have more fine-grained control over which annotations of the group should be downloaded (e.g., annotations written by anyone in the group on this document, but only from this category).

4 System Architecture

Fig. 4 depicts the current Notable system architecture, which is composed of six major components: handheld annotation application, annotation conduit, desktop search application, format conversion service, document/annotation repository, and search service. A simplified version of this architecture may be used if the available handheld devices are wirelessly networked (the "desktop" components are no longer necessary). In this section, we give a brief overview of the data flow among components and also describe each component's functionality in more detail.

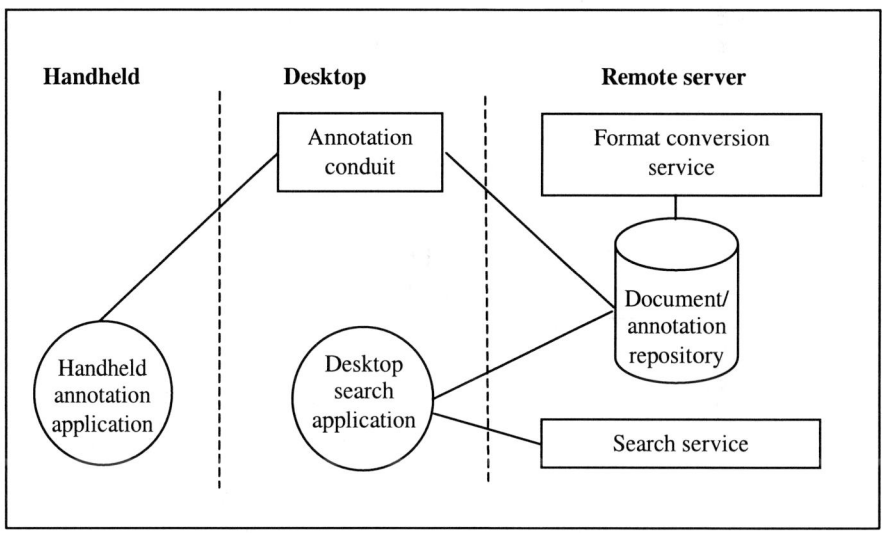

Fig. 4. Notable architecture (version from non-wireless handhelds)

4.1 Handheld Components

Data flow between the handheld annotation application (implemented in C++ for the Palm™) and the annotation conduit takes place at synchronization time. During synchronization, the annotation conduit sends to the annotation application the necessary meta-information (possibly including full text) for the documents the user has selected for future annotation. Any previously existing annotations are sent along with the document metadata. In the opposite direction, the annotation application sends to the conduit all annotations created on the handheld device since the previous synchronization event, together with linking and anchoring information for the annotations.

4.2 Desktop Components

The annotation conduit (implemented in Java) is primarily an intermediary between the handheld annotation application and the document/annotation repository. The conduit locates selected documents by performing a search of the document/annotation repository for documents flagged for download by the user currently performing the synchronization (note that a document might be flagged either because the user selected the document for annotation or because someone in the user's group flagged the document for group annotation).

The conduit is also responsible for sending created annotations to the document/annotation repository for storage. In Notable, annotations are modeled as documents in their own right. This design decision simplifies the activities of annotating annotations and searching for annotations, since annotations differ little from other documents in the repository (they have some special properties, but share many properties in common with other documents).

The desktop search application (also implemented in Java) presents a user interface whereby documents may be located and selected for annotation. The search application sends the entered search parameters to a search service that operates on a remote server. It can receive results from the search service incrementally.

4.3 Remote Server Components

The Notable document/annotation repository is a distributed, property-based system (implemented in Java) that provides transparent document access and remote property-triggered service invocation [10]. Access to all documents stored in the repository is controlled at two levels. At the first level, authentication is necessary for access to the repository. At the second level, property-based access control is possible, though our current implementation does not make use of this feature.

We have defined a schema for the documents and annotations that are created and accessed via the Notable system. By defining a schema (and an accompanying API for submitting and retrieving documents that match the schema), we have built a degree of interoperability into Notable. New annotation reading and viewing platforms can be easily added. Examples of schema properties for documents include type, title, state (indicating if a document is ready for download and by whom), and annotation time. For annotations, the schema defines link and anchor properties in addition to the standard document properties.

The format conversion employed by Notable is invoked by the documents themselves, through the use of active properties. The format conversion service resides outside of the repository on a general-purpose document service bus. This service bus provides numerous services for transforming documents, including summarization, translation assistance, and printing, in addition to format conversion. The format conversion service is invoked by the active property via its Java API.

The search service employed by Notable, also external to the document repository, is capable of performing meta-search across a variety of heterogeneous sources—including the Web as well as local document repositories. The search service satisfies search requests by utilizing a unified interface to numerous existing search engines through the use of proxies [11].

5 Related Work

Annotation systems have been developed for a variety of platforms and media types. Examples include the ComMentor [5] and ThirdVoice™ applications for annotating Web pages, Tapestry [12] features for commenting on e-mail, Microsoft Word™ features for marking up and commenting on text documents, Dynomite [13] features for annotating multimedia documents, XLibris [14] features for marking up documents viewed on a tablet-based computer, and the NotePals [8] application for meeting note taking on both handheld devices and tablet-based computers. More systems are surveyed and analyzed in [2, 15].

Of the annotation systems we have examined, NotePals is the most similar to Notable, even though the focus of NotePals is on supporting note taking at meetings and not comments on documents. Users of NotePals author ink-based notes on a meeting and assign those notes to a particular category and time span that together identify the meeting. At synchronization time, all notes from the group that have the same category and time span are merged together and made accessible to the group. Accordingly, members can take turns authoring notes and can easily share ink-based notes. In addition, NotePals annotations can be linked to particular presentation slides, audio segments, and agenda items based on timestamps. In contrast to NotePals, Notable is tailored to annotating user-selected documents (rather than meetings), uses search for document selection (rather than established category names), relies on keystroke-based annotations (rather than ink-based annotation), and supports phrase-based and region-based anchoring (rather than timestamp-based anchoring).

At the more detailed level of anchoring strategies, there is related work in both the textual and graphical domains. [16] outlines a method for using phrase completion on handheld devices in order to facilitate text entry of Japanese characters. Matches come from a dictionary and are ranked by a variety of factors, including term frequency. Although there is no initial context sensitivity, adaptation to the current document context occurs by virtue of the ranking algorithm giving precedence to previously selected words. [17] uses site-specific auto-completion to inform users about the selectivity of their chosen keywords. Outside of the realm of handheld devices, context-sensitive phrase completion has been used in a variety of products, including text-editing software (e.g., emacs) and personal finance applications (e.g., Quicken™). Similar in spirit to icon-based graphical pinning, Adobe Acrobat Reader™ allows users to select an area of a document for magnification by manipulation of a small rectangle on a thumbnail of a document page.

6 Conclusions and Future Work

A handheld-based annotation system, Notable permits users to author sharable and reusable comments on paper documents in a mobile environment. Key design decisions for Notable include separating the annotation writing platform from the document viewing platform, providing search as the method for document selection, offering context-sensitive phrase completion and icon-based graphical pinning for fine-granularity annotation anchoring, and including some support for coordinating group annotation scenarios.

Our work on Notable has suggested numerous directions for future research. First, we recognize the importance of involving more users in our design process. Conversations with potential users have already resulted in a second iteration of the Notable design. At this point, we believe that a set of qualitative and quantitative user studies would be of great benefit. Questions that we would like to investigate include the usability of the system, the range of scenarios in which Notable is of value, and the effectiveness of our anchoring techniques.

For usability, the design must be extended to allow for the effective viewing of the created annotations and documents on other devices in the user's computing environment. Hybrid graphical/textual/structural anchoring strategies and the development of "icon stationery" are also likely to improve usability. Designing for usability does not stop at interface design. Annotation is part of a wide range of group processes. Accordingly, we foresee the introduction into Notable of active annotations and the integration of better group support.

More generally, we see Notable as an example of an application genre that is rapidly evolving: remote user interfaces that allow users to interact with physically separate objects. With Post-It™ size display areas, keystroke-based text entry systems, and programmable infrastructure, today's handheld devices offer designers the opportunity to orchestrate new interactions between users and the objects they are viewing. At the same time, the limitations in screen real estate, input technology, memory, and bandwidth of these devices (in comparison to desktop computers) impose a complex set of design constraints. Translating desktop applications to this new environment is an increasingly significant design challenge.

7. Acknowledgments

We thank Brian Lee for his implementation work on the first version of the Notable system and Polle Zellweger for her contribution of the idea behind icon-based graphical pinning. We are also grateful to Ken Pier, Mark Stefik, and the HUC2k reviewers for their thoughtful feedback on earlier drafts of this paper.

References

1. Marshall, C.: Toward an Ecology of Hypertext Annotation. In: Proceedings of ACM Hypertext '98. Pittsburgh, PA (June 1998) 40-49
2. Cousins, S. B., Baldonado, M., Paepcke, A.: A Systems View of Annotations. PARC Tech Report P9910022 (April 2000)
3. O'Hara, K. and Sellen, A.: A Comparison of Reading Paper and On-Line Documents. In Proceedings of CHI '97. Atlanta, GA (March 1997) 335-342
4. Baldonado, M., Cousins, S., Lee, B., Paepcke, A.: Notable: An Annotation System for Networked Handheld Devices. In: Proceedings of CHI '99. Pittsburgh, PA (May 1999) 210-211

5. Röscheisen, M., Mogensen, C., Winograd, T.: Interaction Design for Shared World-Wide Web Annotations. In: Proceedings of CHI '95, Vol. 2. Denver, CO (May 1995) 328-329
6. Chalfonte, B. L., Fish, R. S., Kraut, R. E.: Expressive Richness: A Comparison of Speech and Text as Media for Revision. In: Proceedings of CHI '91. New Orleans, LA (April-May 1991) 21-26
7. Phelps, T. A. and Wilensky, R.: Multivalent Annotations. In: Proceedings of the First European Conference on Research and Advanced Technology for Digital Libraries. Pisa, Italy (September 1997)
8. Davis, R. C., Landay, J. A., Chen, V., Huang, J., Lee, R. B., Li, F., Lin, J., Morrey III, C. B., Schleimer, B., Price, M. N., Schilit, B. N.: NotePals: Lightweight Note Sharing By the Group, For the Group. In: Proceedings of CHI '99. Pittsburgh, PA (May 1999) 338-345
9. Zellweger, P., Chang, B., Mackinlay, J.: Fluid Links for Informed and Incremental Link Transitions. In: Proceedings of Hypertext '98. Pittsburgh, PA (June 1998) 50-57
10. Dourish, P., Edwards, K., LaMarca, A., Lamping, J., Petersen, K., Salisbury, M., Terry, D. B., Thornton, J.: Extending Document Management Systems with User-Specific Active Properties. ACM Transactions on Information Systems (in press)
11. Paepcke, A, Cousins, S. B., Garcia-Molina, H., Hassan, S. W., Ketchpel, S. K., Röscheisen, M., Winograd, T.: Using Distributed Objects for Digital Library Interoperability. IEEE Computer Magazine 29:5 (May 1996) 61-68
12. Nichols, D., Oki, B. M., Goldberg, D., Terry, D.: Using Collaborative Filtering to Weave an Information Tapestry. Communications of the ACM 35:12 (1992) 61-70
13. Wilcox, L. D., Schilit, B. N., Sawhney, N.: Dynomite: A Dynamically Organized Ink and Audio Notebook. In: Proceedings of CHI '97. Atlanta, GA (March 1997) 186-193
14. Schilit, B. N., Golovchinsky, G. Price, M.: Beyond Paper: Supporting Active Reading with Free Form Digital Ink Annotations. In: Proceedings of CHI '98. Los Angeles, CA (April 1998) 249-256
15. Ovsiannikov, I. A., Arbib, M. A., McNeill, T. H.: Annotation Technology. International Journal of Human-Computer Studies, 50:4 (1999) 329-62
16. Masui, T.: An Efficient Text Input Method for Pen-Based Computers. In: Proceedings of CHI '98. Los Angeles, CA (April 1998) 328-335
17. Buyukkokten, O., Garcia-Molina, H., Paepcke, A.: Focused Web Searching with PDAs. In: Proceedings of WWW 9. Amsterdam, The Netherlands (May 2000) 213-230

Creating Web Representations for Places

Deborah Caswell and Philippe Debaty

Internet & Mobile Systems Lab
Hewlett-Packard Laboratories
Palo Alto, CA
(caswell@hpl.hp.com, debaty@hpl.hp.com)

Abstract. We believe that the future consists of nomadic people depending upon mobile appliances using World Wide Web protocols to communicate with services offered in real world places. Use of web protocols provides a ubiquitous communication infrastructure and allows interaction with the multitude of existing web-based services. Part of the challenge to realize our vision is to bridge the physical and virtual worlds by creating web representations for people, places, and things that interact virtually as they interact physically. We believe that an interesting set of new services can be provided by bridging the virtual and physical worlds in this way. This paper describes our experience with building a general place manager infrastructure useful for creating web representations for physical places. Although we leverage a general web presence architecture for building all different types of web presence, this paper focuses on the specific needs for building web representations for places.

1 Introduction

We are seeing the convergence of several trends: increasing availability of highly functional portable devices, deployment of wireless networking options, and the explosion in the number of services offered over the World Wide Web. The proliferation in use of mobile devices has increased the number of people who are always connected (or want to be) to the world wide web. Wherever they are, they have access to both a physical reality, and the virtual one presented through their mobile browser (also called its *web representation* throughout this paper). We believe that many useful services can be offered by creating a tighter link between the physical and virtual worlds. The HP Labs Cooltown project (http://www.cooltown.hpl.hp.com) explores this future based on a vision where people, places and things all have web-based representations [9].

In [2] we describe a general infrastructure for building web-present people, places, and things. The infrastructure provides the following capabilities that are necessary for creating the web representations we desire:

- Generates a custom web page for a user considering the user's circumstances.

- Provides an authoring environment for easily creating templates that contain the look and feel of the web representation as well as instruction for dynamic customization.
- Provides a way to store and retrieve information concerning the relationships among web present entities. We call the component that does this the *directory*.
- Provides a configuration interface for defining security policy.

In this paper, we delve into more detail concerning our experience with building web representations for places using this general infrastructure. Whereas [2] concentrates on the similarities among the necessary infrastructures for people, places, and things, this paper focuses on the specific functionality needed in a place manager.

2 Creating a Place Web Representation

A *place* has physical boundaries and semantics assigned to its use. Thus, a virtual chat room is not a place because there are no physical boundaries. A church recreation room might provide the physical boundaries for multiple places, each one with a different use (scout meeting, 12 step program meeting, wedding reception).

A *place manager* is an infrastructure component that provides a web representation for a place. Our goal is to create a general infrastructure from which many different places and kinds of places can be built. We assume that there is a provider of the place with an interest in controlling the functionality offered and how the place appears to its users. It is the combination of provider perspective with the set of user circumstances that are considered for custom web page generation that makes this class of application different from other related work.

A bookstore, museum, conference room, home, and bus stop are some examples of places that become more useful and convenient with a web representation. The majority of web pages today that represent real or physical entities simply describe the place. For example, many retail stores have a web page that describes the merchandise they offer, directions to the store, and store hours. Others might also provide easy email access for asking questions, and still others might offer on-line ordering. Interaction is limited. There is no particular advantage to being physically present in the place and on-line at the same time. We believe that there is great value in providing a dynamic, interactive, and custom web representation for a physical place. It is the bridging of the virtual and physical worlds that makes this vision compelling.

A place's web representation is automatically offered to a browsing device as that device enters the place. The place's web page is generated as a function of the services offered in the place, as well as the devices and people physically in the place at the time of access. The integration of the physical (real) world with the virtual representation of that world is very useful, but not often done today. Imagine a bookstore trying to compete with one of the large online bookstores. In today's world, a connected mobile user could browse the physical book store, read parts of a book to determine whether or not she wanted it, then compare prices online with a vendor who can keep prices lower because of the lower overhead. Now imagine the same physical bookstore integrates the customer's experience with an online presence. If a book is out of stock, it can be ordered and shipped immediately without waiting in line for a store clerk to help. It can give suggestions of related books depending on the section of the bookstore where the user is physically. Some of the search criteria that would otherwise have to be entered manually can be inferred based on the section of the store in which the user is browsing. Another example is a coffee shop whose value to customers, in addition to great coffee, is the ability to telecommute from the shop. Access to office devices such as printers and scanners in the shop can be given to those buying coffee.

There is a good reason why the integration of physical locality and virtual reality has not become pervasive yet, despite the promise it holds for shop owners and other proprietors of physical places. Without a generic infrastructure for building such interactive and dynamic web representations, application building is very time consuming and requires an inter-disciplinary approach of sophisticated programming and web design. This section shows how the generic infrastructure described earlier can be used to create a *Place Manager* that can be customized for a variety of different kinds of places.

The literature is populated with reported efforts to build *context managers*. C*ontext* can refer to any kind of information including location, and the proposals for architecture and prototype applications have different requirements depending on specifically what context is being used. The place manager is a context manager that considers very specific kinds of context for building a specific class of applications: In addition to the user's location, we want the web place representation to be able to reflect the current time, the identity of the user accessing the place, and the capability of the device being used to access the web representation of the place. As a result of these requirements, a place manager is a combination of resource inventory manager and specialized web server that provides the web representation of a place taking all these specific notions of context into consideration.

2.1 Place-Specific Requirements

A place manager has certain requirements that stress a general implementation infrastructure in ways that are different from a person or thing manager.[1]

- *Relationships with other entities*: The web representation of a place needs to represent the people and things present within the place. There is a containment relationship, and for each person and thing within the place, there is a corresponding entry in the place's directory. People and mobile devices enter and leave places, and the current state of the directory must reflect the current state of the place at any given point in time (relative to some small time period of inconsistency). Thus, the implementation of the directory must be able to handle frequent updates.There are several different

---

[1] A person manager is an infrastructure component that provides a web representation for a person. A thing manager is an infrastructure component that provides a web representation for a thing.

service discovery protocols already in existence and several under development. The place manager should be able to support multiple discovery protocols for the purpose of registering entities that offer a service or are physically present within the place.

In addition to having relationships with people and things, places also have relationships with services and other places. Typically services that are particularly relevant to the use of the place are offered as links from the place's web representation. These services can be registered and unregistered dynamically. Therefore, there must be a way to store service information as well as people and thing entities. Inter-place relationships is a topic for further research.

- *Open-ended entity description for programmatic search*: A service might want to dynamically discover other resources it needs to operate. For example, a personal communication service might want to find all the devices in a place with phone, fax, and/or paging capability and then choose one to use as the endpoint for setting up a point-to-point communication. This requires that the directory must support programmatic search where the query is not known ahead of time. We cannot anticipate a priori what information a service might want about the entities within a place. Although standards organizations such as UPnP will be standardizing on entity descriptions that will dictate what attributes can be searched on in the arbitrary queries mentioned above, we believe that new devices and capabilities will be put into use faster than a standards body can update the standard to accommodate new features. Thus, it is important to be able to handle entity descriptions that include both standard and non-standard attributes. Although the place manager will not understand non-standard attributes, it must be able to search for them. Only the services searching on such attributes need know what they are.

- *Security policy*: It is valuable for a place to be able to authenticate a person/device's presence in the place. For purposes of user convenience, revenue protection, and place resource protection, there are times when services should only be offered to those who are physically present in a place, and withhold those services from those viewing the place's web representation remotely. Because there are semantics associated with the use of a place, some services, people, things, and places will be relevant to its web representation, and others will not be. Using the church recreation room as an example, the Karaoke machine that is relevant to a wedding reception place would not be relevant to the AA meeting. It becomes more challenging to specify and control what kinds of relationships are allowed in a place and with which other entities. The place provider needs a way of specifying a policy to determine which other entities may register a relationship in the place's directory, and the implementation must enforce that policy.

2.2 Discovery and Registration

In this section we discuss how relationships are created between a place and people, things, services, and other places. More specifically, we address how descriptions of these entities are entered into the place's directory. There are two parts to the process of establishing a relationship. First is noticing that a relationship exists and second is recording it. *Discovery* is the term we use for the process of noticing that a relationship exists. For a place, discovery usually involves noticing that a person or thing is located in the place and that a service or other place is relevant to the semantics of the place. *Registration* is the term we use for entering the entity description into the directory as a means of recording the relationship. Most industry standard and well known discovery protocols such as SLP [11] and SSDP [12] are standalone services. That is, they contain both discovery and registration mechanisms. Each provides its own silo of information concerning the entities discovered through its protocol, but does not lend itself well to sharing information across discovery mechanisms. Since we decouple discovery and registration, multiple discovery protocols can coexist, and the discovered entity descriptions are recorded in a common directory that is searchable independent of how the entity was discovered.

The place manager provides a registration interface for adding and deleting entity descriptions for entities with a relationship to the place. Registration is accomplished by invoking an *HTTP Get* operation and supplying as an argument the URL of the XML description of the entity to be registered. The place manager uses the URL to contact the entity's description that will be cached in the directory. This same interface is used regardless of how the relationship was discovered.

Now let's examine the various methods that can be used to discover entities in a place.

Manual Registration. There is an html form that allows an administrator to type in the URL of the XML description of an entity that the administrator wants to be in the place's directory. This is especially useful for services or other places that are chosen because of the relevance to the semantics of the place. We do not yet have an automated way to discover such relationships.

Tag Scanning and Recognition. For those things that have a web representation already and which are labeled with a passive tag, an administrator can create an association between the tagged thing and the place by scanning its tag, resolving the tag identifier to its URL, and having associated software automatically invoke the registration interface with its tag. Relationships are determined when an administrator decides which things to scan.

Device and User Self-Registration. The discovery mechanism we assume will be most commonly used is a scheme where a device offering a service registers itself with the place or a user's personal device registers the user in the place on the user's behalf. A place is assumed to have a short-range wireless beacon that announces the URL of the place manager's home page. Alternatively, there could be a passive id tag located in the place that when scanned would yield an id that is resolved to the URL of the place's home page. A device entering the place picks up the place's URL automatically, and uses it to construct the http-based registration invocation. To register, the device sends the URL of the XML description of itself or of the person it is registering.

This mechanism is preferable over manual and tag scanning methods because it requires no administrative intervention at registration time. This protocol also has several advantages over other industry accepted or emerging discovery protocols:

Point-to-point registration. The device contacts the place manager directly. The URL for bootstrapping the registration process is either provided by a short-range broadcast medium that is chosen to match the boundaries of the physical place or by scanning a passive tag whose id can only be read within the place. In either case, the search for a place manager is guaranteed to be confined to the boundaries of the place.

Single point of contact for finding place resources. A service that needs to identify other services, people, and things in a place does not need to broadcast a "is anyone out there? message" and then collate responses as is required by some discovery protocols. Instead, entities can be identified by contacting the place's directory in which information about the entities in the place is cached. That directory can be queried directly.

Caching an XML description avoids the need for fixed schemas. Arbitrary resources can be registered provided their description has the minimal set of information needed by the place manager for storage and retrieval. The XML attributes in the description need to be agreed upon between the entity and the services that will search for that resource based on the attributes. Not every attribute of an entity needs to be standardized across the industry before it can be used.

Other industry standard or emerging discovery systems [1][11][12] make different assumptions about the nature of the environment in which discovery will take place. Their use of client-side multicasting can lead to a mismatch between the network reachability of the multicast medium and the physical boundaries of place that should define the scope of the search. As a result of this mismatch in boundaries, a resource could end up being registered in multiple adjoining places and/or discovering other resources across adjoining places. Avoiding client-side multicasting is also important because mobile devices are likely to be low power. Enabling them to simply listen for a beacon then interact in a simple, point-to-point registration takes less power than multicasting and communicating with individual resources to learn their capabilities.

In order for a device to participate directly in the discovery protocol we define, it must have a beacon receiver or tag scanner, the ability to initiate the http-based registration invocation (e.g. a web browser, programmatic http client capability, or connection to a wap gateway), and the software to construct the registration invocation. That might be a tall order for small, limited-capability handheld devices. Providing they have some way of being discovered by a proxy, the proxy can register such a device on their behalf. Furthermore, the URL of the device's or user's description can be served up by any web server. There is no requirement that the device itself must run the web server that will provide the description.

Discovery Adapters. Some devices will enter a place with client software for some other discovery protocol. These devices can be discovered in a place by providing discovery adapters. A discovery adapter provides the server side of a discovery protocol to establish the relationship with a device, then uses the http-based registration invocation to record the relationship in the place's directory. In this way, industry standard and emerging discovery protocols such as SLP, SSDP, and Jini [7]discovery can coexist within a place, and client devices do not need to have additional discovery software installed that is specific to participating in the kinds of places we describe.

However, due to the limitations described above concerning the potential mismatch of networking technology and place boundaries, the burden is on the place administrator when configuring such adapters to ensure that the discovery mechanism is consistent with the policy of what may enter into a relationship with the place.

2.3 Security

Places have different security requirements. Some public places such as a bus stop will need to offer access without requiring a user to divulge their identity. These places must not rely on any kind of trust relationship. These places primarily offer information services where the user's identity does not affect the presentation or the information they receive. Other public places such as a library will have both information services provided to anonymous users and check-out services offered to authenticated members of the library.

Other places such as conference rooms and general use areas within a private company require more security. Most companies will have a private internal network with a firewall protecting places from access from people without access to the private net. There are many services for which access could be given to anyone on the private network regardless of who they are. However, if meetings are held in a conference room in which outside visitors attend, it might be desirable to provide place services to these guests without having to grant them access to the private network. To do that, the place manager must be cognizant of which network the user is on and issue URL's with the appropriate addresses that can be reached by that user. A proxy that sits on the corporate firewall would recognize the public URLs issued by the place manager and reissue the request to the corresponding private URLs in order to access place resources on the private network. The content available to visitors would be limited to the set of public URLs issued by the place manager and the translation table configured into the proxy.[10]

Then, a reverse proxy would serve the public URLs by translating certain ones to the internal address and let the request pass through the firewall.

Some services must be reserved for designated people who must authenticate themselves to be so designated. For example, a conference room place might establish the policy that only the current speaker is authorized to change the current slide on the overhead projector whereas all other people in the room may view the slide on their personal device. The need for services to be able to provide different authorization levels certainly is not new to places.

2.4 Location Authentication

There is much written about location-based web services: those services whose output is customized based on where the user is located. Examples include mapping programs and yellow pages. Because a place exists in a physical location, it can also offer services that are relevant to its location. For example, imagine that a conference has links to a map showing the floor plan of the building with the conference in the center or directions to the nearest bathroom, coffee station, copier, etc. A place administrator might want to provide such location-specific links only to users who are physically in the conference room and not those who are only virtually present. Those who participate in a meeting remotely would access the place's web representation to view the slides being presented, but would not need directions to the nearest copier. However, there is no adverse affect on the place if remote people were to have access to these links. In this section, we describe a set of scenarios that motivate the need to authenticate a person's physical presence in the place because of the adverse effects remote access could have on the place. There are at least three situations in which a place provider might want to generate a different place web representation depending on the presence or absence of the user in the place: convenience to the user, protecting revenues associated with the use of the place, and protecting place resources. Here we explain these motivations and give examples. Then we explain our basic approach to implementing location authentication.

2.5 Convenience

As explained before, the place manager generates a custom, on-demand web page for the user in his/her current circumstances that include the user's identity, browsing device capability, and time of day. Location is just another user circumstance. Not all web servers use a user's identity for restricting access or protecting resources Some web sites use the user's identity to make the content feel more personal. Similarly, location information can be used to customize the generated web pages. This is accomplished by hiding links to services that require physical presence.

One example is a library place's web page. It is reasonable and common for an employee to access the online card catalogue from their own office. However, it only makes sense to check out a book if one is physically present to take possession of the book. Many times books are expected to be on the shelf according to the inventory system, but cannot be found due to theft or mis-shelving. So, it is convenient to only include the check-out service for a user who is physically present in the library. It also provides some peace of mind to the library staff to encourage the consistency of their inventory system (do not want a book that has been checked out to be on the shelf). However, a user who can spoof their physical location (i.e. can assert that they are in the library when they are really at their desk) risks becoming responsible for a book not in their possession and the library has to deal with the potential inconsistency in their inventory system.

Another example might be selecting the play-list for a communal internet radio. (this is analogous to the old coin-operated jukebox in the local diner). Imagine a casual restaurant allowing their patrons to add selections to be played on the music system in the restaurant and wanting to restrict access to people physically in the restaurant. The reason for such a policy is to raise the probability that real patrons get to hear their own selection before they are finished eating. However, nothing dire happens if someone from outside of the restaurant can add selections to the play-list. It might be annoying, but then if that person were in the restaurant, their selections might be equally annoying.

2.6 Protect Revenues

For places that require an admission fee, providing special services in the place provides motivation for people to enter the place. For example, a rock concert might offer the service of viewing close-ups from different angles that the user chooses. If people not attending the concert were allowed access to this service, there would not be as much incentive to pay to attend the concert in person.

Another example is an amusement park that allows guests inside the park to monitor line lengths but prevents outsiders from doing so. This makes it more difficult for a competitor to gather statistics that could be used in negative advertising against the park.

For both of these examples, the consequences of spoofing presence are more important than the previous examples. However, the negative results of a security breach are not catastrophic. The rock concert will always draw a crowd of people who just enjoy the experience of seeing the band in person and would not find a web-based representation to be an adequate substitute. For the amusement park, word of mouth can already dissuade others from attending the park if the lines are too long. If the park is managed properly, there is nothing to fear from negative advertising.

Protect Place Resources. Many governments are considering making a move towards internet-based voting. Imagine a half-way solution where people must physically come to the polling place in order to be authenticated by a human verifying a picture id but the voting is then done on line, and the counts can be tallied in real time. Imagine that now a polling place can be much more comfortable and informal. One can vote from a mobile handheld device specially configured by the polling place staff that enables voting once and only once. Voting could be done while lounging on a sofa and sipping an iced tea. This step on the path to total internet voting has the advantage of getting results faster and more accurately without having to trust internet security to prevent fraudulent votes[2]. Furthermore, the comfortable atmosphere would make voting a more pleasant experience. In this case, we only want users who are present to access the voting system. The consequences of a breach could invalidate the entire election.

Another example is when supervision of place resources is needed. If a guest comes into Carol's office and she wants to share the contents of her file on the guest's PDA, she might not want the guest to be able to save or print the file. She wants to

---

[2] Voters might even prefer this method to complete on-line voting because the proving identity is divorced from the voting itself. Thus, there should be less worry that there will be a record of how an individual voted.

maintain ownership. She also wants access to the file to go away once the guest leaves her office, where she can no longer supervise their use. The consequence of a security breach could compromise her file system.

Notice that in both examples, identity authentication was very important. Critical place resources were issued only after the user established the trust of someone responsible for protecting the resources. As the owner of her office, Carol gets to discern which guests can access her file system, and she suffers the consequences if she exercises poor judgment.

Our Approach to Authenticating Location. The basic idea is to establish a user's presence by proving proximity to a known reference point within the place. There are several ways to do this. One way is to associate the place manager with a short-range networking access point and require all accesses desiring local status to be invoked over the short-range wireless network. Only users within the reachability of the short-range network could obtain local status, and its assumed that the reachability of the network does not extend outside of the boundaries of the place. However, this solution is too limiting because of the requirements each place would put on the networking infrastructure supported by a user's personal device and the potential mismatch of network reachability and place boundaries. To observe place boundaries, small places would be limited to using very short range networking technologies such as IR or Bluetooth whose bandwidth is quite limited. In a place where a higher speed wireless network coexists with the short range network confined to place boundaries, it is better to limit the use of short-range network to the discovery process and allow normal http traffic to take place over a higher speed medium.

It is desirable to separate the act of obtaining proof of location from the act of requesting the place's web representation. That requires that there be some token of information that can be presented at access time to prove proximity to the place's reference point. However, it is not sufficient for that token to be static because such information can be saved and replayed later at a time when the user is no longer in the place. Therefore, there must be information that can only be obtained by being in the place, and that information must change over time to prove presence within a certain time interval.

The approach we advocate does not require the act of proving location to be atomic with requesting access. A short-range wireless beacon emits a token that contains an encrypted timestamp along with the URL of the place manager. The token is placed in a cookie by the beacon receiver and is presented to the place manager on each access. The cookie is valid until the current time passes the time in the timestamp. When the cookie becomes invalid, the beacon receiver must get a new token and create a new cookie from it.

If location authentication is being used for convenience, we do not care that a user could retransmit the token over a wider-area network and those receiving the token could spoof presence in the place. However, if we are trying to protect revenues, the place manager would require that all communication be done over a secure link, and that individual tokens be generated for specific users. By encrypting the token in a secret shared between the user and the place manager, retransmitting the token will not enable outsiders to spoof location. Since server-only authentication can be used to secure the communication link and the beacon receiver can choose a random secret key for the personal device and place manager to share, the identity of the user can remain anonymous. It is important to note, however, that although the user's identity is not disclosed, the use of the secret key maps all accesses using that key to a single session. The key can be tied to other information about the access such as an internet address. The place manager can use this information to limit the extent of a security breach by only acknowledging one IP address associated with a secret key. If the IP address changes while still in the same place, a new secret key would have to be negotiated through authentication location again.

The remaining problem needing to be solved to protect place resources is that a person inside the place with malicious intent could retransmit both the token and the secret key to an outsider. If it is important to guard against an inside attack, then client authentication must be required as well, and the secret key is tied to the user's identity. In that way, although the place resources were violated by the outsider, the security breach would be traceable to the accomplice.

2.7 Scalability

Places come in various sizes and purposes. We have thought about all different kinds of places from personal office places to amphitheatre places where large concerts are held. The directory needs to scale from recording descriptions of just a few entities to recording several thousand entities. In addition, a general place manager infrastructure must be able to scale from serving a single isolated place (it might be embedded in a special purpose device) to having a centrally run and administrated place manager serving up the web representation of many places simultaneously. An example of that is having the IT department support a single place manager deployment serving all the conference rooms in the building.

We have built a stand-alone office place manager consisting of printing and personal communication services. We are in the process of building a single place manager with industrial database support to serve up an entire building's conference room web representation. We expect to deploy this version internally in Fall '2000.

3 Related Work

The team of Dey, Abowd, and Salber at Georgia Tech has been working to define architecture and toolkits for building context-sensitive applications where context is defined very broadly. In their paper *A Context-Based Infrastructure for Smart Environments*[0], the emphasis is on the architecture for context sensing. The important concept is the abstraction and aggregation of context information sensed in the environment. The architecture they describe could provide an infrastructure for implementing a place manager, as it meets the requirement of hiding the discovery details from the application. However, they do not describe the coexistence of multiple discovery schemes or manual and automatic discovery. Another paper from Georgia Tech [4] describes a context sensitive application that they built using their context toolkit. The Conference Assistant they describe requires application-specific code running on the user's mobile device.

In their paper Scalable and Flexible Location-Based Services for Ubiquitous Information Access [8], Jose and Davies from University of Minho and Lancaster University respectively present a generic architecture for building location-based applications. Their goal is providing information associated with a location context. The emphasis is on how to translate location into the semantic information of place. The location hierarchy they describe might be useful for providing a place manager that has relationships with other place managers (where the relationship is based on proximity or containment). However, there could be other kinds of relationships among places that would not be represented by a location hierarchy. Jose and Davies describe their tourist guide application as an example of the kind of service that can be built using their location-based service infrastructure. The tourist guide considers the user's location when displaying relevant information. However, all users are treated the same by the tourist guide. Thus, user identity is not used as context, and the infrastructure does not support describing and enforcing access control rules. In addition, it assumes a homogeneous browsing device. They do not deal with accommodating differences in the capabilities of the user's browsing device.

The Microsoft-sponsored Universal Plug and Play Forum has the notion of proximity networking. Proximity networking allows a mobile device to enter a new logical or geographic area and be able to interact with local resources without requiring pre-loaded applications specific to the area.[5][6] Unfortunately, there is not enough concrete information available yet on proximity networking to determine whether it will meet our requirements for supporting or providing place management.

4 Future Work

The work described in the paper is currently in progress. We have demonstrated the use of a place manager in an embedded, isolated application. Next, we will demonstrate the scalability of the place manager by using it to manage all the conference rooms in our building, several of which are large auditoria. In addition, we will implement a secure place that offers services to visitors not on the private company network and use location authentication for creating custom content on the basis of a user's presence or absence in the place.

Automatic discovery of relevant services and places is an area that requires future work as well.

5 Conclusions

We have built rudimentary place managers using a general implementation infrastructure. The specific requirements for creating a web representation for places have emphasized specific implementation issues. Our place managers interact with person managers and thing managers to create the powerful and useful web-based services envisioned in Cooltown.

6 Acknowledgements

We wish to recognize and thank the following people for their contributions to this paper. Our reviewers Tim Kindberg, John Schettino, Jeff Morgan, and Gary Herman gave us invaluable suggestions for improvement and support. Our technical consultants included Jean Tourilles, Bill Serra, Jeff Morgan, John Schettino, Marcos Frid, Venky Krishnan, Tim Kindberg, and John Barton.

References

1. Czerwinski, S.E. et al. *An Architecture for a Secure Service Discovery Service*, Mobicom '99, Seattle Washington.
2. Debaty, P. and D. Caswell. *Uniform Web Presence Architecture for People, Places, and Things*. Hewlett Packard Laboratories Technical Report HPL-2000-67, June 2000.
3. Dey, A.K., G.D. Abowd, and D. Salber. *A Context-Based Infrasructure for Smart Environments*. Proceedings of the 1st International Workshop on Managing Interactions in Smart Environments, Dublin, Ireland; Dec. 13-14, 1999.
4. Dey, A.K., M. Futakawa, D. Salber & G. D. Abowd. *The Conference Assistant: Combining Context-Awareness with Wearable Computing*. Proceedings of the 3rd International Symposium on Wearable Computers, San Francisco, CA, October 20-21, 199
5. http://www.microsoft.com/HOMENET/uPnP.htm
6. http://www.upnp.org/resources/UPnPbkgnd.htm
7. Jini Discoveryhttp://developer.java.sun.com/developer/Books/CoreJini/chapter6.html
8. Jose, R. and N. Davies. *Scalable and Flexible Location-Based Service for Ubiquitous Information Access*, Handheld and Ubiquitous Computing; Proceeding from the First International Symposium, HUC'99, Karlsruhe, Germany, September 1999.
9. Kindberg, T. et al. *People, Places, Things: Web presence for the Real World*, http://www.cooltown.hpl.hp.com HPLabs Technical Report HPL-2000-16.
10. Morgan, J. Internal technical memo entitled *Security in Cooltown*.
11. RFC 2165: Service Location Protocol, J. Veizades, E. Guttman, C. Perkins, S. Kaplan: ftp://ftp.isi.edu/in-notes/rfc2165.txt..
12. Simple Service Discovery Protocol, IETF Internet Draft, Y.Y. Golund, T. Cai, P. Leach, Y. Gu, S. Albright: http://www.upnp.org/download/spec-ssdp.doc.

A Context-Sensitive Nomadic Exhibition Guide

Reinhard Oppermann and Marcus Specht

GMD - German National Research Center for Information Technology Institute for Applied
Information Technology (FIT-HCI) 53754 Sankt Augustin
{reinhard.oppermann, marcus.specht}@gmd.de

Abstract: The paper describes a nomadic guide that considers the context of use (CoU) for information selection and presentation. A nomadic system is defined by continuous access to information spaces independent from specific devices. The CoU is defined by the location and characteristics of the user. Interests of the user deduced from the navigation in the physical and information space are the main goal of information adaptation in the paper. A prototype of a nomadic system that adapts the information to the user needs is presented.

1 Introduction

The paper describes the goal and practice of the nomadic exhibition guide Hippie[1]. Hippie takes into account the context of use of the nomadic system. An information system is said to be nomadic when users have access both to their personal information and to the public information from wherever they are, independent from specific devices. For nomadic information systems no one particular (small, wearable, mobile) appliance is crucial. Nomadic information systems include mobile devices as well as stationary desktop computers or kiosk systems, with all having access to information spaces relevant for the user. Users will increasingly be nomads [1]. Just as they always wear a bundle of keys in their pocket to have access to physical spaces future nomads will have an electronic appliance to get access to information spaces no matter which device they currently are working with.

To be useful for the user, information content and information presentation should take into account the context of use. The context of use is defined by the physical environment, the geographical position, social partners, user tasks and personal characteristics. The more context parameters are considered for the information selection and presentation, the more effective, efficient and satisfactory the user interaction will be. Users are most competent in specifying the context of use, but the more complex and the bigger the information spaces the more effort users need for information selection and presentation. A context-sensitive information system can help users to

---

[1] The prototype Hippie was developed by GMD within the project Hyperinteraction within Physical spaces (HIPS), an EU-supported LTR project in ESPRIT I[3]. The partners of the consortium are University of Siena (co-ordinating partner), University of Edinburgh, University College Dublin, ITC, SINTEF and GMD, CB&J, and Alcatel. Within the consortium, GMD is responsible for the user modelling component. A concerted prototype has been developed for the Museo Civico in Siena.

pre-select and appropriately present information automatically. In this paper we introduce and discuss new potentials of nomadic information systems to exploit the context of use for interest-specific information selection and presentation. Nomadic information systems create some new possibilities to identify the needs of users. A nomadic system can follow the stream of activities over the process of usage at different locations, and can take into account the specific context of use [2-6]. Furthermore a nomadic information system can integrate these new parameters into the consideration of the user's needs already evaluated by traditional user-model based systems.

2 Modeling Approach

The nomadic information system to be presented in this paper contains three models to identify the context of use. A *domain model* describes and classifies which objects of the domain information are to be presented and processed. A *space model* describes the physical environment where the nomadic system is used and the location of the domain objects in the physical space. A *user model* describes the knowledge, the interests, the movement, and the personal preferences of the user. The domain model and the space model are assumed to be static, i.e. the domain objects are described and their location are identified before the systems are used. If changes occur in the environment, the domain model or the space model has to be updated explicitly. The user models are dynamic, i.e. the users' interactions with the information system and their movements in physical space are evaluated to update the user model automatically.

The nomadic information system Hippie has been developed for a cultural environment, providing information about an art exhibition and a fair. The nomadic user is supported by adaptive information during the entire process of a visit in a museum, i.e., for the preparation at home, the visit in the museum and its evaluation at home again. The main purpose of the electronic guide presented in this paper is to support the actual visit of a museum, i.e., to enrich the understanding and enjoyment of exhibits, not to replace a real visit by a virtual one. The electronic guide provides the information access at home via normal internet connection for the preparation and evaluation of a visit. Inside the museum, information access is provided via wireless technologies. The latter allow the user to access information by moving in the physical space and concurrently navigating in the information space. A Web-based client-server approach allows for adaptive selection and presentation of information based on a user model, evaluating the history of the usage of Hippie with respect to knowledge, interests, movement and preferences. The user can accelerate and modify the adaptation by explicitly specifying interests and preferences in a user model dialog.

2.1 Domain Model

The domain model contains a taxonomy allowing the classification of the objects of the art gallery used for the exhibition guide. The taxonomy is mainly based on the structure of "ICONCLASS" – an ICONographic CLASsification System, which was published in 1974 to 1985 in Amsterdam [7].

The taxonomy structures all pictured topics of occidental graphic art in nine main groups of genres, divided in at most nine subgroups, again divided in at most nine subgroups and so on. The classification is not an exclusive one, where artworks can only be classified once. It is possible that an artwork shows combined characteristics of several categories. The nine main (not exclusive) groups are: Religion&Magic, Nature, Human Being, Man in General, Society, Civilisation, Culture, Abstract Ideas and Concepts, History, Bible, Literature, Classical Mythology & Ancient History.

For our experiential gallery of artworks used for the Hippie prototype, we have introduced some more detailed categories to obtain an acceptable distribution of given artworks. We also classified the artworks according to their kind: paintings, sculptures and arts-and-crafts.

2.2 Space Model

To locate the user in the physical space, several techniques can be applied. For the location, infrared installations are used for small (indoor) environments; the Global Positioning System (GPS) can be used for large-scale outdoor environments. The former can use a proprietary map; the latter uses the geographic latitude and longitude co-ordinates. Beside the location, the orientation of the user is also needed to identify the direction of his or her focus of attention. For orientation, an electronic compass is used in combination with the infrared receiver attached to the user.

2.3 User Model

The user model is the most complex for context modeling in our approach. Adaptive hypermedia systems adapt the information selection and presentation to the user's goals, preferences, knowledge, and interests. In most cases, the user-model acquisition is based on activities of users in the information space and an analysis of connection and device characteristics. Additionally, nomadic information systems can make use of the user's current position in the physical space and his/her movements within.

The knowledge model of the user can be built by monitoring the user's interaction with the user interface. Positive evidence for gaining knowledge about exhibition objects comes from listening or watching presentations. Negative evidence comes from skipping or stopping presentations. Furthermore, other diagnostic components can be used, like interactive games or questionnaires. The adaptation of the information to the assumed current knowledge of the user provides an optimal fit to the perception capability and avoids unnecessary repetition. Repetition is helpful for in-depth learning. For information presentation during nomadic activities, e.g. an exhibition visit, it tends to be boring.

The interests of the user are the most difficult part to model, especially because they are highly dynamic. On the one hand we are assuming an underlying relatively stable interest trait structure of a visitor, on the other hand we take into account the current situation and a multiplicity of environmental factors that have an impact on the actual activation (the state) of the interest structure. The concept of interest is important in particular in a context of user self-directed behaviour. This is not typical for the work environment where tasks define the goals and the process of user behaviour. In an entertainment or cultural environment there are no predefined tasks but at most arranged attractions that catch or do not catch the people's attention. A visit in a museum is a good example for exploiting the navigation of the visitors matched with the taxonomy of the exhibits to predict visitor interests in types of artworks.

Interest as a concept relevant to explain and predict human behaviour is used in several fields of psychological research. We shall only give a very short overview about the approaches to explain human behaviour with references to interest. According to Lewin's field theory, human behaviour is a function of environmental and personal factors (see a summary of Lewin's theory by [8]). Environmental aspects can be perceived as demands and affordances in a given situation. Personal aspects can be perceived as the needs and motivation of the individual. Social aspects are part of and influence the environment and influence the development of the individuals needs and motivations.

Motivation theories refer to interest as a tendency to focus the attention towards objects or issues in a specific environment [9]. Interest can be more specifically characterised by three elements, a directness of attention, an object or issue toward which the attention is directed, and learning about the object or issue. Interest is a conscious direction to an object or issue; it determines the degree to which an individual is occupied with the object or issue by perception, by communication or by interaction. Interest is a latent variable that can be activated by external conditions, in particular by the presence of the object or issue of interest. Interest is not a constant concept, but develops according to the personal history of experiences and external affordances.

The dynamic character of interest as a condition for learning has a long history in *educational psychology* [10]. The readiness for learning, i.e., for the acquisition of knowledge, depends on the interest of the learner. The more the individual knows and learns about an object or issue, the higher the interest grows. The higher the interest is, the more effectively the individual learns about an object or issue. Both variables are interdependent. The individual's need for change defines the saturation point when the individual relaxes or directs the attention to another object or issue. As interest can be invoked by the presence of an object or issue, interest also tends to decrease after a period of occupation.

Psychological *perception theories* have shown that interest triggers perception behaviour in a quantitative and qualitative way [11]. The more the individual is interested in an object or issue, the more likely it is that he or she becomes aware of the object or issue, and the more likely it is that he or she will also search for and perceive information. Perception theories have also shown that interest determines the kind and content the individual perceives about the object or issue of interest. Perception is selective and interpretative. The interest determines what content will be selected, perceived and memorised about the object or issue of interest.

In *social psychology* interest has been studied in terms of attitude formation and social expectations [12]. Attitudes describe how an object or issue is evaluated by an individual. Social factors, e.g. peers and significant others, influence the formation of attitudes and the relevance of attitudes in an environment where the individual feels to be under social observation. A museum study [13] showed the relevance of social formations for the physical movement and the information behaviour of visitors.

For an adaptive exhibition guide like Hippie, the goal of a user model is to predict the information needs of a user in a given episode of a visit. The inferences to be made are the next exhibit to be recommended and the next information content to be presented. These two predictions have to be inferred from the previous navigation in the physical and in the information space. We now shall discuss how the concept of interest can help for this task.

Studies of human perception show that there is an interrelation between the interests of an individual and the attraction of a perceived object. Weidenmann (1988, 39, 42f., 89f.) and Kowalski (1970, 68ff.) showed this interrelation in the context of visual perception of artworks. The attraction of an artwork can be described by several variables, including but not limited to novelty, complexity, and abstractiveness. These variables are no absolute determinants but depend partly on the perceiving individual [14]. Roughly, children can be described by a holistic perception, adolescents by representational perception and adults by reflective perception following the competence and interest of the individual [15]. The more the individual grows up and the more opportunity he or she has had to have experience in the domain, the more are perception and interpretation of art objects determined by individual preferences and evaluation [16]. The more the individual matures in the understanding of a domain the more he or she can proceed in the process of perception.

Perception is not limited to cognitive determinants. Affective dispositions of the individual and affective cues of the object also determine perception [16] [17] [14]. The length of time spent viewing artworks can be limited by the subject's need for diversity [14] but additional external stimuli (ibid., 92) like explanations or stories can re-activate the occupation.

The studies cited above support the assumption that the perception of exhibition items can be predicted by the position of the perception episode within the individual life history (child, adolescent or adult), within the individual domain maturity (naive viewer or experienced viewer) and within the current visit sequence (at the beginning or after reaching a saturation point viewing an artwork or an exhibition). The more the user is experienced in a domain, the more the concept of interest can contribute to the prediction of the user's information needs. A user model of an information system has access to the exhibits and to the content of information selected by the individual to make inferences to his or her interests.

3 Exploitation of User Navigation for User Interests

In the context of nomadic information systems, we shall discuss the potential of localization to evaluate the user's interests during his or her navigation in physical space. Besides navigation in the information space, we also use the user's navigation in the physical space as an additional indicator for his or her interest in particular objects and particular content about the objects.

In the context of an exhibition visit, there is a great chance for a nomadic information system to evaluate the physical navigation of the visitor. The visitor using a position aware device can be observed during the visit with respect to the objects he or she directs his or her attention to. The position and the time spent at the position are indicators of attention in the particular exhibit. If the time spent in the critical position is very short it may be assumed that the visitor is not interested in the exhibit. If the time increases and the number of information pieces that the visitor selects from the information guide increases, then the probability that the visitor is interested in the exhibit can be assumed to be higher.

In a nomadic usage context, the user's navigation in the information space of the system and his or her navigation in the physical space may be coincident. The user walks to an object in the physical space and selects information about the object in the information space. In a location-aware system the user model can evaluate both the user's navigation in the physical space and his or her navigation in the information space. In the positive case where the user selects information about the objects seen in the physical space there is redundancy; both forms of navigation tell the user model that the user has approached a particular object. From both indicators, the user model may infer that the user is interested in the approached object.

Interest in objects: From the type of an exhibit, i.e. from the genre or style of an exhibit identified in the taxonomy of the domain model, it can be inferred which next exhibit or which series of exhibits (a tour) can be proposed to the visitor. By navigating through the physical space, the visitor implicitly communicates to the user model the prevalent interest in a kind of exhibit. The interest evaluation can even be enriched by assessing the approach to the exhibit, whether the visitor only views an exhibit from a general position or whether he or she chooses several positions to see different views and details. There is evidence about visitors' differentiated navigation behaviour. Varying distances and direction to view artworks have been found in an empirical study [18] where over 500 visitors of five European museums were asked for their actual navigation approach to exhibits.

Interest in attributes: Visitors not only communicate their interest in particular kinds of exhibits; they also communicate their interest in specific content about the exhibits by selecting pieces of information. If the information about exhibits has been structured in a content taxonomy, inferences can be made from the selected content to a content class of interest. The more explicit the information structure is, the more effectively the information can be adapted to the interest of the user. The information can be structured by classes of information about the general meaning of the exhibit, the historical background, the domain-specific value (i.e., artistic details), and stories. The most preferred information class can be proposed to the visitor automatically.

Until now, movements of visitors have been used to infer their interest in objects or content. Evaluations of visitor movements have been proposed without referring to underlying interests [19]. The authors rely on the approach by [20], who propose a classification of visitors according to their "visiting style" while evaluating the sequence of exhibits in the exhibition (ibid., 18). The type of visitor movement is observed and styles of stereotypical movements are classified. Twenty-one visitors could be classified by four categories: ANTS, FISHES, BUTTERFLYS and GRASSHOPPERS; 4 visitors showed a "mixed" style of navigation [20]. In the reception of the approach by [19], the classification of a visitor is no longer made stereotypically by describing a visitor uniquely as one of the four animals, but as an estimation of the "degree of compatibility between the user's movement pattern and the four stereotypes" at a given point of time [21]. The characterisation of a visitor is a list of probabilities, e.g., FISH 20%, ANT 30%, BUTTERFLY 50%, GRASSHOPPER 10%. In this reception, the visiting style is assumed to be dynamic, i.e., the style can develop during the visit from one pattern to another. No explanation is made why the visitor follows a particular visiting style, and no prediction is made when the visiting style changes. For a given visiting style, a particular information is said to be appropriate: long presentations for an ANT, short presentations for a GRASSHOPPER and medium for a FISH and a BUTTERFLY.

[22] presents another approach that tries to classify the visiting navigation. Visitors were observed and also interviewed about their visit and their perception of the exhibition and of the exhibits they have actually seen to identify the cognitive strategy of the visiting behaviour. The author identifies 4 cognitive strategies of visitors: a pragmatic reception strategy, a critical reception strategy, utopian reception strategy, and a diversionary reception strategy. The classification can be derived from movement patterns in the physical space, but it also refers to subjective interpretation of the experience by the visitors given in an interview. In the description of movement patterns the author refers to the visiting style model by [20] combining the BUTTERFLY and the GRASSHOPPER to one visiting style "leaping". So, three movement patterns are distinguished: crawling, leaping, swimming. Crawling is defined as a "steady, systematic, movement from beginning to end"; "leaping pattern (is) characterised by a more erratic jumping back and forth between displays in different parts of the gallery" and "swimming pattern" is described as "one where the visitor flows through the centre of the gallery space with almost no stops" and his or her "refusal to negotiate the intended meanings of the gallery" [22]. She uses a behaviour property metaphor rather than an animal being metaphor as more appropriate to describe a visiting style. [22] shows the relation of the cognitive styles to the movement patterns in the following table (marginal sums added by the authors):

Table 1: Movement patterns of different groups of visitors adapted from [22]

N=41	Pragmatic (29%)	Critical (17%)	Utopian (22%)	Diversionary (32%)
Crawling (46%)	50%	71%	56%	23%
Leaping (44%)	25%	14%	44%	77%
Swimming (10%)	25%	14%	0	0

The two navigation approaches were originally meant to be analytic. The visiting style model has been adopted by [19] as a pragmatic model for inferences of information length of a mobile information guide. Long and detailed presentations are proposed for ANTS, short presentations are proposed for GRASSHOPPERS. The inference of information presentations is limited by the unknown persistence of a visiting style. It is supposed to be subject to change: An ANT may mutate to a GRASSHOPPER from one minute to another or from one exhibition hall to another. Temporary physical obstacles or other visitors (crowds) in the room may determine visiting navigation. Or the kind of artworks relevant to the interests or the knowledge of the visitor acquired during the visit may determine the visiting navigation. As far as the physical movement of the visitor is not reflected together with the domain model (taxonomy of the artworks) the space model (location of the artworks) and the user model (the visitor's interests), the predictive power of the visiting style approach is poor. It may be a first guess if no knowledge about the taxonomy of the artworks, about the location of the specific artworks in the physical space and about the interests of the visitor (types of artworks) is available. But the predictive power of the evaluation of the movement of the visitor will considerably increase once all these factors are considered in a combined visiting model. Figure 1 shows a process model for information presentation of the adaptive system.

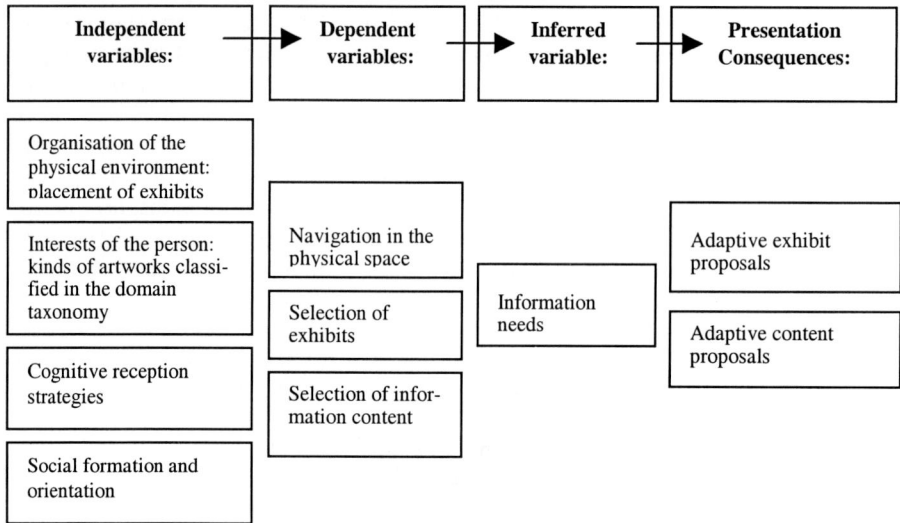

Fig. 1. A process model for user's information needs in a mobile environment

The process model in figure 1 shows measurable variables (independent variables) on the left side. The organization of the physical environment, the interests of the individual, cognitive perception strategies, and the current social formation and orientation have an impact on the dependent variables (the navigation in spaces, the selection of exhibits, and the selection of contents). The inferred variable of the users information need is the basis for the presentation consequences as exhibit and content proposals.

4 A Prototype of a Context-Sensitive Nomadic Information System

Hippie offers added value to current information facilities by supporting all along the process of mobile activities. Process support is made possible by the nomadic characteristic of the system that allows the user to have access to his or her personal information space from wherever they are, independently from specific devices. The information selected and presented to the visitor reflects the location (at home or in front of an exhibit), the interests, the knowledge and the presentation preferences of the user. Dynamic elements for animated interpretation and audio presentations complement the visual modality preoccupied by the physical environment. The user is equipped with a handheld computer and a headphone to listen to explanations of the current object and environment to immerse into the subject of interest. The user is left alone with the physical environment, and the complementary explanations; via the communication function of the system, he or she can also get in touch with other individuals present in the real or virtual exhibition for appointments or suggestions.

In the following we describe the main features of the system to explain the benefit for the users: the process support by permanent system accessibility, the location awareness of the system to present information suitable to the current position of the visitor, multimodal information presentation to exploit the range of human perception, and information adaptation to the user's knowledge and interests.

4.1 Internet Connectivity for Continuous Information

Internet connectivity provides access to the information basis from all over the world. At home, the user can access the system with a desktop computer with high resolution representations to study the site of interest, e.g., a content list and pictures of an exhibition, descriptions of individual artworks and artists as well as practical information about opening hours, ticket prices, etc., and to prepare an actual visit. The visit in the exhibition is supported by a handheld computer with wireless LAN connection. Access points provide the network connection within the museum. In the museum, the user can access the same information space he or she is already familiar with from sessions at home. The same richness of information is available, although the visitor will not see a high-resolution representation. On a small screen, only a thumbnail icon will be presented to reassure the visitor that the information that is presented is about the artwork he or she is in front of.

4.2 Location Awareness

The user of the nomadic system is free to roam in the physical space. The system identifies the user's position in two ways. It knows about the type of computer and the technical infrastructure the user is connected to. At home a big computer with high resolution and high bandwidth is used. In the museum a small computer with a small screen and lower bandwidth requires an adaptation of information presentation: less explicit interaction, more implicit interaction by navigation in the physical space, more audio presentation than text, less detailed graphical presentations and more thumbnails.

The second type of location awareness means the current co-ordinates of the visitor within the museum. By infrared infrastructure the position and by an electronic compass the direction of the visitor are identified and transmitted from the handheld computer to the server, so that the server can automatically send the appropriate information for the visitor about the current exhibit. The infrared infrastructure consists of emitters being installed on the walls underneath each exhibit. The emitters send an ID to a receiver fastened on the jacket of the visitor or attached to the user's headphones and connected to the handheld computer. Additional emitters are installed above each door of the museum, allowing the identification of the visitor passing through the entrance of a room before entering into the cone of an exhibit emitter. By these means, a continuous localisation of the visitor can be used for information selection and be displayed on an electronic map of the museum, if the visitor requires support for the navigation in the physical space, e.g., to find an exhibit of interest.

If a new item of interest is detected by infrared the system presents an "earcon" combined with a blinking click sensitive "News" icon on the screen. On request the system displays the name and a thumbnail presentation of the current exhibit; with a follow-up hyperlink the user can start the presentation. (In case of exhibit groups an infrared emitter is connected to several exhibits so that the user receives a list of items.). An example of the sequence of the "News" notification, the display of close paintings to be selected and the artwork Cupid & Mercury are shown in figure 2.

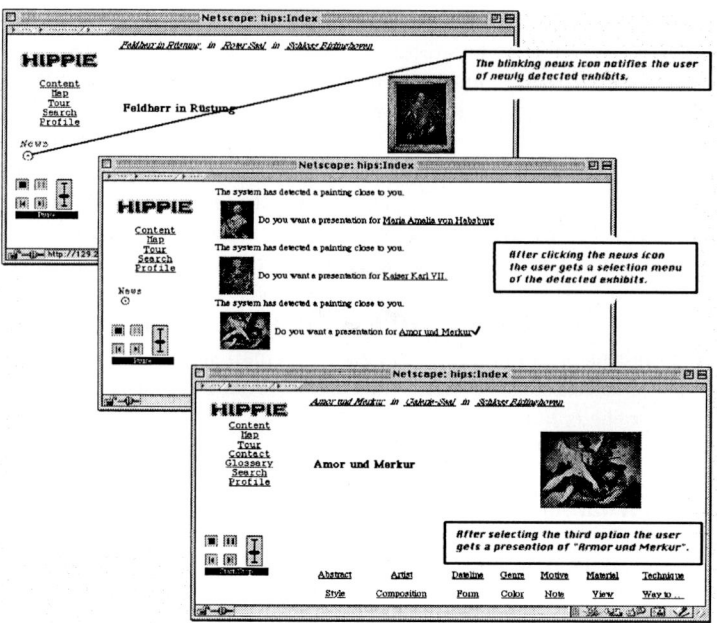

Fig. 2. Notification of a new exhibit next to the wandering visitor

4.3 Multimodal Information Presentation

The default information presentation for visitors during the preparation and evaluation phases is unimodal, containing pictures and text. This default type of presentation reflects the typical interaction and perception style of a user at a desktop and enables easy reading and printing, including scanning and browsing of the information space. The default information presentation during the visit is multimodal containing written text on the screen *and* spoken language via headphones, and multicodal, including text, graphics and animations. The visitor's visual attention is free for the physical environment, especially for viewing the exhibits. Most information is presented aurally without requiring the visitor to look at the screen. The audio information to be presented is currently composed of snippets of canned text spoken by a human speaker. In the future, computer-generated language can also be used, once it is of sufficient quality. At present 819 audio objects are included in the system. For paintings, between 160 and 300 sec of presentations of 7 to 25 attributes are offered with an average time of 207 sec. For all artworks, including sculptures and art-and-crafts, the average presentation time is 90 sec.

There are some cases when it is necessary for the visitor to look at the screen. A first incident is navigation support. Orientation in the physical space and the location of oneself and of exhibitions of interest may require a graphical map with indicators for the visitor and for the exhibitions. The second incident where visitors may need screen displays are visual aids to understand an artwork, e.g., its composition, its form design or its colour design. The electronic guide provides explanations of such features of artworks not only by textual descriptions but also by graphical illustrations and videos. Figure 2 shows an example of a graphical form design explanation together with the explaining text displayed to the right of the graphical illustration (the text is also presented aurally via headphones).

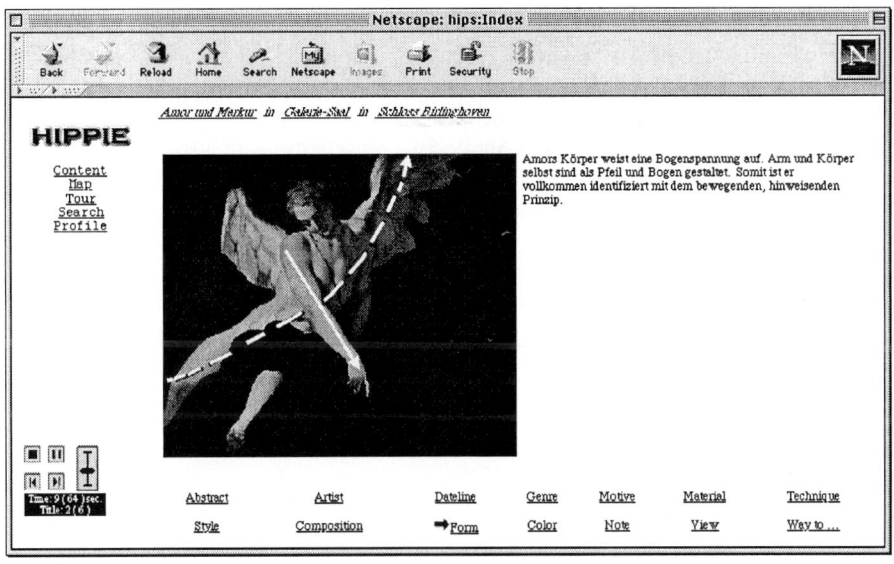

Fig. 3. Form design description by auxiliary lines combined with written and spoken text

4.4 Information Adaptation to User's Knowledge and Interest

As described above, information selection and presentation is adapted to the currently used device, to the network connection, and to the location of the user. Now we will describe the adaptation of information selection and presentation to the individual user. The user can be more or less competent of and interested in the domain in question. The adaptive component runs a user model describing the knowledge and the interests of the user. The user model contains a history of the user's information selection from the system and the user's roaming in the museum. The history is continuously evaluated for user-preferred items or user-preferred attributes to identify particular interests comparing the user's selection with the taxonomy of the domain.

If the user has used the system to select information about an exhibition, an artist, an artwork, particular attributes of an artwork and so on, the system updates the user model for seen entities and seen topics. For the following presentations it can adapt the information to the user's assumed prior knowledge and interests. The adaptation to assumed prior knowledge is performed by avoiding redundancy—see also [23]. A painting that has already been seen by the user and explained to him or her will only be reminded of its name when the user selects it a second time; more information about author, dateline, style, etc. are available on explicit requests of the user.

Adaptive tips provide adaptation to the assumed interests of the user. If a user selects a number of exhibits, the user model identifies common attributes of the selection in terms of, e.g., artist, style or genre. When it exceeds a rule-defined threshold, the system initiates a click-sensitive "Tip" displayed by a light blinking on the screen three times. The system presents its observation as a list of objects the user has selected, e.g., paintings from the genre "mythology", and a recommendation of a tour the user can start encompassing other paintings of the genre "mythology" to be seen in the museum. Two screenshots with a blinking light notifying the user of available tour proposals and a set of three tours with the system's observations and inferred tour proposals are shown in figure 3.

The same rule-based mechanism is applied for presentations of attributes of the artworks. If the user selects a set of particular interesting attributes, the system recommends presenting the set of attributes as a default sequence of topics for the given class of artworks. A user who is more interested in the history and social background gets a sequence of topics like biography, while a user who is more interested in art-analytical topics gets a sequence of composition and form and colour design.

By adaptation of the information selection and presentation, the benefit of a visit for the user is expected to be higher, especially his or her knowledge and understanding of the exhibition in general and the exhibits in particular, but also the richness of experience, which can be intensified by personalised information.

4.5 Annotation, Explanation, and Communication

Hippie provides additional features to support the individual user and a user group. For the process of a visit at different times and places it is helpful for the user to make notes attached to exhibitions or to individual artworks in order to store personal explanations or bookmarks available during a visit. An annotation button "Notes" attached to the presentation of the exhibits supports this goal.

For definitions of terms and descriptions of names, a "Glossary" is available that can be addressed from the main menu; short explanations as excursions in the context of content description are available via hyperlinks on the fly.

The "Contact" function of the system allows the user to communicate with other users. The communication can be directed to a dedicated addressee (a partner, a family, a group). A list of currently present users is offered as well as the possibility to enter a full e-mail address to contact a remote user. Recommendations can be exchanged while moving independently through the physical space, or appointments can simply be made to meet in the cafeteria in half an hour. Messages can also be directed to the public as a contribution to a growing knowledge base about the environment.

By the combination of features described above, Hippie makes use of Weiser's vision, call calm technology by ubiquitous computing [24]. The equipment used in the museum and the information and communication interface is designed to let the visitor walk in the physical space of the museum while getting access to a contextualized information space tailored to the individual needs and the current environment.

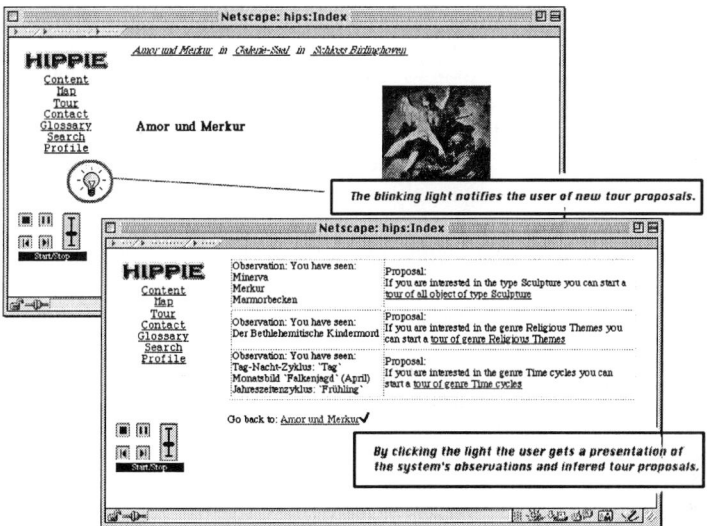

Fig. 4. Notification of an adaptive tour proposal

5 Evaluation

The added value of the system compared with current information media has received positive feedback from experts from computer science and the cultural heritage domain (museum curators, art educators). During the development of the system, formative evaluations have been conducted with human factor experts and an art educator. The input has been used to improve the content and the user interface of the system.

Summative evaluations of the system have been performed with domain experts, i.e., artists, art educators, and museum curators during a one-day demonstration and feedback workshop. The experts confirmed the added value of the nomadic information system both for the process support of preparing, conducting, and evaluating a museum visit, and for the understanding of artworks with respect to the wide spectrum of information provided by the system.

Evaluations with real users are currently being conducted. Four media are compared to analyse the relative value of information-presentation methods: the mobile guide Hippie, a stationary kiosk information system placed in the centre of the exhibition, an audio guide playing back descriptions with simple play and skip controls, and a book guide with texts and pictures. All media present identical content but different modalities and forms of interactivity. The richest modality and interactivity are provided by the mobile Hippie and the kiosk system, the former identifying the position and history of the user automatically, the latter requiring all controls to be used manually by the user. The most restricted but the most comfortable and easy to use media are the audio guide and the book, the former being familiar from CD-players and the latter from catalogues.

Limited numbers of visitors supported by the mobile Hippie showed that users with extensive interest and prior knowledge in art immersed into the perception of the exhibits on the wall and the information presented by the system. They exploited the richness of the information space both quantitatively, with an average presentation time of 2.5 min. per exhibit, and qualitatively, with audio and text presentation and additional graphical support for the art-analytical understanding of aspects like composition, form or colour design. Visitors with only curiosity and low prior knowledge used the system for short snippets of information while wandering through the exhibition. Visitors using the other media were less engaged in system interaction and more relaxed with presentations. Whether the average visitor can be stimulated to perceive a more intensive presentation and develop a more extensive understanding of artworks will be investigated in the in-depth evaluation study.

6 Conclusion

The approach described in the paper exploits user navigation in physical space (roaming) and in information space (selection of presentations) to enrich the adaptation of an exhibition guide to user needs. Interests are the most important criteria used in the study because they can be deduced from the user's navigation in physical space and in information space, and because interests are the main criteria for information selection. The prototype based on the theoretical approach has been implemented and tested in an art gallery. The results of evaluations with art experts and real visitors are encouraging. More suitable multimodal presentations and rich interaction facilities of the adaptive guide compete with the simplicity and ease of use of conventional guides.

References

1. Makimoto, T. and D. Manners, *Digital Nomad*. 1997: John Wiley & Sons.
2. Brézillon, P., *Introduction to the Special Issue "Using context in applications"*. International Journal of Human-Computer Studies, 1998. 48: p. 303-305.
3. Abowd, G.D., et al., *Cyberguide: A Mobile Context-Aware Tour Guide*. Baltzer Journals, 1996(September 23).
4. Abowd, G.D., et al. *Context-awareness in wearable and ubiquitous computing. Poster.* in *1st International Symposium on Wearable Computers ISWC'97*. 1997. Cambridge, MA.
5. Schmidt, A., M. Beigl, and H.-W. Gellersen, *There is more to Context than Location*. Rostock, . 1998.
6. Wallace, M.D. and T.J. Anderson, *Approaches to Interface Design*. Interacting with Computers, 1993. 5(3): p. 259-278.
7. Heusinger, L., *Marburger Informations-, Dokumentations- und Administrations-System (MIDAS) Handbuch*. 3 ed. Literatur und Archiv, ed. G. Jäger, et al. Vol. 4. 1994, München: K.G. Saur. 593.
8. Deutsch, M., *Field Theory in Social Psychology*, in *The Handbook of Social Psychology*, G. Lindzey and E. Aronson, Editors. 1968, Addison-Wesley: Reading Mass. p. 412 - 487.
9. Rubinstein, S., *Die Interessen*, in *Die Motivation menschlichen Handelns*, H. Thomae, Editor. 1970, Kiepenheuer &Witsch: Köln, Wien. p. 136 - 144.
10. Bruner, J.S., *Bereitschaft zum Lernen.*, in *Pädagogische Psychologie.*, F. Weinert, Editor. 1961, Kiepenheuer &Witsch: Köln, Wien. p. 105 - 117.
11. Schulz von Thun, W., *Kommunikationsprozeß.*, in *Publizistik.*, E. Noelle-Neumann, Winfried Schulz von Thun, Editor. 1971: Frankfurt am Main. p. 89 - 109.
12. Fishbein, M. and I. Ajzen, *Belief, Attitude, Intention and Behavior: An Introduction to Theory and Research*. 1975, Reading, Mass.
13. McManus, P.M., *Making sense of exhibits*, in *Museum Languages: Objects and Texts*, G. Kavanagh, Editor. 1991, Leicester University Press: Leicester, London and New York. p. 35 - 46.
14. Weidenmann, B., *Psychische Prozesse beim Verstehen von Bildern*. 1988, Bern: Hans Huber.
15. Kowalski, K., *Praxis der Kunsterziehung 2. Werkbetrachtung*. 1970, Stuttgart: Klett Verlag.
16. Kayser, T. and C. Körner, *Abiturwissen Malerei*. 1997, Stuttgart: Klett Verlag.
17. Hofer, M., R. Pekrun, and W. Zielinski, *Die Psychologie des Lernens*, in *Pädagogische Psychologie*, B. Weidenmann, Andreas Krapp et al., Editor. 1994, Belz: Weinheim. p. 219 - 272.
18. Specht, M., *HIPS Questionnaire result report*, . 1998, GMD: Sankt Augustin. p. 13.
19. Gabrielli, F., P. Marti, and L. Petroni, *The environment as interface*, in *Proceedings of the i3 Annual Conference: Community of the Future, October 20 - 22, 1999 in Siena*, M. Caenepeel, D. Benyon, and D. Smith, Editors. 1999, The Human Communication Research Centre, The University of Edinburgh: Edinburgh. p. 44 - 47.
20. Véron, E. and M. Levasseur, *Ethnographie de l'exposition: L'espace, le corps et le sens*. 1991, Paris: Centre Georges Pompidou Bibliothèque Publique d'Information.

21. Bianchi, A. and M. Zancanaro, *Tracking Users' Movements in an Artistic Physical Space*, in *Proceedings of the i3 Annual Conference: Community of the Future, October 20 - 22, 1999 in Siena*, M. Caenepeel, D. Benyon, and D. Smith, Editors. 1999, The Human Communication Research Centre, The University of Edinburgh: Edinburgh. p. 103 - 106.
22. Umiker-Sebeok, J., *Behavior in a Museum: A Semio-Cognitive Approach to Museum Consumption Experiences.* Signifying Behavior, 1994. 1 (1994)(1).
23. Not, E., et al., *Person-Oriented Guided Visits in a Physical Museum. In: D. Bearman/J. Trant eds.: Proceedings of the Museum Interactive Multimedia 1997: Cultural Heritage Systems. Design and Interfaces. Paris, 3 - 5 September 1997, pp. 69 - 79.,* . 1997.
24. Weiser, M., *The Computer for the 21st Century.* Scientific American, 1991. 265(3): p. 94 - 104.

Exploiting Location-Based Composite Devices to Support and Facilitate Situated Ubiquitous Computing

Thai-Lai Pham, Georg Schneider, and Stuart Goose

Multimedia/Video Technology Department, Siemens Corporate Research, Inc.
755 College Road East
Princeton, NJ 08540
001 609 734 6500
{pham, gschneider, sgoose}@scr.siemens.com

Abstract. Small screen appliances, such as cellular phones or Personal Digital Assistants (PDAs), enjoy enormous popularity as is evidenced by the tremendous commercial success. One focus of the ubiquitous research community is the potential utility of this class of devices beyond that of a basic organizer or communication device. The pocket-sized requirement imposes constraints upon the computational power and user interface of these small screen devices. This paper describes the Composite Device Computing Environment (CDCE) that offers a framework for supporting nomadic users with small screen devices for the retrieval of rich contents and the access of diverse services. CDCE provides a communication network infrastructure for seeking, unifying and exploiting any surrounding devices as a means to overcome the small screen client constraints. This paper describes the architecture and reports the current status of the ongoing realization of CDCE.

1 Introduction

Recent years have witnessed the remarkable commercial success of small screen devices, such as cellular phones and Personal Digital Assistants (PDAs). Recent market studies predict an inexorable growth for mobile computing devices and wireless communication for the future. Recent studies by International Data Corporation [16] report that the current number of cellular phone users outnumbers households in the USA with an Internet connection.

The World Wide Web (WWW) has enjoyed phenomenal growth over recent years and now accounts for a significant proportion of all Internet traffic. The unmitigated success of the WWW bears testimony to the previously unsatisfied need for a system able to integrate and deliver distributed information. Users can access a wealth of information and associated services over the WWW, ranging from international news to local restaurant menus.

Mobile and ubiquitous computing research has attracted much attention within the information technology community by making advances in breaking away from the desktop-centric world into one that surrounds the mobile user. A common use of the current generation of small screen devices is as electronic organizers, able to read synchronized emails (PDA) or simply to use as a mobile communication device (cellular phone). However, it is possible to extrapolate from current trends a rising demand for mobile access to rich multimedia content and diverse services from small screen devices. Unfortunately, the constraint of small screen appliances being pocket-sized impairs the computational power and optimal user interface. As such, there exists a mismatch that requires resolution before such devices are suitable for accessing rich multimedia content and diverse services.

Acknowledging this mismatch of capabilities, one research focus at Siemens Corporate Research (SCR) has been to investigate a ubiquitous framework that provides an infrastructure to resolve this problem. Our primarily goal is to unify the high ubiquity and personalization nature of small screen entities with the powerful capabilities of static and location-based computing devices. As such, we have built a user-centric and small screen device-centric system called the *Composite Device Computing Environment (CDCE)* [21]. In the CDCE project the surrounding available computing resources are considered as another facet of situated computing and hence provides mechanisms for seamlessly exploiting and interacting with the available surrounding computing resources (e.g., PCs, workstations, TVs, telephones) to augment the PDA. Based upon the user's request, the CDCE framework dynamically creates a unified composite, or virtual, device composed of an appropriate mix of the surrounding resources. That is using the small screen appliance as a personal companion and unique system access interface, whereas the execution of service request is outsourced to the most appropriate composite unit(s). Hence, depending upon the availability of hardware resources at user's actual *location,* the CDCE framework provides a network infrastructure to seek these resources in order to create virtual compositions of composite devices and to exploit it. As such, CDCE flexibly combines the positive aspects of mobility with static computing resources in the vicinity.

The remainder of this paper is structured as follow: Section 2 describes related research activities. The motivation of CDCE and the main CDCE characteristics are discussed in section 3 and 4. Section 5 describes a potential application scenario. Section 6 illustrates the high-level CDCE system architecture and describes its components. Section 7 describes the control interface and composite device interactivity models. The current implementation status of the CDCE framework and infrastructure is reported in section 8. Finally, we conclude this paper with future activities in section 9.

2 Related Work

Much research has been conducted since the first discussions and the pioneering work in mobile and ubiquitous computing was published by Weiser in the early 90s [26, 27, 28]. Much research effort has also been dedicated to building context-awareness computing systems, such as the tourist guiding and information systems Cyberguide [1] and GUIDE [5,6]. These systems both use location context to provide guidance through a university campus. Location context is also utilized by the Active Badge

System [25] to determine the current position of people wearing badges in an office environment. However, these systems differ from CDCE in our fundamental objective to provide a small screen device-centric and ubiquitous computing system with the ability to access multimedia services and rich content. The PC tablet hardware of the GUIDE system is heavy and bulky in comparison to small screen devices and service diversity as well content richness aspects are lack in the Cyberguide and the Active Badge system.

Meyers et al [19] describe the Pebbles framework, which supports multiple PDAs connecting to a PC for collaborative working. Pebbles provides a simple method for a group of people to, in turn, control applications running on a PC. Although, in Pebbles PDAs are simply used as an additional input device for a group of people to conduct meetings, it demonstrates a new perspective of using this class of devices for a purpose other than the typical organizer functionalities, such as address book, calculator or memo pad.

The Portolano project [8] at the University of Washington provides an excellent vision of the future computer, which will be invisible, ubiquitous and highly specialized on particular tasks. Esler et al make recommendations about research issues that further need to be addressed in order to make the vision become reality. Accordingly, the authors identify the user interface, the distributed services and the infrastructure as three essential research areas. However, Esler et al do not describe either a conceptual framework or propose a high-level system architecture to illustrate their vision and scenario.

The UbicompBrowser project by Beigl et al [2] express similar ideas to the CDCE framework. The UbicompBrowser was specifically designed to enable ubiquitous WWW access and to use a PDA to control environmental resources. Like the CDCE framework, Beigl et al recognize the possibility of using location-based computing resources in combination with a small screen device. Yet, the CDCE framework differs from the UbicompBrowser in several aspects. Most importantly, the CDCE framework provides a network and communication infrastructure that enables the small screen device to seek for location-based resources and to redirect server requests to these resources. That allows the user to create different compositions of composite devices depending upon the current location, to access diverse services and to interact with processes redirected to the composite devices by using the small screen device.

3 Motivation of the CDCE Project

The CDCE project has been mainly inspired by the challenges of building a small screen device centric system that enables the ubiquitous access to rich content and multiple services. We have in particular observed and acknowledged the trends of future mobile and computing technology as well as carefully studied the activities of the ubiquitous research society. Therefore, we conclude that:

- Small screen device capabilities will change towards more processing power and high-resolution displays.

- Wireless networks and protocols will improve towards higher bandwidth. That is underlined by the introduction of next generations of wireless network protocols GPRS (General Packet Radio Service) [11] and UMTS (Universal Mobile Telecommunications System) [24], with higher bandwidth in comparison with today's available cellular network such as GSM (Global System for Mobile Communications) [14].
- The multimedia content and services will change, e.g. trend from desktop-centric *e*-Commerce towards to *mobile*-Commerce or mobile interactive shopping.
- However, the maximum display size of the small screen devices will remain the same due to the requirement being pocket-sized. While it is likely that the screen resolution and quality will improve, the display size is anticipated to remain constant for a longer period.

The limited user interface as well as the poor CPU performance and low memory space however overstrain the capabilities of a single small screen device to access rich and diverse contents/services. Thus, we propose the inclusion of available location-based computing resources as a means to overcoming the limitations of a single small screen device. This is possible since our daily living environment, at work as well as at home, is evermore equipped with a diverse number of electronic and computing appliances. Therefore, the CDCE infrastructure provides the fundamental prerequisite for mobile users to actively exploit and to create dynamic virtual compositions of computing resources available at the user's current location.

4 CDCE Main Characteristics

CDCE is characterized by number of different aspects. Due to the highly mobile attribute the small screen device is used as a unique access/control interface to request services or content, whereas the request is outsourced to the composite device in the close vicinity for processing. The exploitation of the positive aspects of each composite element ensures appropriate accomplishments of requests. Thus, the CDCE client/server architecture requires an underlying network and communication infrastructure that satisfies the redirection of server responses to composite elements for the completion.

Hence, a number of design goals have been determined to build the CDCE framework that:

- enables the detection of available location-based composite devices and the recognition of the capabilities and availability of each output device.
- has the ability to organize, arrange, manage and synchronize multimedia content in order to ensure reliable service deliveries to output clients.
- offers the interactivity with rich content and the control of services on composite clients via small screen units.
- allows the redirection of server responses to the most appropriate composite devices in the close vicinity of the user for the rendering process.

- permits the server instance to invoke processes on output devices to deliver requested services.

The next section describes in brief an application scenario that demonstrates potential usage areas of the CDCE framework.

5 CDCE Application Scenario: Healthcare Environment

In order to have a better appreciation of the CDCE framework, this section provides a potential application scenario that CDCE network can support.

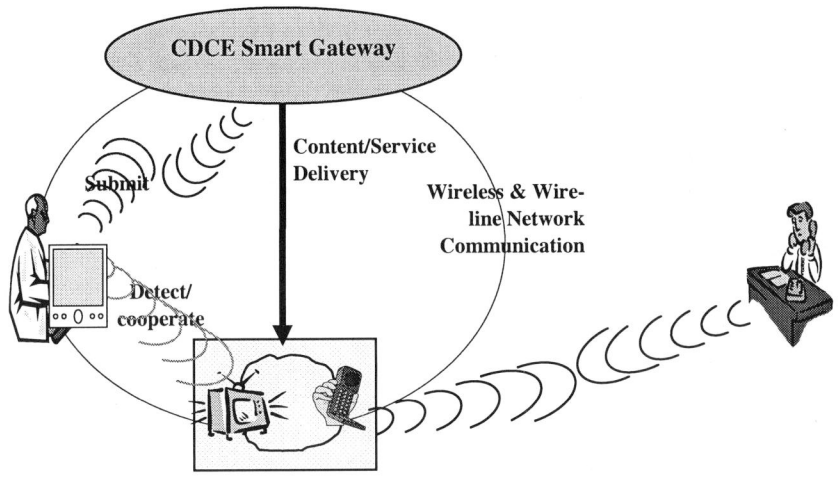

Fig. 1. CDCE system for healthcare

Hypertext-based infrastructure, as proposed by Hsu *et al* [15], may one day replace the paper-based structure of healthcare environments. Concurrent, dynamic multimedia annotation system, as described by Sastry *et al* [23], can be used to create multimedia reports including annotations. Doctors and nurses equipped with PDAs can access this multimedia data at any time while roaming within the hospital vicinity (see figure 1). For example, when in a patient room, doctors can request the patient's medical history, including symptoms, diagnoses, prescriptions and x-rays via the PDA. The presence of the location-based composite elements, TV and telephone, is detected by the PDA. Being aware of the PDA limitations, the CDCE Smart Gateway (SG) intelligently routes the x-ray and multimedia annotations to the TV for viewing. Via the PDA the doctor can control the playback of the annotation created by the patient's primary care physician and annotate critical areas of the x-ray. Depending upon request, the CDCE SG establishes a telephone call to the patient's primary care physician for further consultation.

6 CDCE High-Level Architecture

Figure 2 illustrates the CDCE system high-level architecture. As can be appreciated from this picture, the architecture is comprised of five major components: the CDCE Smart Gateway (SG), the CDCE Access Point, the System Control Interface, the Virtual CDCE Resource Mix and the Network Communication Infrastructure. Accordingly, the server side consists of the CDCE SG and the CDCE Access Point whereas the Control Interface and the CDCE Resource Mix represent the client side of the system. The next sections describe each component in further details.

6.1 CDCE Access Point

The System Entry Server is the entry point for the control interface to access services and contents provided by CDCE. It manages the connectivity between the different devices and offers a choice of available services and information that users can select from. Therefore, it provides the user interfaces for the selection of different information/services. The realization by using standard markup language structured interface, such as HTML, XML [10], WAP/WML (Wireless Application Protocol/Wireless Markup Language) [29] and the ability to interpret server side scripting commands have been evaluated.

6.2 CDCE Smart Gateway (SG)

The Smart Gateway (SG) is an essential component of the CDCE system. The main effort was to redirect heavy computing tasks on the small screen unit and to location-based composite clients for the rendering process. Hence, the SG is primarily responsible for the assignment of selected information/services to the most appropriate composite element(s). As depicted in figure 2 the essential components of the SG are:

- *Composite Device Repository:* In principal the *composite device repository* maintains the number of composite elements that are available in the vicinity and can be utilized to process certain computing tasks. Important is the exact knowledge of the capabilities of each composite element in order to facilitate the assignment of selected services to the most appropriate output device(s) by the *media-composite device manager* (see description below). The capabilities can be gathered using technologies such as Jini [18], CC/PP (Composite Capability/Preference Profiles) [7] or simply via static storage in a database. In addition, the control interface is further used to update the SG about the number of available output resources and its availability.

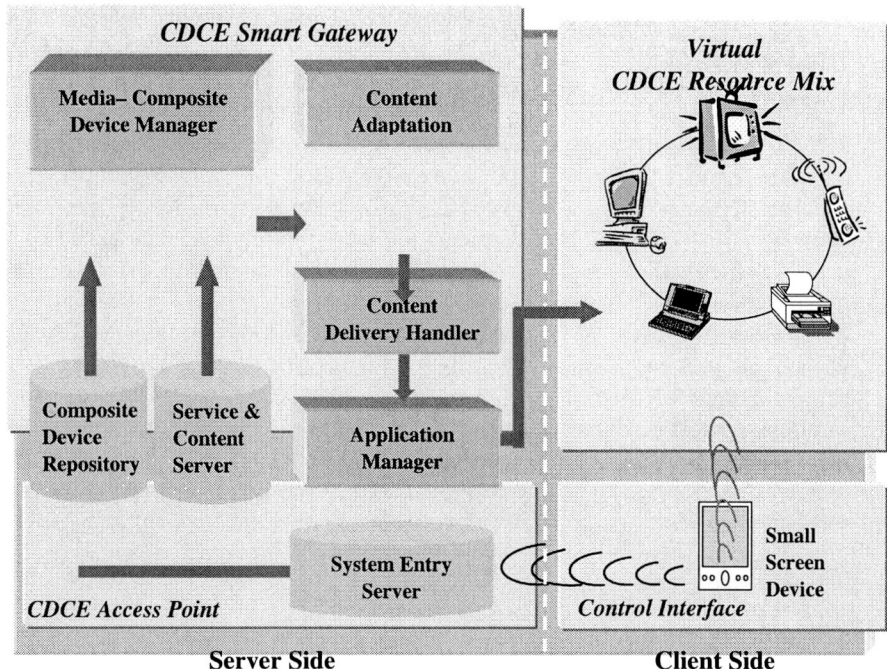

Fig. 2. CDCE High-Level Architecture

- *Multimedia Service & Content Server:* The *multimedia service and content server* provides and manages the pool of multimedia services and information available to CDCE network users. Depending upon the selection and requested content it handles the communication with the responsible content/service storage server. E.g., in the described medical scenario it enables specific applications based on the doctor's location, identity and privileges.
- *Media - Composite Device Manager:* This component is an important entity of the SG. It is responsible for the assignment of requested services and information to the composite element(s) that is (are) most appropriate to perform requested tasks. As suggested in the application scenario, the x-ray image is redirected to the TV for display instead sending it to the PDA. Hence, depending upon the selected service or content type, the *media-composite device manager* determines the most appropriate devices available in the repository for the execution of the request.
- *Multimedia Content Adaptation:* In situations, when the actual composition of the composite device is lack of the capability to handle the request type, a content adaptation process is taking place to adapt/match the content to the capabilities of the available element(s) of the composite device. E.g. a user queries a multimedia video message via her PDA, but only a PC without speakers and a telephone are available. The *multimedia content adaptation* component will split the video into a visual part for the PC and an audio part for the telephone.

- **Content Delivery Handler:** The consequence of offering service diversity and rich multimedia contents requires the consideration of an appropriate service delivery order and sequence. That is crucial when multiple services are requested at the same time. The exploitation of location-based computing devices with arbitrary spatial orientation even complicates the appreciation of multiple services on different output devices simultaneously. Thus, the implementation of a sophisticated *content delivery handler* prevents the performance of the entire requests at once. The situated consideration of certain criteria, such as *message priority*, *user preference*, *privacy concern* etc., can essentially contribute the process of determining an ideal service delivery order.
- **Application Manager:** A diverse number of functionalities are assigned to this unit of the SG. A substantial capability of the SG is the ability to invoke computing processes to run remotely on composite elements dispersed in different locations. That is necessary to deliver service requests redirected to a virtual pool of location-based output devices for the accomplishment. Thus, the SG is the only entity within the CDCE infrastructure with privileged security authorization for remote process invocation on output clients. Further, the *application manager* provides applications to control and interact with the invoked application on the output clients via the small screen unit.

6.3   CDCE Control Interface

This component of mainly comprises of the small screen device. Three main functions are primarily designated to the control interface:

- First, it is used as a unique device to access information and services provided by the CDCE system.
- Second, it detects and reserves available composite devices in the close vicinity and informs the SG about the number of potential output clients.
- Third, it controls the invoked services on composite devices and offers alternative input possibilities for users to interact with requested information and services (see section 7).

6.4   Virtual CDCE Resource Mix

The Virtual CDCE Resource Mix describes the current physical location of the system users and a pool of available composite elements that are characteristic for this environment and is also defined as a *Composite Device*. The number and types of devices varies considerably from location to location. E.g. the office environment typically consists of high performance computing devices and high-resolution monitors. Whereas, the home area is more likely equipped with entertainment devices, such as TV or VCR.

6.5 Network Communication Infrastructure

The network communication infrastructure is illustrated in figure 2 and is responsible for managing the convergence of wireless and wire line networks, as well as the corresponding communication protocols. It comprises of short-range wireless communication used by the small screen client for detection, cellular or wireless network to support the interaction between the PDA and the SG, and wired network technologies enabling the communication of the SG and location-based composite devices. This is necessary to ensure a seamless inter device communication and reliable data transmission. Hence, it contains sensing technologies, such as WLAN (wireless LAN), Bluetooth [3] or Infrared, required to enable the small screen client to detect available output resources in user's close vicinity as well as wireless technologies (e.g. CDPD (Cellular Digital Packet Data) [4], GSM [14], UMTS [24]) for the communication with the SG. Further, it provides the essential infrastructure prerequisite, such as Java RMI (Java Remote Method Invocation) [17], DCOM (Distributed Component Object Model) [12] or CORBA [20], that enables the SG to manage processes running on remote composite clients.

7 System Interactivity

One attribute of the CDCE framework is the interactivity and control of invoked processes on composite client via the control interface as well as the interaction with the CDCE system, since in many cases, users cannot rely upon the interactive possibilities provided by the location-based output clients (e.g. TV set has limited input capability). The next sections describe the alternative models supported.

7.1 Interactivity with Invoked Processes

It is clear that the physical constraints of the screen mean that the information to be rendered on the PDA imposes limitations not experienced on a desktop machine. Interaction with the environment is crucial and, in view of this requirement, we anticipate three alternative modes:

- *Abdicative*: In this case the control interface hands over the control to the output unit that currently processes the request. E.g. once an application is invoked on the PC mouse and keyboard can be used as input devices.
- *Cooperative*: Control interface and input capabilities of the output device can jointly be utilized to control the application. E.g. a slideshow can be annotated either using the mouse and keyboard of the output device or through a control interface on the control interface.
- *Exclusive*: The only input device is the small screen. This is especially important for output devices where no input facilities are available (e.g. a TV).

The cooperative and the exclusive modes require a special *mobile user interface* on the control interface. The functionality that these interfaces must provide depends strongly on the scenario.

We are also experimenting with three modes of interactivity:

1. Wireless Mouse Cursor Control via Control Interface
In this case, it is anticipated that the application control interface and the application are operating on the output device. The mouse cursor of the output device is controlled wireless via the small screen element such as the PDA. Thus, all mouse commands are entered on the PDA display using the PDA stylus. Such a solution as proposed by Meyers *et al* [19] can be deployed, but need to be modified to support wireless communication ability.

2. Representation of the Application Control on Control Interface
Unlike the first approach, the application control part of the application is represented on the display of the small screen unit. Users can directly operate the application from the control interface and all the commands are transferred wirelessly to the output client running the application.

3. Speech Technology
We are also currently experimenting with using speech recognition on both PDAs and cellular phones, to evaluate its suitability as a technique to control remote services on the composite device.

7.2 CDCE Process Management

Furthermore, interactivity is significant on a higher system interaction level as well. As important to the ability to execute and redirect a process, it is also necessary to explicitly stop a working task. This differs to the above interactivity models in cases e.g. users wish to roam, a network interruption occurs or the composite client owner wishes to use her device. Therefore, a session handler is required to automatically manage these interruptions. Thus, stopping the process means that the ad-hoc network between the claimed output clients is resolved respectively the link to the SG. As a consequence, these resources need to be released again for other users or processes. The possibility to pause/resume sessions and a unit to track these instances are helpful in cases of occurred interruptions. This avoids repeated device detection and service selections thus allowing the user to continue working from the point the interruption occurred. It further provides an alternative instrument to incorporate "new" devices joining the virtual pool of composite clients.

8 Implementation

This section describes the implementation of a demonstrator to verify the CDCE framework that has been deployed for an office environment. Unlike the situation for traditional computing systems, the situation for research and development for small screen devices is more immature and cannot rely upon standard components. The support of small screen clients for standards is still very limited. Thus, for the initial realization of the CDCE framework we decided to choose much de facto standard elements, such as a wireless IR or RF interface and HTTP/HTML or WAP/WML [29], that is flexible enough to adapt upcoming technologies. Up to current stage, much development efforts were dedicated to build a multi-tier communication infrastructure that enables us to conduct experimental tests as well as providing a fundamental basis for deployments of further modules of the CDCE framework.

8.1 Current Implementation Status

At the current implementation, a WWW server is the CDCE Access Point for small screen clients. The user interface is realized using HTML with embedded server side scripting commands that is accessible to system users via HTTP over the deployed wireless network CDPD/WLAN. Due to lack of support on small screen clients, HTML was selected over XML/XSL/CSS [10]. A commercial scalable database system manages the detected available composite devices that are submitted via the small screen device to the SG. The database maintains information and capabilities of each composite element. We have implemented Microsoft Exchange Webmail, streaming media and Netmeeting videoconferencing as test services.

The *media-composite device manager* calculates the assignment of selected services to the most appropriate composite client(s) and represents it in HTML, which the user can either confirm or manually modify. The computed assignment schema is used by the *application manager* to ensure the delivery of the requested services/content to the composite device. DCOM [12] is used to remotely invoke processes on the composite elements.

The Cassiopeia E-105 PDA running Windows CE 2.11 was selected to represent the class of small screen devices. The composite device comprises of multiple PC workstations and a TV set. The PCs are operating different Windows versions, such as Windows 98, Windows NT and a Windows 2000. The TV set consists of a TV that is attached with a camera, a RF wireless mouse and is connected via RF link to a Windows 98 running desktop. All composite elements are equipped with JetEye PC IR serial interface adapter by Extended Systems [9] that periodically broadcasts its configuration data, such as device name and configuration.

The standard PDA Infrared interface facilitates the decision to use IR technology for short-range detection and communication until technology such as Bluetooth [3] is available. We have developed a detection software for the PDA that receives the broadcast sequences of the composite elements. PDA and SG communication is enabled via the CDPD network.

8.2 Prototype Technical Experiences

The deployed network communication infrastructure and integrated test services provide a suitable environment with which to experiment with the CDCE framework. The demonstrator allows the user to request the streaming of media files to one workstation, to redirect the Webmail service to another and to conduct a videoconferencing session on the TV.

Although still at the early stage of the framework realization, we could verify the robustness of the network communication infrastructure. It ensures reliable client server communication and more importantly the remotely invocation of server responses redirected to composite clients that are not initiator of the server requests. This result is essential for further activity and realization of the CDCE project. The device detection via IR technology proves to be a very simple but powerful alternative. Yet, we are keen to integrate Bluetooth technology instead. The selected services are properly delivered to the most appropriate composite devices. The design decision of outsourcing any computing task from the PDA and concentrating all components on the server side was the right step, since e.g. the calculation process of the service-device assignment could be time consuming. Further it requires much computing power and dependent on the operating system. We test the calculation on Pentium 200 MHz running Windows NT and the same machine operating Windows 2000. The difference was several seconds.

9 Conclusion and Future Work

This paper has presented a conceptual framework and network infrastructure architecture that allow the class of small screen devices to access rich multimedia information and diverse services. In comparison to related activities the CDCE framework consequently avoids performing heavy computing tasks on a single small screen device or to shrink and tailor services and information badly to match the limitations of these devices. The CDCE approach solves several problems of using small screen devices for ubiquitous rich multimedia information access. First, the outsourcing of requests to appropriate devices for the performance allows offering a diverse range of services and information. Second, the user interface limitation of such devices is overcome by a better exploitation of available location-based hardware resources. Third, it suggests models to enable the control and interactivity with the processes invoked on the composite devices via the small screen device. Fourth, it provides a network communication infrastructure to ensure detection of location-based composite resources and request redirection.

Our technical tests with the current prototype verify the requirement to control and to interact with invoked process as proposed in section 7. That is one focus of the CDCE project. Further, we recognize the importance of the system to be flexible and to adapt media intelligently in cases when no appropriate composite client is available. Our current work is focusing on the integration of different techniques such as *splitting*, *conversion* or *filtering* to adapt the media type to multiple output devices with varying capabilities as well as the changing number of devices. Also, we acknowledged the need for a smart service delivery order due to the multi-tier architecture of the CDCE framework. The initiator of server requests is not the recipient of server responses. Instead, the server needs to redirect the responses to multiple clients. That makes the situation for the user to appreciate the services even more complicated, when all the responses are distributed simultaneously. Standard values such as *frequency of service request, content urgency, type of requested media* and *type of output device* could be considered to calculate an optimal delivery sequence. We further acknowledge that a single CDCE user should not be allowed to monopolize devices in use by owners, or when they wish to use devices while a CDCE services is invoking on their devices. Thus, in these cases we consider the ability of the CDCE system to reserve resources in advance. We aim to realize this by using the standards CC/PP [7] and the Resource Reservation Protocol (RSVP) [22]. Finally, we are working on the deployment of the CDCE framework into different specific application scenarios and to gather and evaluate user experiences.

References

1. Abowd, G. D., et al. Cyberguide: A mobile context-aware tour guide. ACM Wireless Networks Vol 3 (5), 1997, pp. 421-433
2. Beigl, M., Schmidt, A., Lauff, M., Gellersen, H.-W. The UbicompBrowser, Proceedings of the 4th ERCIM Workshop on User Interfaces for All, 1998, Sweden
3. The Bluetooth Forum, http://www.bluetooth.com
4. Cellular Digital Packet Data (CDPD), http://cdpd.org/cdpd/
5. Chervest, K., Davies, N., Mitchell, K., Friday, A., The Role of Connectivity in Supporting Context-Sensitive Applications, Proceedings of the First International Symposium on Handheld and Ubiquitous Computing 1999, pp. 193-207, Springer Verlag
6. Chervest, K., Davies, N., Mitchell, K., Friday, A., Efstratiou, C., Developing a Context-aware Electronic Tourist Guide: Some Issues and Experiences, ACM CHI 2000 Conference Proceedings, pp. 17-24
7. Composite Capability/Preference Profiles (CC/PP): http://www.w3.org/TR/NOTE-CCPP/
8. Esler, M., Hightower, J., Anderson, T., Borriello, G. Next Century Challenges: Data-Centric Networking for Invisible Computing, *The Portolano Project at the University of Washington*, The Proceedings of MOBICOM '99, Seattle, WA August 1999
9. Extended Systems, http://www.extendsys.com/products/infrared/
10. The Extensible Markup Language (XML), http://www.w3.org/XML/
11. General Packet Radio Service (GPRS)http://www.gsmworld.com/technology/gprs.html
12. Grimes, R. Professional DCOM Programming. *Wrox Press*, 1997.
13. Goose, S., Wynblatt, M. and Mollenhauer, H., 1-800-Hypertext: Browsing Hypertext With A Telephone *Proceedings of the ACM International Conference on Hypertext*, June, 1998, pp. 287-288.
14. The Global System for Mobile Communications (GSM) http://www.gsmworld.com/index1.html
15. Hsu, L.-H.; Johnson-Laird, B; Vjaygiri, S. Authoring, Managing and Browsing of Large-Scale Hyperlinks in Multimedia Product Documentation, Markup Technologies Conference, November 1998.
16. International Data Corporation IDC, http://www.idc.com/default.htm

17. Java RMI, http://www.javasoft.com/products/jdk/rmi/index.html
18. The Jini Org, http://www.jini.org/homepage.html
19. Myers, B. A., Stiel, H., Garggiulo, R., Collaboration Using Multiple PDAs Connected to a PC, Proceedings CSCW 98: ACM Conference on Computer-Supported Cooperative Work, November, 1998, pp. 285-294
20. The Object Management Group, http://www.omg.org/
21. Pham, T-L., Schneider, G., Goose, S., Pizano, A. Composite Device Computing Environment: A Framework for Augmenting the PDA using surrounding Resources, ACM CHI 2000 Conference Online Workshop Proceeding "Situated Interaction in Ubiquitous Computing", The Hague April 2000, http://www.teco.edu/chi2000ws/
22. Resource ReSerVation Protocol (RSVP), IETF RFC 2205
23. Sastry, C., Lewis, D., Pizano, A. Webtour: A System to Record and Playback Dynamic Multimedia Annotations on Web Document Content, Proceedings ACM Multimedia 99, pp 175-179.
24. The Universal Mobile Telecommunications System (UMTS), http://www.umts-forum.org/
25. Want, R. et al. The Active Badge Location System, ACM Transactions on Information Systems, Vol. 10, 1992
26. Weiser, M. The Computer for the 21st Century, Scientific American 1991
27. Weiser, M. Some computer science issues in ubiquitous computing. *CACM*, 36(7): 74-83, July 1993. In Special Issue, Computer-Augmented Environments
28. Weiser, M. Hot topic: Ubiquitous computing. *IEEE Computer*, pp 71-72, October 1993
29. Wireless Application Protocol Specification and Wireless Markup Language specification, http://www.wapforum.com/what/technical.htm

Location-Aware Information Delivery with *ComMotion*

Natalia Marmasse and Chris Schmandt

MIT Media Laboratory
20 Ames Street
Cambridge, MA 02139, USA
{nmarmas, geek}@media.mit.edu

Abstract *comMotion* is a location-aware computing environment which links personal information to locations in its user's life; for example, *comMotion* reminds one of her shopping list when she nears a grocery store. Using satellite-based GPS position sensing, *comMotion* gradually learns about the locations in its user's daily life based on travel patterns. The full set of *comMotion* functionality, including map display, requires a graphical user interface. However, because it is intended primarily for mobile use, including driving, the core set of reminder creation and retrieval can be managed completely by speech.

1 Introduction

It is evidence of our hectic and mobile lives that many of us carry portable computers and wireless communication devices everywhere we go. Yet, these devices provide few services which are responsive to location, and location matters; I want my list of books recommended by friends when I have time to browse and am at the bookstore. *comMotion* seeks to address this problem, so that we are reminded about the important meeting on the way to work and told that we need to buy milk as we are about to drive by the grocery store on the trip home, thus providing just in time information delivery. The user interface is critical for systems which are meant to be always on and available; *comMotion* presents both graphical and speech interfaces to its core set of functions.

    comMotion knows its latitude and longitude from the satellite-based Global Positioning System (GPS). But coordinates must be translated into positions that are relevant to the user, and these obviously vary greatly from person to person. Users neither know nor care about such coordinates; rather they identify "home", "work", "school", "post office", etc. Although a map could be used to specify such points, why should users spend valuable time filling out detailed property lists for a system which has yet to prove its value to them? Instead, *comMotion* learns salient locations by observing its user's travel over time, and periodically inviting him to name or classify a frequented coordinate.

    comMotion keeps "to do" lists for each location, or class of locations (a user may shop at multiple "grocery stores", for example). These lists consist of text and voice entries. Other users may also send reminders to the user at some specific location, and (with consent) query the user's position. *comMotion* also provides mobile access to location-based information from the Web, such as locations of nearby banks, and delivers other information at specified times and days of the week.

A graphical user interface is most appropriate for display of map data and allows full control of administrative functions. But because *comMotion* is meant to be used while mobile, it also demands both alerting and a user interface which function while the user's hands and eyes are otherwise busy, such as while driving or cycling. To this end, core *comMotion* functionality is available through a non-visual speech and auditory user interface.

Modest user evaluation suggests that *comMotion*'s promise is attractive, but user interface design, including multiple modalities, is as important as size. For example, speech is well suited for driving, but at least initially some users find it embarrassing to call attention to themselves while speaking to their computer on foot in a public locale.

2 Related Work

Most previous location-aware applications have used predefined content and/or locations.

C-Map [1] is a tour guidance system which, based on location and individual interests, provides information to visitors at exhibitions. CyberGuide [2] is a collection of intelligent tour guides which provide information to tourists based on knowledge of their position and orientation. Metronaut [3] is an application developed for schedule management and guidance instructions for a visitor to a university campus. City Guide [4] enables a user to see his position on a map and request restaurant and hotel information. These applications have predefined content based on location and they are user-independent.

The Olivetti Active Badge [5] was used in several systems, for example to aid a telephone receptionist by dynamically updating the telephone extension a user was closest to. Augmentable Reality [6] allows users to dynamically attach digital information such as voice notes or photographs to the physical environment. Audio Aura [7] provides information via auditory cues based on people's physical actions in the workplace. These systems use predefined locations and are designed for users to find each other or objects in the environment.

The Forget-Me-Not [8] was a wearable device which recorded interactions with people and devices, and stored this information in a database for later query. The Remembrance Agent [9] provides text information relevant to the user's context, for example class notes when entering a specific classroom. These applications remind the user of past events associated with a location whereas *comMotion* associates events in the future.

comMotion can have predefined content associated to locations, however its main feature is user-defined content and the possibility to subscribe to Web content based on location. To the best of our knowledge no other system observes the user's mobility data to independently learn the frequented locations.

3 Overview

A user's interaction with *comMotion* begins with the location-learning agent. It observes the user's frequented locations over time and allows them to be labeled.

Once a location has been defined, a to-do list is associated with it. A to-do list is a set of text items or digital audio recordings; these may be ticked off once completed. When the user is in the relevant location, he will hear an auditory cue alerting him that he has items on the associated to-do list. In addition, other users can also send him reminders to his virtual locations. These reminders resemble the common 3M Posts-its™ and can be sent via regular e-mail.

The user can also subscribe to information services, such as headline news, weather reports and current movie listings; the subscription is per location and different schedules can be made for different days. For example, the user could request to receive a list of the movies showing at the local cinemas when leaving work on Fridays. In addition, *comMotion* can provide maps showing the user's current position together with neighbourhood locales, such as banks, movie theatres or grocery stores.

The data types and functionality of *comMotion* require a multi-modal user interface. Its alerting function reminds the user to, for example, buy milk when nearing a grocery store. Since we can rarely view a screen while travelling, this cue cannot be visual so an auditory alert is used. Map information, on the other hand, is best displayed visually; although we have in the past explored giving driving directions by voice [10], this requires a detailed and up-to-date street database, not just maps. *comMotion*'s reminders are either voice or text. Although its graphical interface is more extensive, *comMotion*'s core functions are accessible by speech input to allow mobile use.

comMotion, with the appropriate hardware, and with some modifications in the software, could accommodate different architectures. A number of scenarios can be envisioned, each adapted for different life-styles, or different modes of mobility: a wearable on-the-go architecture for the highly active, such as, cyclists; a car architecture for the more sedentary; a briefcase architecture for the mobile individual, for example, knowledge workers; or a stripped down kids architecture. These are all variations on the same *comMotion* system, tailored to different needs. What changes is the hardware, the user interface and the features included in the system, which range from full-fledged to stripped down variations. A first *comMotion* prototype was built in order to evaluate its feasibility and usefulness. In highly active situations, such as cycling, the components are put in a fanny pack or carried in a shoulder bag.

4 Architecture

The hardware includes a portable PC, a GPS receiver, a CDPD modem and a Jabra earphone speaker with a bone conductive microphone.

The human-computer interface, on the client side, is composed of both speech and graphical user interfaces. The former includes speech recognition and text-to-speech synthesis and was developed using AT&T's Watson SDK (software development kit). The Watson product is an integrated, Automatic Speech Recognition (ASR) and Text-to-Speech (TTS) synthesis system which complies with the Microsoft Speech API (SAPI). The ASR engine uses phoneme-based sub-word analysis and, therefore, supports speaker-independence and continuous speech recognition. The *comMotion* speech server, developed with the Watson SDK, operates on the client device.

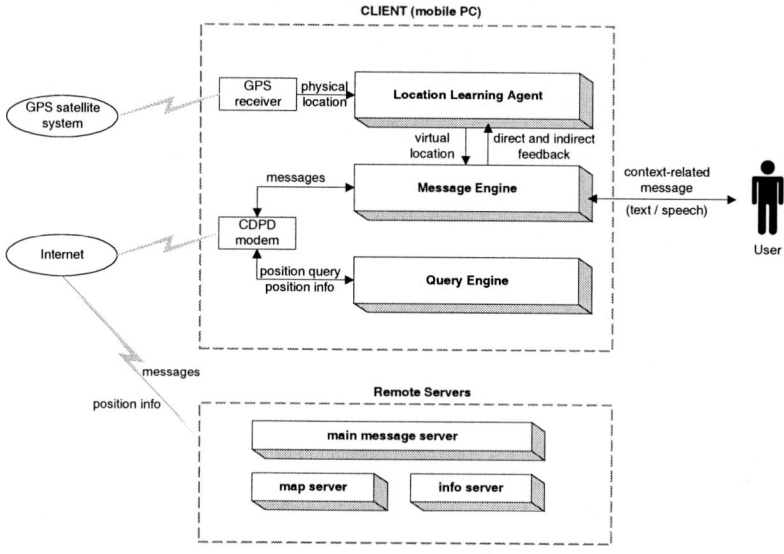

Fig. 1. The architecture of comMotion showing the three main modules of the client application and its connection to the remote servers

The client application communicates via TCP/IP sockets to all the different server processes, hence, these processes could easily be transported to the client device or to any other computer with Web-server capabilities. In the current setup, with only the speech server on the client device and all other servers on a remote station (Figure 1), even if connectivity were lost the user would still have full access to his to-do lists and any reminders which had previously been downloaded. Furthermore, since all position tracking and analysis are done on the client device, these would not suffer from lack of connectivity. Reminders sent from other users are immediately downloaded to the client device where they are stored until delivery time. If the server cannot access the client, these new reminders are saved until connectivity is re-established and they can be downloaded. Lack of Internet connectivity means information from on-line sources will not be accessible; likewise, no maps or related information can be downloaded.

5 Location and Learning

When designing location-aware applications it is vital to know where people are. *comMotion* focuses solely on outdoor tracking by means of a GPS (Global Positioning System) receiver; indoor tracking requires an additional location sensing system. GPS, until very recently, had an accuracy of less than 100 metres due to a deliberately induced error signal, preventing hostile military applications. Although position information is still inexact, it is often sufficient to know the vicinity (within 10 m) in which the user is located.

It is essential to design location-aware applications to take into account the accuracy and reliability of available location. Not only is GPS data not very accurate, but it is also not always available. GPS signal is lost when entering most buildings and the so-called concrete canyons in urban areas make reception difficult. The fact that most buildings are GPS opaque was exploited advantageously, permitting a simple learning mechanism for the locations of buildings.

Latitude and longitude coordinates are obtained via a GPS receiver connected to the client's serial port, using the NMEA-0183 protocol. All data is analysed for frequented locations, however, at present, only locations such as buildings can be identified, since the system recognizes locations where GPS signal is lost. After losing signal within a given radius on three different occasions the agent infers that this must be a building and marks it as a salient location. The user is prompted for a location name, which he can either designate or tag at a later stage by seeing the location on a map. Once tagged, the virtual location has a to-do list associated with it. However, if the location is of no interest, the user can indicate that it is to be ignored. For example, a frequented T-stop (metro) would be identified by the agent but the user would typically not want to have context-related information (to-do list items, electronic reminders, etc) delivered there.

To compute its position, a GPS unit must receive a signal from various satellites: three for a 2D fix (latitude and longitude) and four in the case of a 3D fix (latitude, longitude, and altitude). In urban areas, shadowing from tall buildings often occurs, and leads to long delays in position acquiring. Initially, locations were identified both upon user arrivals and departures. However, it was found that the GPS receiver often took several minutes to acquire its location when exiting a building and, therefore when the signal was regained, the user was no longer at the place he had left. Depending on his mode of transportation, this could be a considerable distance; hence false locations were identified.

The GPS receiver is polled for data every ten seconds but does not return a coordinate until it "sees" satellites. In the examples which follow, each line begins with the time of polling. If the data is returned immediately, the next line is ten seconds later. A longer delay indicates a poll waiting for the GPS data.

Date	Poll time	Latitude/longitude data
03/30	09:43:53	4223.351,N, 07104.613,W
03/30	09:44:03	4223.153,N, 07104.625,W
03/30	09:44:13	4223.092,N, 07104.641,W
03/30	09:44:23	4221.867,N, 07103.786,W
03/30	09:54:14	4221.870,N, 07103.787,W
03/30	09:54:24	4221.872,N, 07103.789,W

Fig. 2. GPS data showing how signal is lost when arriving at a building

As can be seen in the GPS data (Figure 2), at 9:44:13 the user arrived at location (4223.092N, 7104.641W). Ten seconds later the receiver was polled for data but a signal was received about 10 minutes later, locating him at (4221.867N, 7103.786W).

If the GPS receiver loses signal two more times within a given radius of (4223.092N, 7104.641W), then this is understood to be a building and, consequently, a frequented location.

Date	Poll time	Latitude/longitude data
03/29	16:34:09	4221.686,N, 07105.339,W
03/29	16:42:24	4221.687,N, 07105.341,W
03/29	16:42:34	4221.685,N, 07105.392,W

Fig. 3. GPS data showing how signal was acquired only several minutes after departing from a building

In this second example (Figure 3), the user turned on the unit and left the office at 16:34:09, however, the GPS receiver took several minutes to acquire a position after exiting the building. Data was received ten seconds before the next entry, that is, at exactly 16:42:14. So in this case, data was received eight minutes and five seconds later –this includes the time it takes to descend three flights of stairs besides the acquiring time once outside the building. The user was identified at location (4221.686N, 7105.339W), several hundred metres from the building he exited.

The algorithm was modified to detect only arrivals. So from the data in the first example, (4223.092N 7104.641W) would be considered a location to analyse, however (4221.867N, 7103.786W) would be ignored. It takes the agent twice as long to identify a location but the false ones formerly recognized were eliminated. If previously your "home" location could be identified in two days, that is, after a sequence of arrive-depart-arrive or depart-arrive-depart, with the new algorithm it takes a sequence of three arrivals.

It will be necessary to further modify the learning algorithm since not all buildings were found to be GPS-opaque, that is, the GPS signal is sometimes received while within a building. Therefore, the data must also be analysed for stationary points. Even when a GPS receiver is static, the data indicates fluctuations of many metres; this requires compensation. The analysis to identify a stationary receiver is also necessary for the *comMotion* car architecture, where the GPS receiver will be permanently installed in the car, as opposed to in a mobile device with the user. When the car is stationary, such as in the grocery store's parking lot, it may be in a salient location. Also, a parking lot may be large enough to cause confusion between multiple trips.

Any monitoring system raises many privacy issues, that is why in *comMotion* all the location tracking and analysis is done solely on the client device. Hence, the user's privacy is safe to the extent that the client device is safe.

6 Graphical User Interface

comMotion consists both of a GUI and a speech user interface which complement each other and are appropriate for different modalities.

Location-learning Module. When a frequented site has been identified, the user is prompted to tag it with a virtual location name. A speech dialogue is followed by the appearance of a visual interface through which the user specifies the location name and associates a to-do list with it.

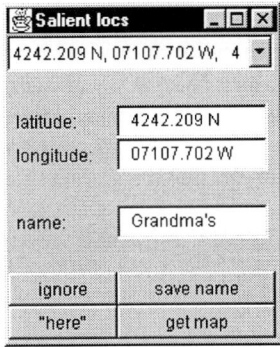

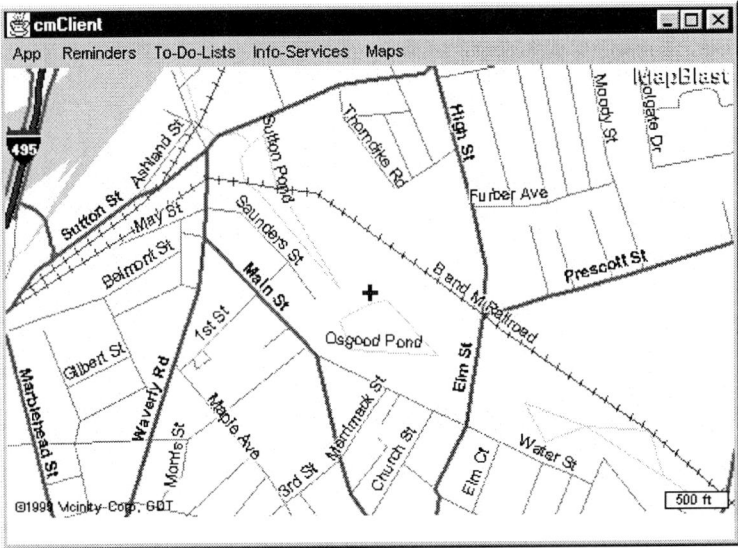

Fig. 4. Visual interface used to see a salient location on a map and tag it with a virtual location name

A visual interface is essential since the location name must be text, and not audio. By default, the associated to-do list name is identical to the location name, however, an existing to-do list can also be chosen, since these lists can either be site specific or shared. A user who shops at three different grocery stores would probably only want one shared grocery list. On the other hand, places such as "home" and "work" would presumably have very different tasks associated with them, and, therefore, separate to-do lists would be preferable.

The speech dialogue occurs only when in situs however the tagging can also be done later; the user can see the exact location on a map (Figure 4). If the location is of no interest the user can indicate that it is to be ignored.

To-do Lists. A to-do list is associated with each defined virtual location. When the user is in the relevant location, he will hear an auditory cue ("psst") indicating that he has items on the associated to-do list and the visual interface will be displayed (Figure 5). Visually, the list resembles its real world paper parallel, on which items are simply listed and can be checked once they have been done. However, in *comMotion*, the to-do items can either be text, typed in using the graphical interface, or recorded audio.

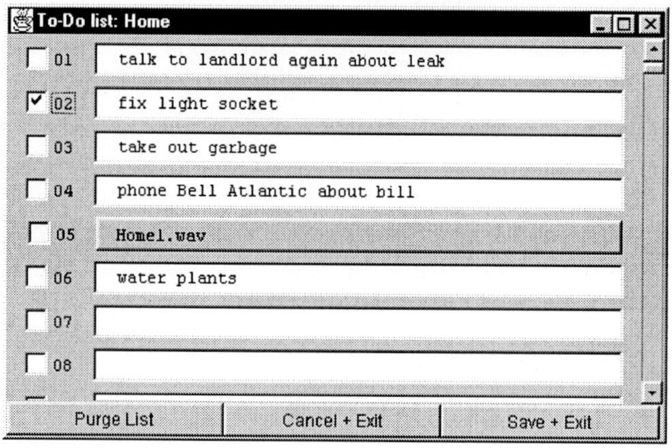

Fig. 5. A to-do list with both text and audio items

The list items can be viewed and scanned using the visual interface or heard and scanned using the speech interface. Text items are synthesized to speech, whereas audio items are played. The recorded audio items are not transcribed to text, rather they appear as a button in the list, and can only be retrieved in the form of audio. Once the task has been completed, the item can be checked-off and the list purged.

The audio items can be recorded using either a visual interface or through speech commands. Although a file name is shown in the interface, the user simply specifies the list name. In the graphical interface, the user can start and stop the recording, and play back the audio until satisfied with the recording. Saving the file will automatically insert an audio item button in the specified to-do list, enabling future playback.

Reminders. The metaphor used for the reminders is the widespread 3M Post-its™; the visual component resembles them in shape, size and colour (Figure 6).

Context-aware reminders for *comMotion* mobile users can be sent via the regular e-mail system by specifying the location name in the subject line. This is important since the mobile user must be accessible to the rest of the world. Reminders, or electronic Post-it notes, can also be sent from another *comMotion* client, however, unlike the to-do items, they are text-only.

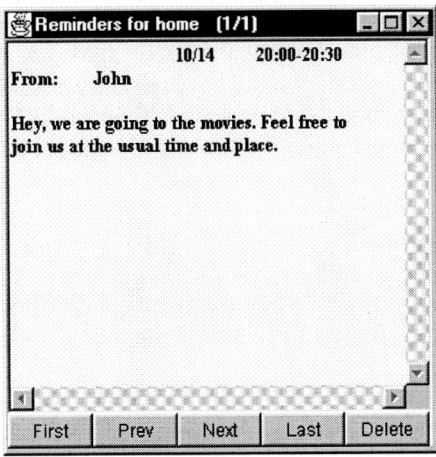

Fig. 6. Visual interface component to view and scan reminders

The reminders are posted to a specific location and can be constrained to a certain date or date and time range. When the user is in the relevant context, he will hear an auditory cue indicating that he has some relevant reminders and a visual component resembling a Post-it note will appear on the display (Figure 6). These notes can then be viewed and scanned using the visual interface or heard and scanned as synthesized audio by means of the speech interface.

When creating a new reminder, the user can specify the frequency of repetition (daily, weekly, monthly, or none), the repeat increment, the day of the week, and the date range. For example, one could create a reminder for a certain event that takes place on Mondays, every other week, for the next three months. All these parameters can be defined whether sending the reminder from a *comMotion* client or via e-mail, however, the *comMotion* client provides a more convenient interface for this task. When sending a reminder via the *comMotion* interface, both the user and the location are chosen from a list, which is composed of all this particular user's locations, as well as all the locations of other *comMotion* users to which he has privilege. When sending the reminder through e-mail, if the format cannot be parsed out correctly, the e-mail sender will receive a reply indicating the problem and the correct format to be used.

Map Module. The user can view a map of his current location showing features such as banks, movie theatres, grocery stores, etc, acquired from MapBlast's [11] Web database. The display shows a map as well as the address and telephone number of the sites of interest. The input necessary for this module are latitude and longitude coordinates, hence it is not limited to the locations that *comMotion* has already learned. Undoubtedly it will be more useful when the user is in an unfamiliar neighbourhood.

Information Services. The message engine can also deliver content such as headline news, weather reports and current movie listings from information sources on the Web. As the requested information may vary depending on context, the user can subscribe to different information services based on location, and special schedules can be made for different days. For example, the user might request to receive a list of the movies showing at the local cinemas when leaving work on Fridays.

When the user is in the relevant context, he will hear an auditory cue indicating he has location-based information that he has subscribed to. The data will be displayed in the visual interface and may also be synthesized to speech.

Headline news is downloaded and parsed from the msnbc.com site; weather reports are taken from wunderground.com, and the movie listings are from the sidewalk.com site. The default city for the weather information is Boston but this can be modified by the user. Likewise, the default city for the movies (Cambridge) can be changed. The weather site supports most large cities in North America as well as several others around the world. However, the sidewalk.com site only supports a subset of the larger, or most important cities in the US. The data is parsed out and formatted for the visual display. Although the text can be synthesized to speech, its format was not specifically adapted for that purpose.

Query module. A user can be queried for his whereabouts via a *comMotion* client or through the regular e-mail system. In either case, the request goes to the main server where the priorities are checked. A *comMotion* user can establish priority levels per location and per user and can log by whom and when location information was requested. The log file includes: by whom he was queried, where the queried user was at the time, what information was released, and the date and time of the query. Querying from a *comMotion* client is done by choosing from a list of other *comMotion* user names. If the request was sent by an authorized person, a reply such as "Jane is at work" will be received; however, if queried by someone unauthorized, the response will be "Jane is incognito!". A query request via e-mail is performed by sending a message, to the *comMotion* user who is being queried, with "cm query" as the subject.

7 Speech/Auditory Interface

comMotion is meant to be carried by its user at all times, and, almost by definition, location-based reminders will arrive while the user is busy doing something else – driving, walking, biking, etc. These factors suggest that the core memo management functions and alerting be speech input and auditory cues.

Speech is suitable for portable applications as speakers and microphones are small and require little power. Auditory input and output can be performed while the user's hands and eyes are busy, while driving or biking. More importantly, performing multiple tasks is more effective in terms of cognitive resources, if the tasks are performed using different sensory modalities [12].

The main downside of the auditory interface is that speech recognition is difficult, and its accuracy remains poor, especially in noisy environments. In addition, speech is transitory and serial in nature; it is difficult to take an auditory "glance" at a list to pick out the important item. Also, if the presentation is via text-to-speech synthesis, an even greater cognitive load is placed on the user [13].

Effective speech user interfaces must exploit its advantages while minimizing user frustration due to error and cognitive load. This influenced *comMotion* in several ways. Only a limited set of functions are made available by voice; these are related to hearing and modifying to-do lists and reminders. Limiting functionality allows for smaller speech recognizer vocabularies with resulting better recognition performance. Even if the less frequently used *comMotion* functions were speech accessible, users would most likely forget what to say to invoke them, increasing frustration with the recognizer. Actual reminders created by voice are simply saved as digitized audio; attempting dictation to text without visual feedback would be tedious at best. Although we have in the past explored giving spoken driving directions [10], *comMotion* limits map-based features to the graphical interface for simplicity.

Different auditory cues are associated with the various types of information (to-do lists, reminders and subscribed content information). Whenever the user has pending messages relevant to his context, the pertinent audio cue is heard. As the purpose of these cues is to alert the user without distracting him from his primary task, different ones can be chosen and in this way they may be as subtle as he wishes. The system default cues are currently a "psst" for the to-do list, a "ding" for the reminders and chimes for subscribed information. In the future new default cues may be chosen, based on the consensus of several users' preferences.

The user interacts with the system via speech commands, which are mostly two-word commands and should be intuitive. *comMotion* can be run in terse or verbose mode. When in verbose mode, the user will receive much more auditory feedback: after each speech command is recognized the system will repeat the command before performing the task. For example, if the user says "read item", the system will repeat "read item", before it synthesizes or plays back the relevant to-do list item. Once an auditory cue has been given, it will explain the reason for the cue. For instance, "You have five items on your grocery list". When choosing one of the locations from the list of names, after the user says "yes", the system will respond, for example, "bank".

Speech recognition is fragile; speech commands might not be recognized or they could be mis-recognized causing an unwanted action to be performed. Unlike in a visual interface, where the user can generally perceive what the system is doing, an audio interface is not transparent to the user. Therefore, explicit feedback is beneficial, especially for novice users. For example, when marking a to-do item as checked: in a visual interface the user will easily see if the wrong item was ticked, however in a speech interface he has no way of knowing unless the system gives explicit feedback, or he has enough experience with the system to trust it.

In *comMotion,* speech recognition is not continuously enabled since ambient conversation is often picked up and misinterpreted as direct input. However, since the objective of the speech interface is to enable system functionality in a hands and/or eyes busy situation, the user cannot be expected to manually activate the recognition by means of a push-to-talk button. Consequently, *comMotion* automatically activates the continuous recognition when it expects to receive speech commands. As long as the user interacts with the system, the continuous recognition remains enabled. For example, if the system alerts the user (with an auditory cue) regarding pending messages, the continuous speech recognition is activated, giving the user the opportunity to ask for the messages to be read. As long as the user gives speech commands, the recognition stays on. However, unanticipated speech interaction requires manually initiating the recognition. Once activated, it will remain enabled as long as it picks up audio.

Location-learning Module. When a new salient site has been identified, the user is prompted for a virtual location name. The system initiates the speech dialogue with: "This is a frequented location. Would you like to name it?". A negative answer (speech command: "no" or "nope"), or no answer whatsoever, terminates the dialogue, whereas a positive answer (speech command: "yes", "yep", "sure" or "okay") from the user causes a visual component to appear, through which the user specifies the location name and associates a to-do list with it. The user can indicate that the location is to be ignored by saying "Ignore this location", when prompted for a location name.

To-do Lists. The speech commands used to navigate within a specific list are: "first item", "last item", "next item", "previous item" and "read item". If operating in verbose-mode, after each command the system repeats the command before actually performing it. The command "check item" is used to toggle the check mark next to an item. If operating in verbose-mode, after performing the command, the system says, for example, "Item: fix light socket, is now checked". The verbose feedback is useful for the user to gain confidence in the system and to understand the system's behaviour in the case of mis-recognitions when a command is misunderstood for another. If the command is not recognized, the system answers: "Say that again".

The user can initiate the dialogue to record an audio item by saying: "Choose list". The system then recites the names of the lists, one at a time, until the user says "yes" to one of them. If the user does not want a specific list, he can say "no", or simply say nothing –if no response is heard after five seconds, the next list name is recited. When recording an audio item via the speech commands, it is not possible to stop the recording once it has started. The system automatically records during 20 seconds. An auditory cue, a beep, is heard just before the recording begins, and once again after the 20 seconds timeout.

More sophisticated list management and audio browsing, inspired by VoiceNotes [14], will be implemented in future prototypes.

Reminders. The speech commands used to navigate between the reminders are: "first reminder", "last reminder", "next reminder", "previous reminder", "read reminder" and "delete reminder". If operating in verbose-mode, after each command the system repeats it before actually performing the command.

Speech Levels. The speed of the audio output can be modified with the commands "speak faster" and "speak slower" and the volume level with "speak louder" and "speak softer". The system defaults can be reset by "reset speech levels".

8 Evaluation

For *comMotion* to be most effective, it should be used on a regular basis over a period of time. The system must first learn the user's frequented locations as only after these virtual sites have been established can location-related information be delivered. Therefore, two different parts of the system must be evaluated: the location learning feature and the delivery of information.

8.1 Location Learning

GPS data was collected over a couple of months by the authors. This data was used to evaluate and make iterative improvements to the location learning algorithm. For instance, *comMotion* initially identified locations based on when the user arrived and when he departed; however as GPS can take several minutes to regain its location after leaving a building the user often "reappeared" at quite some distance. This gave rise to problems so the algorithm was modified and now locations are only identified when arrived at. The problems encountered and how they were resolved are described in detail in the section on learning. At present, the *comMotion* learning algorithm effectively identifies GPS opaque buildings after they have been visited three times.

8.2 Information Delivery

Preliminary tests were carried out to evaluate the effectiveness of information delivery and to refine the initial interface design.

The *comMotion* system was taught three virtual locations: a local post office, a bookstore and a bank; all are within the same two blocks. The users were told that they had pending items on their to-do lists and reminders specific to each location. They were asked to walk in the general area of the different locales, choosing whichever route they preferred.

Feedback was received from 4 different people –two of whom are non-technical with very little experience with mobile computing devices, and two members of the Speech Group who have a deep understanding of the concepts used. Their comments can be divided into different categories:

Hardware. The hardware must become smaller and lighter, to be truly mobile, and the earphone must be wireless. One person noted that even a wireless speaker is unacceptable since it is uncomfortable and most of the time the system is not "speaking"; loud-speakers could be integrated into clothing or the frame of eye-glasses. The device should not be larger than the size of a PalmPilot and should perhaps be integrated into a device which already is carried around, such as a cellular phone.

Speech Input. Speech as a form of input is beneficial when in a hands and/or eyes busy situation. However, using speech commands can raise both social and privacy issues. People do not want to appear to be talking to themselves and may not necessarily want others to know what they are doing. One person refused to use the speech commands while walking around with the system. Speech recognition is still problematic and one of the users with a non-American accent had great trouble being understood. Ambient noise levels also proved to be a problem. In a car situation, both ambient noise and self-consciousness would be much less of a problem.

Precision and Alert Timing. GPS data is intentionally imprecise –when the user evaluation was done, accuracy was within 100 metres. For this application, exact position information is not required. When two different virtual locations are physically within metres of each other, however, due to the inaccuracy of the position data, one location is identified and not the other –that is, location shadowing. This can be solved by clustering the virtual locations and providing alerts for all the locations within the cluster. The lack of precision of position data also strongly affects the alert timing and auditory cues were sometimes given too late. Loss of GPS signal due to shadowing by tall buildings was also experienced.

Alerts and Data. Users indicated that the auditory alerts, when given at the right time, were useful since it enabled them to be doing something else, such as walking down the street and talking, and still draw their attention without losing their thread of thought. Since certain users didn't want to use the speech interface to retrieve the location-specific information, upon receiving an alert, they pulled out the visual display and intuitively navigated amongst the reminders. A couple of people suggested a tactile vibra-alert as an alternative to the audio one. It was also suggested that to-do list items could be prioritized and a deadline indicated.

The results are non-conclusive and more extensive evaluation must be done, however it seems clear that there is place and desire for such a system.

9 Future Work

The current prototype allowed us to develop location learning algorithms and do preliminary user evaluations. Based on these, the next version will include a more sophisticated speech UI on more portable hardware, allowing longer term evaluation of *comMotion* utility in daily life. We will also explore ways to increase location awareness of a community and the sharing of information, for example, between the members of a family.

References

1. Sumi, Y., T. Etani, S. Fels, N. Simone, K. Kobayashi and K. Mase. "C-MAP: Building a Context-Aware Mobile Assistant for Exhibition Tours". *Social Interaction and Communityware*, Japan, June 1998.
2. Long, S., D. Aust, G. Abowd, C. Atkeson. "Cyberguide: Prototyping Context-Aware Mobile Applications". *Proceedings of the conference on Human Factors in Computing Systems, CHI'96.*
3. Smailagic, A. and R. Martin. "Metronaut: A Wearable Computer with Sensing and Global Communication Capabilities". *Proceedings of the International Symposium on Wearable Computing,* IEEE, 1997.
4. Kreller, B., D. Carrega, J. Shankar, P. Salmon, S. Bottger, and T. Kassing. "A Mobile-Aware City Guide Application". *ACTS Mobile Communication Summit,* Rhodos, Greece, 1998.
5. Want, R., A. Hopper, V. Falcao, and J. Gibbons. "The active badge location system". *ACM Transactions on Information Systems,* 10(1): pp. 91-102, January 1992.
6. Rekimoto, J, Y. Ayatsuka and K. Hayashi. "Augmenta-able Reality: Situated Communication through Physical and Digitial Spaces". *Proceedings of the International Symposium on Wearable Computing,* IEEE, 1998.
7. Mynatt E., M. Back, R. Want. "Designing Audio Aura". *Proceedings of the conference on Human Factors in Computing Systems, CHI'99.*

8. Lamming, Mik and Mike Flynn. "Forget-me-not: Intimate computing in support of human memory". *FRIEND21: International Symposium on Next Generation Human Interface*, pp. 125-128, 1994
9. Rhodes, B. "The Wearable Remembrance Agent: a system for augmented memory." *Proceedings of the International Symposium on Wearable Computing,* IEEE, 1997.
10. Davis J.R. and C. Schmandt. "The Back Seat Driver: Real Time Spoken Driving Instructions". *Vehicle Navigation and Information Systems*, 1989.
11. Mapblast. http://www.mapblast.com/mapblast/start.hm
12. Allport, D., B. Antonis and P. Reynolds. "On the Division of Attention: a Disproof of the Single Channel Hypothesis". *Quarterly Journal of Experimental Psychology*, 24:225-235, 1972.
13. Luce, P. A., T. C. Feustel, and D. B. Pisoni. "Capacity Demands in Short-Term Memory for Synthetic and Natural Speech". *Human Factor*, 25(1):17-32, 1983.
14. Stifelman, L., B. Arons, C. Schmandt and E. Hulteen. "VoiceNotes: A Speech Interface for a Hand-Held Voice Notetaker. *Proceedings of INTERCHI '93*

CybreMinder: A Context-Aware System for Supporting Reminders

Anind K. Dey and Gregory D. Abowd

Future Computing Environments Group
College of Computing and GVU Center
Georgia Institute of Technology, Atlanta, GA, USA 30332-0280
{anind, abowd}@cc.gatech.edu

Abstract. Current tools do not provide adequate support to users for handling reminders. The main reason for this is the lack of use of rich context that specifies when a reminder should be presented to its recipient. We describe CybreMinder, a prototype context-aware tool that supports users in sending and receiving reminders that can be associated to richly described situations involving time, place and more sophisticated pieces of context. These situations better define when reminders should be delivered, enhancing our ability to deal with them more effectively. We describe how the tool is used and how it was developed using our previously developed Context Toolkit infrastructure for context-aware computing.

1 Introduction

A reminder is a special type of message that we send to ourselves or others, to inform us about some future activity that we should engage in. For example, a colleague might send us a reminder asking us to bring a copy of a paper to our next meeting.

We use reminders to signal others and ourselves that a task still exists to be worked on and/or that a task is ready for further processing We use reminders to re-establish needed information in short-term memory so that the trigger conditions for these reminders can be satisfied [14].

Reminders have two main features — a signal and a description. The signal is used to indicate something is to be remembered. An example of an audio-based signal is an alarm on an alarm clock. Lights flashing in a theatre or a note pinned to a door are examples of visual signals. The description is used to explain what needs to be remembered. This can vary from being non-descriptive, in the case of the alarm clock, to being partially descriptive, in the case of a icon which provides only a few cues as to what needs remembering, to being fully descriptive, in the case of an e-mail message or handwritten note that provides all relevant details of the reminder.

We currently have a number of tools and strategies at our disposal to help us keep track of reminders. However, studies have shown that users still have difficulty dealing with reminders [6]. Difficulties stem from a number of issues regarding the use of signals. Current reminder systems, acting as a form of externalized memory, do not present appropriate signals at appropriate times. More specifically, these tools are not sufficient because they are not proactive and do not make use of rich contextual information to trigger reminders at appropriate times in appropriate locations. Herstad *et al.* claim that in order to build useful, functional and powerful tools for supporting human-human interaction, we must take context into account [9]. For example, to be most effective, a reminder to bring a paper to a meeting should be delivered when we are leaving our office and heading towards the meeting, and not when we happen to read our e-mail. We will investigate this idea further by looking at traditional ways of handling reminders, indicating how insufficient use of context causes problems.

By reviewing existing reminder tools, we will show that users have trouble dealing with reminders due to the lack of use of rich context. We will then propose a list of features that an ideal reminder should support. We describe CybreMinder, a reminder tool that supports these features and some scenarios that it currently supports. Finally, we describe CybreMinder's system architecture and how it leverages off an existing context-sensing infrastructure (the Context Toolkit [4,16]) to allow the specification of situations in which reminders can be delivered.

2 Current Reminder Tools

We use a variety of tools that help us in creating and managing our reminders. In this section, we examine these tools and investigate our claim that they do not use enough context information to adequately support our needs. This brief review of reminder tools will lead us to a list of desirable features for a context-aware reminder system.

2.1 Paper To-Do Lists

A common reminder tool is a to-do list written on a piece of paper. The to-do list may contain both traditional calendar/scheduler information and a set of tasks that need to be completed. While it is simple to create a list, it is not so easy to remember to use it in the appropriate situation. A to-do list lacks the ability to proactively remind us when an item on the list needs to be accomplished. Instead, the list creator must remember to check it often, to determine which items need/can be accomplished. In other words, a to-do list provides reminders with descriptions, but no signals.

2.2 E-Mail Mailbox

An e-mail mailbox is often used as an informal to-do list. Some people send themselves e-mail as a reminder to perform some activity at a later date. A study of e-mail tool usage showed that when checking their e-mail, people often flag messages containing to-do items to create a visual reminder [8]. Another strategy is to file them in a special mail folder, creating the electronic equivalent of a paper-based to-do list. As with the paper-based to-do list, e-mail tools cannot proactively remind us of to-do items. We are forced to repeatedly review these flagged or stored messages, in an attempt to ascertain which to-do items can be handled at the time. Again, this is an example of a reminder with descriptions, but no signals. One advantage of e-mail over paper is that people can use e-mail to create and send reminders to others. However, it suffers from the disadvantage of not being as readily available as paper.

2.3 Post-It Notes

Another common strategy is to use post-it notes, paper or virtual [2,15], placed in locations where the intended recipients can view them. The visibility of post-it notes in the environment provides a signal to recipients that something needs to be remembered. The content of the note provides the description of what is to be remembered. Because post-it notes are always visible to the intended recipients, there is no way to determine when they are valid. For example, a reminder to call someone may only be valid before 10 p.m. but the reminder is still visible after 10 p.m., unless it is explicitly removed. The paper post-it notes also have the disadvantage that they can also be viewed by anyone, not just the intended recipients. This is another example of a reminding tool with inappropriate signaling capabilities. Post-it notes can only provide a signal based on their location in the environment, indicating that they are only useful for location-based reminders. An additional disadvantage of post-it notes is that they do not support the ability to collect all reminders in a single artifact, unlike email folders or to-do lists.

2.4 Personal Information Management Tools

Personal information management (PIM) tools such as electronic calendar and to-do list programs suffer from a similar problem as post-it notes. While post-it notes are useful for reminders where location is the only useful context, these PIM tools only have affordances for temporal context: a meeting is at a certain time or a task must be completed by a certain date. Current PIM tools can only provide a signal based on the current time, making them no more intelligent than a simple alarm clock. The tool provides an audio or vibration signal and it is our responsibility to retrieve the description or content of the reminder. Both types of cues may be inappropriate in various situations (e.g. audio cues in a meeting are disruptive and vibration cues while jogging may not be noticed). This suggests that the manner in which reminders are delivered is also extremely important.

2.5 Human Assistant

Another "tool" used to manage reminders is a human assistant. We often rely on a personal assistant (secretary, spouse, etc.) to remind us of scheduled events and tasks that require attention. The assistant acts as a mediator between the actual set of things to be remembered and ourselves, creating reminders from a variety of communication media (phone messages, faxes, e-mail, etc.), presenting them in the appropriate situation and using an appropriate delivery mechanism. However, even a personal assistant may not be enough. In most cases, personal assistants can only present reminders when they are co-located with us. They can provide two types of reminders, those that are relevant right now and those that are relevant in a future context when they will not be with us. It is the second case that is troublesome. How many of us have been reminded to pick up an item from a grocery store as we are leaving for work, only to forget to stop at the store on the way home? An ideal assistant would provide the reminder in the context that maximizes the chance for appropriate action.

2.6 Desired Features of a Reminder System

The externalized memory tools we have discussed are simple to use, but all take limited advantage of context for signaling; or for indicating that a reminder is relevant in our current *situation*. Human assistants come closest to being the ideal reminder tool, but as shown, there are opportunities to improve on their capabilities, and we cannot all have human assistants. Based on our analysis of current tools, here is a list of the features an ideal reminder tool should support:

- the use of rich context for specifying reminders, beyond simple time and location and for proactively determining when to deliver them;
- the ability for users and third parties to submit reminders;
- the ability to create reminders using a variety of input devices;
- the ability to receive reminders using a variety of devices, appropriate to the user's situation;
- the use of reminders that include both a signal that something is to be remembered and a full description of what is to be remembered; and
- allowing users to view a list of all active reminders.

3 Related Work

There has not been a lot of previous work in the area of context-aware reminders. As discussed in the previous section, commercial efforts have focused on e-mail tools that use no context or PIM tools that use only time. Another system that uses time-aware reminders is Lifestreams [6]. Lifestreams is a system for organizing documents that is intended to replace conventional files and directory structures. Instead, Lifestreams organizes documents temporally, based on when they were created, received, and/or modified. The beginning of a stream contains the oldest documents while the end of a stream contains the most recently created documents. The interface allows users to even visit the future portion of the document stream. When a user creates a document in the future portion of the stream, they are effectively creating a time-based reminder. When they return to present time, these documents are hidden and only appear when present time matches the future time of the documents.

The comMotion project [13] moved beyond this by using a combination of location and time information to deliver relevant messages. When a reminder message is created, a location is associated with it. Then, when the intended recipient arrives at that location (work or a grocery store, for example), the messages associated with that location are delivered via speech synthesis. In addition, when a user arrives at work, her calendar events for that day are delivered, taking advantage of time as well as location information.

Proem is a wearable computer-based system that supports profile-based cooperation [11]. Wearers can write simple rules that indicate their interests in other people. When someone physically close to the wearer has a profile that matches one or more of his interests, Proem can alert him. Interests are limited to fairly static pieces of information such as names and personal interests and hobbies.

Memory Glasses is a wearable computer-based context-aware reminder system [3]. It proposes the use of time, location, and activity to deliver reminders. It focuses on personal context and uses body-worn sensors (a camera and a microphone) to determine what activity the wearer is engaged in, including walking down stairs or taking part in a conversation. When Memory Glasses determines the current activity, reminders associated with that activity are presented to the using audio output. Memory Glasses proposes that knowledge of this activity may be used to better determine when it is appropriate to interrupt the wearer with a reminder.

While these systems address many of the features of an ideal reminder tool, they are limited by their restricted use of context. The notion of context is quite rich and encompasses many information types beyond location, time and activity, such as identity, physical/environmental conditions, as well as information about other individuals besides the user [5,18]. As the context associated with a reminder is made richer, the system's ability to deliver the reminder in the appropriate situation is improved. The CybreMinder reminder tool we will present in the next section attempts to address all the features of the ideal reminder tool, concentrating on increasing the variety of context used to associate with reminders. It is not intended to replace existing calendar or to-do list tools, but to augment them.

4 The CybreMinder Tool

To aid our investigation of reminder tools and interfaces, we built the Java-based CybreMinder tool. It has two main parts — reminder creation and reminder delivery.

4.1 Reminder Creation

When users launch CybreMinder, they are presented with an interface that looks quite similar to an e-mail creation tool. As shown in Figure 1, users can enter the names of the recipients for the reminder. The recipients could just be themselves, indicating a personal reminder, or a list of other people, indicating a third party reminder is being created. The reminder has a subject, a priority level (ranging from lowest to highest), a body in which the reminder description is placed, and an expiration date. The expiration date indicates the date and time at which the reminder should expire and be delivered, if it has not already been delivered.

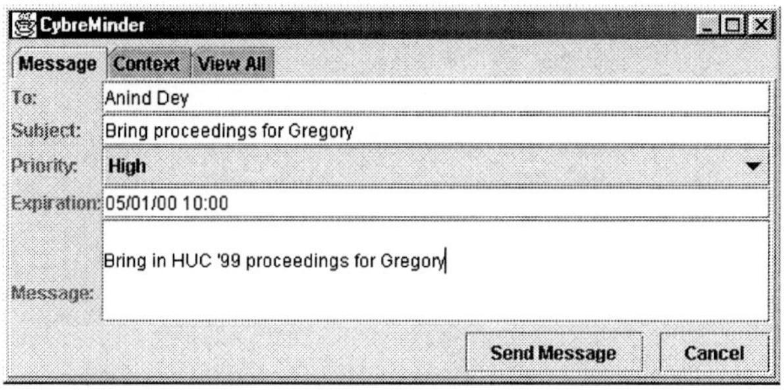

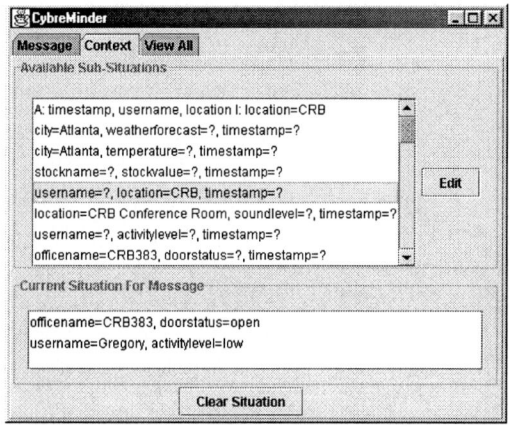

Fig. 1. CybreMinder reminder creation tool

Fig. 2. CybreMinder situation editor

In addition to this traditional messaging interface, users can select the Situation tab and be presented with the situation editor (Figure 2). This interface allows dynamic construction of an arbitrarily rich situation, or context that is associated with the reminder being created. The interface consists of two main pieces for creating and viewing the situation. Creation is assisted by a dynamically generated list of valid sub-situations that are currently supported by the CybreMinder infrastructure (as assisted by the Context Toolkit described later). When the user selects a sub-situation, they can edit it to fit their particular situation. Each sub-situation consists of a number of context types and values. For example, in Figure 2, the user has just selected the sub-situation that a particular user is present in the CRB building at a particular time. The context types are the user's name, the location (set to CRB) and a timestamp.

In Figure 3, the user is requiring the user name to be "Anind Dey", and is not using time. This sub-situation will be satisfied when Anind Dey is in the location 'CRB'.

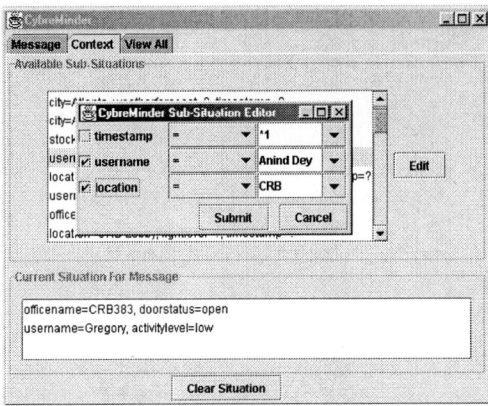

Fig. 3. Sub-situation editor

The user indicates which context types are important by selecting the checkbox next to those attributes. For the types that they have selected, users may enter a relation other than '='. For example, the user can set the timestamp after 9 p.m. by using the '>' relation. Other supported relations are '>=', '<', and '<='. For the context value, users can either choose from a list of pre-generated values, or enter their own.

At the bottom of Figure 2, the currently specified situation is visible. The overall situation being defined is the conjunction of the sub-situations listed. Once a reminder and an associated situation have been created, the user can send the reminder. If there is no situation attached, the reminder is delivered immediately after the user sends the reminder. However, unlike e-mail messages, sending a reminder does not necessarily imply immediate delivery. If a situation is attached, the reminder is delivered to recipients at a future time when all the sub-situations can be simultaneously satisfied. If the situation cannot be satisfied before the reminder expires, the reminder is delivered both to the sender and recipients with a note indicating that the reminder has expired.

4.2 Reminder Delivery

Thus far, we have concentrated on the process of creating context-aware reminders. We will now describe the delivery process. When a reminder can be delivered, either because its associated situation was satisfied or because it has expired, CybreMinder determines what is the most appropriate delivery mechanism for each reminder recipient. The default signal is to show the reminder on the closest available display, augmented with an audio cue. However, if a recipient wishes, they can specify a configuration file that will override this default.

A user's configuration file contains information about all of the available methods for contacting the user, as well as rules defined by the user on which method to use in which situation. If the recipient's current context and reminder information (sender identity and/or priority) matches any situation defined in his configuration file, the specified delivery mechanism is used. Currently, we support the delivery of reminders via SMS on a mobile phone, e-mail, displaying on a nearby display (wearable, handheld, or static CRT) and printing to a local printer (to emulate paper to-do lists).

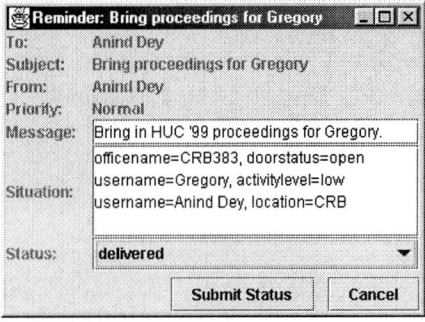

Fig. 4. Delivered reminder

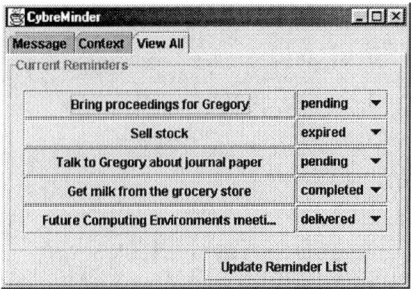

Fig. 5. List of all reminders

For the latter three mechanisms, both the reminder and associated situation are delivered to the user. Delivery of the situation provides additional useful information to the user, helping them understand why the reminder is being sent at this particular time. Along with the reminder and situation, users are given the ability to change the status of the reminder (Figure 4). A status of "completed" indicates that the reminder has been addressed and can be dismissed. The "delivered" status means the reminder has been delivered but still needs to be addressed. A "pending" status means that the reminder should be delivered again when the associated situation is next satisfied. Users can explicitly set the status through a hyperlink in an e-mail reminder or through the interface shown in Figure 4.

Since SMS messages have limited length, only the subject of a reminder is delivered when using this delivery mechanism. Users receiving such an SMS message have the option of going to a networked device and launching their interface (Figure 1) to CybreMinder. By selecting the View All tab, users can view a personalized list of all reminders and can change the status of any of these reminders (Figure 5).

5 Example Reminders

In this section, we describe a range of reminders and situations that users can create using CybreMinder, moving from simple situations towards more complex situations. The situations are only limited by the context that can be sensed. Table 1 gives the natural language and CybreMinder descriptions of the illustrated situations below.

Table 1. Natural language and CybreMinder descriptions of scenarios in Section 5

Situation	Natural Language Description	CybreMinder Description
Time	9:45 am	Expiration field: 9:45 am
Location	Forecast is for rain and Bob is leaving home	City = Atlanta, WeatherForecast = rain Username = Bob, Location = Bob's front door
Co-Location	Sally and colleague are co-located	Username = Sally, Location = *1 Username = Bob, Location = *1
Complex #1	Stock price of X is over $50, Bob is alone and has free time	StockName = X, StockPrice > 50 Username = Bob, Location = *1 Location = *1, OccupantSize = 1 Username = Bob, FreeTime > 30
Complex #2	Sally is in her office has some free time, and her friend is not busy	Username = Sally, Location = Sally's office Username = Sally, FreeTime = 60 Username = Tom, ActivityLevel = low

5.1 Time-Based Reminder

Like many of the other systems previously described, CybreMinder allows reminders to be triggered based on a simple time context. In this scenario, Sally has a meeting at 10 a.m. tomorrow. She wants to send a reminder to herself fifteen minutes before the meeting occurs, so that she has time to walk to the meeting. She can simply set the expiry date to be tomorrow's date and 9:45 a.m.

5.2 Location-Based Reminder

In this scenario, Bob wants to remind himself to take his umbrella to work because it is supposed to rain this afternoon. He keeps the umbrella near his apartment door, so he wants to receive the reminder as he approaches the door. Here, he can simply create a situation with only one sub-situation: he is at his front door. In CybreMinder terms, he sets the username to his name and location to his front door. This situation can be made slightly more complex. If Bob is sending the reminder the night before, then he may want to add a time attribute and set it to be greater than 7:00 a.m. By doing so, the reminder will not be triggered and displayed each time he leaves his apartment that night. It will only be displayed when he approaches the door after 7:00 a.m. the next morning. Pushing on this scenario a little more, Bob does have to know ahead of time that it is going to rain. He can simply create a reminder that is to be delivered whenever the forecast calls for rain and he is leaving his apartment.

5.3 Co-location-Based Reminder

Of the systems we reviewed, only Proem [11] supported proactive reminders when two or more people were co-located in an arbitrary location. It can be argued that post-it notes could be used in this setting, although it currently breaks normal social conventions to stick post-it notes to people. An example co-location scenario follows: Sally wants to engage a colleague in a discussion about an interesting paper she read, but forgets when she sees her colleague. She can create a context-aware reminder that will be delivered when she is in close proximity with her colleague. The situation she creates is slightly more complex than the ones we have discussed so far, and it makes use of variables. Variables allow users to create relationships between sub-situations. First Sally creates an initial sub-situation where she sets the user name to be her colleague's name and the location to be variable (indicated in Table 1 by *1). Then, she creates a second sub-situation, where she sets the user name to be her name and the location to the variable used in the first sub-situation. Now when Sally and her colleague are in the same arbitrary location, the reminder will be delivered.

5.4 Complex Reminder

CybreMinder supports the unlimited use of rich context, allowing users to create as rich a situation as can be sensed. We describe two such situations. In the first scenario, Bob owns stock in Company X and has decided to sell that stock when it is valued over $50 per share. He only wants to be reminded to sell, however, when he is alone and has free time. To create this situation to signal a reminder to sell, Bob creates a number of sub-situations: stock price of company X > $50, Bob is the only occupant of his location, and Bob's schedule shows that he has > 30 minutes before his next meeting. When this situation occurs, Bob receives the reminder to sell his stock.

In our second complex scenario, Sally needs to make a phone call to her friend Tom. She wants to receive a context-aware reminder when she arrives at her office, has some free time in her schedule, and her friend is not busy. To create this situation, she creates three sub-situations: Sally is in her office, Tom's activity status is low, and Sally has at least one hour before her next appointment.

6 The CybreMinder Architecture

In the previous two sections, we described how CybreMinder works from the user's perspective. Here, we discuss how CybreMinder was built. When users write situations to be associated with reminders, CybreMinder must have a way to determine when they have been realized. It uses the Context Toolkit[1] for this purpose.

---

[1] The Context Toolkit and tutorial can be downloaded from http://www.cc.gatech.edu/fce/contexttoolkit.

6.1 The Context Toolkit

The Context Toolkit is a software toolkit that aids in the building of context-aware applications [4,16]. It promotes three main concepts for building context-aware applications; separation of context sensing, or acquisition, from context use; context aggregation; and context interpretation. It relieves developers from having to deal with how to sense and access context information, allowing them instead to concentrate on how to use the context. It provides simplifying abstractions like aggregation and interpretation to make it easier for applications to obtain the context they require. Aggregation provides "one-stop shopping" for context about an entity, allowing application designers to think in terms of high level information, rather than low-level details.

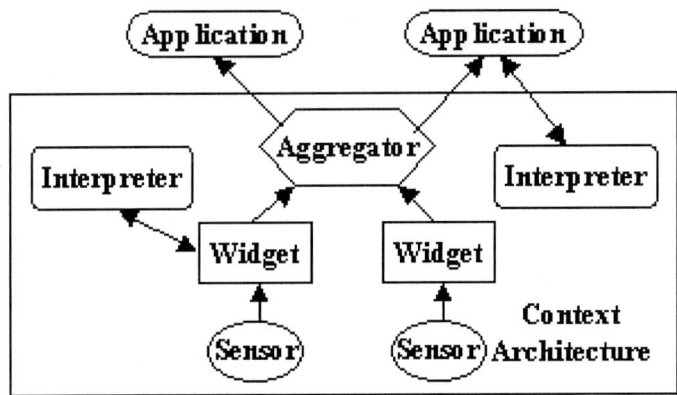

Fig. 6. Context Toolkit components: arrows indicate data flow

The architecture makes it easy to add the use of context to existing applications that don't use context and to evolve applications that already use context. In addition, the architecture makes context-aware applications resistant to changes in the context-sensing layer. It encapsulates changes and the impact of changes, so applications do not need to be modified.

The Context Toolkit consists of three basic building blocks: context widgets, context aggregators and context interpreters. Figure 6 shows the relationship between the context components and applications. Context widgets encapsulate information about a single piece of context, such as location or activity, for example. They provide a uniform interface to components or applications that use the context, hiding the details of the underlying context-sensing mechanism(s). They allow other components to both poll and subscribe to the context information they maintain. Widgets are mainly responsible for collecting information about the environment. However, they also support services that allow them to affect the environment. For example, a Light widget that detects the intensity of the light in a particular location, and have a service that controls a lamp to change the intensity.

A context aggregator is very similar to a widget, in that it supports the same set of features as a widget. The difference is that an aggregator aggregates multiple pieces of context. In fact, it is responsible for the entire context about a particular entity (person, place, or object). Aggregation facilitates the access of context by applications that are interested in multiple pieces of context about a single entity. A context interpreter is used to abstract or interpret context. For example, a context widget may provide location context in the form of latitude and longitude, but an application may require the location in the form of a street name. A context interpreter may be used to provide this abstraction.

Context components are intended to be persistent, running 24 hours a day, 7 days a week. They are instantiated and executed independently of each other in separate threads and on separate computing devices. The Context Toolkit makes the distribution of the context architecture transparent to context-aware applications, mediating all communications between applications and components. A discovery protocol allows components to communicate with each other without knowing about the existence of each other at compile or instantiation time.

6.2 CybreMinder and the Context Toolkit

When CybreMinder launches, it uses the Context Toolkit discovery protocol to detect what context components are currently available. It analyzes this and determines what sub-situations are available for a user to work with. The sub-situations are simply the collection of subscription callbacks that the context widgets and context aggregators provide. For example, an IdentityPresence context widget contains information about the presence of individuals in a particular location (specified at instantiation time). The callback it provides has three attributes: a user name, a location, and a timestamp. The location is a constant, set to "home", for example. The constants in each callback are used to populate the menus from which users can select values for attributes.

When the user creates a reminder with an associated situation, the reminder is sent to the aggregator responsible for maintaining context about the recipient. CybreMinder can be shut down any time after the reminder has been sent to the recipient's aggregator. The recipient's aggregator is the logical place to store all reminder information intended for the recipient because it knows more about the recipient than any other component and is always available. This aggregator analyzes the given situation and creates subscriptions to the necessary aggregators and widgets so that it can determine when the situation has occurred. It also creates a timer thread that awakens when the reminder is set to expire. Whenever the aggregator receives a subscription callback, it updates the status of the situation in question. When all sub-situations are satisfied, the entire situation is satisfied, and the reminder can be delivered.

The recipient's aggregator contains the most up-to-date information about the recipient. It tries to match this context information along with the reminder sender and priority level with the rules defined in the recipient's configuration file. The recipient's context and the rules consist of collections of simple attribute name-value pairs, making them easy to compare. When a delivery mechanism has been chosen, the aggregator calls a widget service that can deliver the reminder appropriately. For example, a display widget provides information about the display capabilities of a device. It also provides a service that allows other components to display information on that device. Similarly, e-mail and SMS services exist in the Context Toolkit.

Services can also return information to the component that calls them. For example, the display service not only shows the reminder and associated situation, but also a form allowing the user to set the state of this reminder. The user input to this form is sent back to the recipient's aggregator, which can update the reminder status. In the case of SMS, when the user must set the status using the CybreMinder, the application contacts the user's aggregator and queries for all the reminders and associated information. The application sends any updated status information to the aggregator.

7 Conclusions and Future Work

The goal of CybreMinder is to provide users with a tool that provides appropriate support for dealing with reminders. In particular, our objective is to support all the features of an ideal reminder tool:
- use of rich context for specifying reminders, beyond simple time and location and for proactively determining when to deliver them;
- ability for users and third parties to submit reminders;
- ability to create reminders using a variety of input devices;
- ability to receive reminders using a variety of devices, appropriate to the user's situation;
- use of reminders that include both a signal that something is to be remembered and a full description of what is to be remembered; and
- allowing users to view a list of all active reminders.

We believe that we have been mostly successful in this objective. We provide some support for all of these features, except for the ability to create reminders using a variety of input devices. We will discuss each of these features in turn.

The first feature, allowing for the use of rich context in reminders, is the most important feature for a reminder tool and is the one that is most lacking in existing reminder tools. By leveraging off of the Context Toolkit's ability to acquire and distribute context, we allow users to create arbitrarily complex situations to attach to reminders and to create custom rules for governing how reminders should be delivered to them. Users are not required to use templates or hardcoded situations, but can use any context that can be sensed and is available from their environment. From initial use of the system, we have found that while the interface supports the specification of complex situations, it can be complex to use, particularly when variables are involved. We would like to find the correct balance of sophistication and simplicity in an effort to improve the interface. One potential solution is a suite of special-purpose reminders with highly simplified interfaces that suit their specific use.

By using a discovery protocol for determining what context is available, we attempt to limit users in creating situations that CybreMinder is able to detect. However, it is possible for users to create situations that CybreMinder cannot detect. Some of these situations can be caught by the aggregator, but not all. We intend to improve the checking ability of CybreMinder.

Part of the reminder creation process is the specification of recipients. A user can set the recipients of the reminder to be herself, herself and others, or just others. In this way, CybreMinder supports the ability to send reminders to yourself or third parties. Currently, users can only create reminders using the Java-based CybreMinder. This application can run on any networked device that can support Java, including desktop computers, WinCE devices and wearable computers. However, the Context Toolkit does not require that applications be written in Java. We envision, in the near future, creating simplified versions of CybreMinder that can be executed on a Palm Pilot, a pager, or a mobile phone, which a user interacts with not only using text, but also pen and speech input. We would also like to support the automatic creation of reminders from user's calendars and to-do lists.

On the delivery side, CybreMinder sends both the reminder and the associated situation to a service for display (via e-mail, available screen, or SMS). The quality of the reminder signal and the completeness of the reminder description depend on the service being used. E-mail provides a poor signal if the user is not at reading their e-mail at the reminder time, but does present a complete description. Displaying a reminder on a nearby screen with an audio cue provides both a good signal and a complete description. SMS provides a very good signal but only a partial description. Likewise, there are advantages and disadvantages to automatically printed reminders.

By supporting a greater variety of devices and display services, we can allow users to make better personal choices about how they want to receive reminders (both in terms of the signal and description) in various situations. CybreMinder delivers a reminder when the associated situation has been realized, and chooses the delivery mechanism/service based on the recipient's current context. However, it does not take into account how interruptible the recipient is. We realize that the use of static user configuration files is not the answer, but determining interruptiblity is an enormous unsolved research problem [10,14,17,19], and as researchers make progress in this area, we would like to improve CybreMinder accordingly.

Initial responses to CybreMinder have been promising. We intend to expand our current user population and perform an objective evaluation of CybreMinder and comparison to existing reminder tools. We would also like to examine the use of the CybreMinder reminder tool as part of a larger context-aware messaging system.

8 Acknowledgements

We would like to thank the Future Computing Environments research group for contributing to these ideas. This work was supported in part by a NSF CAREER Grant # 9703384, a Motorola University Partnerships in Research grant and the ITO division of DARPA through the Expeditions/Ubiquitous Computing program.

References

1. Bergqvist, J., Ljungberg, F.: ComCenter: A Person Oriented Approach to Mobile Communication. Extended abstract In *Proceedings of CHI 2000* (2000) 123–124

2. Brown, P.J.: The Stick-e Document: A Framework for Creating Context-Aware Applications. Electronic Publishing (1996) 259–272
3. DeVaul, R.W., Clarkson, B., Pentland, A.: The Memory Glasses: Towards a Wearable Context Aware, Situation-appropriate Reminder System. In *CHI 2000 Workshop on Situated Interaction in Ubiquitous Computing* (2000)
4. Dey, A.K., Abowd, G.D., Salber, D.: A Context-Based Infrastructure for Smart Environments. *1st International Workshop on Managing Interactions in Smart Environments (MANSE'99)* (1999) 114–128
5. Dey, A.K., Abowd, G.D.: Towards a Better Understanding of Context and Context-Awareness. In *CHI 2000 Workshop on the What, Who, Where, When, and How of Context-Awareness* (2000)
6. Fertig, S., Freeman, E., Gelernter, D.: "Finding and Reminding" Reconsidered. SIGCHI Bulletin, Vol. 28 (1996)
7. Gellersen, H-W.: EMC: Environment-Mediated Communication. *International Workshop on Interactive Applications of Mobile Computing (IMC'98)* (1998)
8. Gwizdka, J.: Timely Reminders: A Case Study of Temporal Guidance in PIM and Email Tools Usage. Extended abstract in *Proceedings of CHI 2000* (2000) 163–164
9. Herstad, J. Van Thanh, D., Audestad, J.A.: Human-Human Communication in Context. *International Workshop on Interactive Applications of Mobile Computing IMC'98* (1998)
10. Horvitz, E.: Mixed-Initiative User Interfaces. In *Proceedings of CHI 99* (1999) 159–166
11. Korteum, G., Segall, Z., Thompson, T.G.C.: Close Encounters: Supporting Mobile Collaboration through Interchange of User Profiles. In *Proceedings of HUC'99* (1999) 171–185
12. Ljungstrand, P.: Context-awareness in distributed communication systems. In *CHI 2000 Workshop on the What, Who, Where, When, and How of Context-Awareness* (2000)
13. Marmasse, N.: comMotion. Extended abstract in *Proceedings of CHI'99* (1999) 320–321
14. Miyata, Y., Norman, D.A.: Psychological Issues in Support of Multiple Activities. User Centered Design, edited by Norman, D.A., Draper, S.W. Chapter 13 (1986) 265–284
15. Rekimoto, J., Ayatsuka, Y., Hayashi, K.: Augment-able Reality: Situated Communication through Physical and Digital Spaces. In *Proceedings of 2nd International Symposium on Wearable Computers (ISWC'98)* (1998) 68–75
16. Salber, D., Dey, A.K., Abowd, G.D.: The Context Toolkit: Aiding the Development of Context-Enabled Applications. In *Proceedings of CHI'99* (1999) 434–441
17. Sawhney, N., Schmandt, C.: Nomadic Radio: Scaleable and Contextual Notification for Wearable Audio Messaging. In *Proceedings of CHI'99* (1999) 96–103
18. Schmidt, A., Beigl, M. Gellersen, H-W. There is More to Context than Location: Environment Sensing Technologies for Adaptive Mobile User Interfaces. *Workshop on Interactive Applications of Mobile Computing IMC'98* (1998)
19. Stringer, M., Eldridge, M, Lamming, M.: Towards a Deeper Understanding of Task Interruption. In *CHI Workshop on Situated Interaction in Ubiquitous Computing* (2000)

Using Handheld Devices in Synchronous Collaborative Scenarios

Jörg Roth and Claus Unger

University of Hagen
Department for Computer Science, 58084 Hagen, Germany
{Joerg.Roth, Claus.Unger}@Fernuni-hagen.de

Abstract. In this paper we present a platform specially designed for groupware applications running on handheld devices. Common groupware platforms request desktop computers as underlying hardware platforms. The fundamental different nature of handheld devices has a great impact on the platform, e.g. resource limitations have to be considered, the network is slow and unstable. Often, personal data are stored on handheld devices, thus mechanisms have to ensure privacy. These considerations lead to the QuickStep platform. Sample applications developed with QuickStep demonstrate the strengths of the QuickStep environment.

1 Introduction

Collaborative applications help a group to, e.g., collaboratively create documents, write agendas or schedule appointments. A common taxonomy [3] classifies collaborative applications by time and space, with 'same place' and 'different places' attributes on the space axis and 'same time' (*synchronous*) and 'different time' (*asynchronous*) ones on the time axis. Synchronous groupware supports real-time group activities, i.e. events are distributed to group members without considerable delay. In contrast, asynchronous activities may happen at different times.

To develop groupware, especially synchronous groupware, is a difficult and time-consuming task. Usually, groupware is not developed 'from-scratch', but with the help of a groupware toolkit. In this paper, we introduce a groupware platform for synchronous collaborative applications with handheld devices. Our approach assumes that group members operate in a close neighbourhood, i.e. long distance connections between users are not supported.

Although several groupware toolkits are available already, they can hardly be adapted to handheld devices. Straight-forward approaches, i.e. simply cross-compiling existing applications, fail because of the specific properties of handheld devices and the connecting network:
- Handheld devices have low computational power, small memory and usually no mass storage devices (e.g. hard disks).
- Handheld operating systems (e.g. PalmOS [1], Windows CE [2], EPOC [11]) do not offer the same variety of services as desktop operating systems. PalmOS, e.g.,

- does not support threads or processes for background tasks, a common technique for desktop computer applications.
- Handheld applications follow a different usage paradigm: they are designed for a small display, have to provide short start-up and response times and are developed for gathering and presenting small pieces of information rather than processing large amounts of data.
- Network connections to handhelds have low bandwidths and are considerably unstable.

The notions of *handheld device*, *palmtop*, *PDA* and *organizer* are often interpreted in different ways. One (older) interpretation distinguishes between *pen-based devices* and *palmtops*, where the latter have keyboards. In contrast, Microsoft divides Windows CE devices into *handheld PCs* (H/PC) with a keyboard, *palmsize PCs* (P/PC) which are controlled by a pen and *handheld PC Pro* devices, which are subnotebooks [2]. In the following, we understand by *handheld devices* pen-based devices with small displays (e.g. 160x160 pixels). Popular examples for such devices are 3Com's Palm III and Casio's Cassiopeia.

2 Collaboration in Mobile Environments

Collaborative applications significantly differ from single-user applications. Many users provide input (often simultaneously), output has to be processed for many users and shared data have to be kept consistent. Groupware applications have to provide a kind of 'group feeling', called *collaboration awareness*: users have to be aware of other users involved in the collaborative task. Collaboration awareness is provided by elements inside the application called *awareness widgets*.

A similar concept applies to the mobility aspect of handheld devices. Mobile devices can be connected to a network at different places. Depending on the location, different information is available. Users should be aware of their current location, including the geographic location as well as the location in the network, e.g. the actual domain. This kind of awareness is called *context awareness*.

We call an application *aware* of something, if it explicitly takes care of a special situation, otherwise we call it *transparent*. *Collaboration aware* applications are especially designed to support a group, i.e. they contain special code for group functions. *Collaboration transparent* applications are original single-user applications, which, with the help of a group toolkit, can be used by many users simultaneously. Collaboration transparent applications do not offer awareness widgets. A similar notion can be applied to the mobility aspect: *mobility aware* applications contain code to handle mobility, e.g. react on unstable network connections and changing network locations. *Mobility transparent* applications cannot handle such problems explicitly, but rely on an underlying platform.

The QuickStep platform is designed to develop both, collaboration aware and mobility aware applications. It provides awareness widgets for collaboration awareness as well as for context awareness. Before we describe the QuickStep approach, related work is presented.

3 Related Work

Collaborative as well as mobile applications have to keep data consistent. Applications which are collaborative and mobile at the same time double the problem of data consistency. Collaborative applications have to synchronise concurrent data manipulations, mobile applications have to keep data consistent when devices are moved inside the network or are disconnected from the network.

Several toolkits have been developed to address the problem of data distribution in mobile environments. Coda [5] provides a distributed file system similar to NFS, but allows disconnected operations. Applications based on Coda are fully mobility transparent, i.e. run inside a mobile environment without any modification. Disconnected mobile nodes have access to remote files via a cache. Operations on files are logged and automatically applied to the server when the client reconnects. Coda applications can either define themselves mechanisms for detecting and resolving conflicts or ask the user in case of conflicts. A follow-on platform, Odyssey [9], extends data distribution to multimedia data such as video or audio data. To support real-time data, bandwidths and available resources have to be monitored. Odyssey applications are mobility aware.

Rover [4] supports mobility transparent as well as mobility aware applications. To run without modification, network-based applications such as Web browsers and News readers can use network proxies. The development of mobility aware applications is supported by two mechanisms: *relocated dynamic objects* (*RDOs*) and *queued remote procedure calls* (*QRPC*). RDOs contain mobile code and data and can reside on a server as well as on a mobile node. During disconnection, QRPCs are applied to cached RDOs. As in Coda, operations are logged and applied to server data after reconnecting.

Bayou [12] provides data distribution with the help of a number of servers, thus segmented networks can be handled. In contrast to Coda, replicated records are still accessible, even when conflicts have been detected but not resolved. Bayou applications have to provide a conflict detection and resolution mechanism, thus no user intervention is necessary. Bayou is not designed to support real-time applications.

Sync [7] allows asynchronous collaboration between mobile users. Sync provides a collaboration based on shared objects which can be derived from a Java library. As in Bayou, data conflicts are handled by the application. Sync applications have to provide a *merge matrix*, which contains a resulting operation for each pair of possible conflicting operations. With the help of the merge matrix, conflicts can be resolved automatically.

Lotus Notes [6] has not primarily been designed for mobile computers, but allows replicated data management in heterogeneous networks. Nodes can be disconnected and merge their data after reconnection. Data in Lotus Notes have a record structure. Fields may contain arbitrary data which are transparent to Notes. Records can be read or changed on different nodes simultaneously. When reconnecting, conflicting updates are resolved by users.

With the help of handheld devices, Pebbles [8] allows to remotely control applications running on a server. It follows a collaboration and mobility transparent concept. Instead of using the mouse and keyboard directly, input is taken from the handheld device's touchscreen and handwriting area. From the application's view, input comes directly from the server's keyboard and mouse respectively. In turn, the server window output is transferred to handheld devices. With these mechanisms it is possible to remotely control off-the-shelf applications (e.g. MS Word) with handheld devices.

Most of the toolkits above request their mobile clients to be notebook computers with, e.g., hard disks. Only Pebbles is designed for handhelds. The focus of the other platforms is to maintain data consistency in a weakly connected environment. Problems related to handheld devices, such as small memory and reduced computational power, are not handled satisfactorily. Automatic conflict detection and resolution need a considerable amount of resources on the handheld devices. We believe that such mechanisms are (currently) not suitable for handheld scenarios.

Concepts, such as the Rover toolkit, which require mobile code and marshalling/unmarshalling mechanisms currently cannot be adapted to handheld devices, since these are significantly different from their servers. The concept of mobile code requires platform independent code and identical runtime libraries on both platforms. Even though languages such as Java are running on many platforms, handheld portings will provide other runtime libraries, thus mobile code mechanisms will fail.

Looking at typical data types stored in handheld devices we mostly find well structured and textual data. Real-time data such as video or audio data provided by the Odyssey system are currently inadequate due to small network bandwidths, low computational power and reduced peripheral equipment of handheld devices. Even graphical data such as freehand sketches or diagrams are difficult to handle because of inaccurate and inconvenient screen devices.

Data stored inside a handheld device are usually viewed as *private*. Even more than desktop computers, such devices are viewed as personal ones [10]. Personal data, e.g. telephone numbers, birthdays and leisure-time activities are stored inside such a device. If a handheld device is connected to an untrusted network, a platform has to offer mechanisms to guarantee privacy of individual data. None of the platforms above contains such mechanisms.

4 The QuickStep Approach

The QuickStep platform supports developers of collaboration and mobility aware handheld applications. They can use communication and collaboration primitives provided by the platform and can concentrate on application-specific details. A set of predefined awareness widgets can be integrated into an application with a few lines of code.

The QuickStep approach can be described as follows:
- QuickStep supports applications with well-structured, record oriented data, as being used by built-in software for handheld devices (e.g. for to-do lists, memos, telephone lists). QuickStep has explicitly not been designed for supporting multimedia data, graphical oriented applications or continuous data streams.
- QuickStep is mainly designed for supporting synchronous collaboration.
- QuickStep provides awareness widgets for collaboration awareness as well as context awareness.

- QuickStep comes along with a generic server application which allows to support arbitrary client applications without modifying or reconfiguring the server.
- The QuickStep architecture ensures privacy of individual data.

Before we describe the QuickStep platform itself, we present a sample application developed with QuickStep.

4.1 A Sample Application

Consider a scenario in which members of a meeting want to schedule appointments for future meetings. Each member owns a handheld device, which already contains a list of appointments as well as entries indicating the time one is unavailable because of, e.g., vacations or travels. Figure 1 presents an application that can help to find a date, when all members are available.

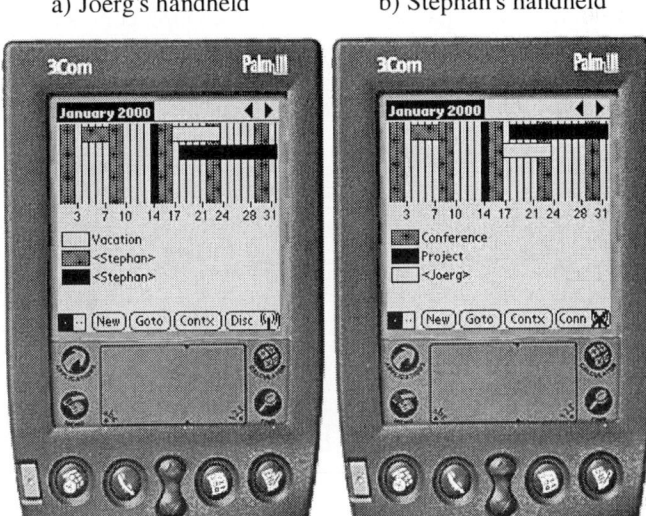

Fig. 1. A collaborative calendar tool

The figure shows two users' views on their personal handheld devices. The upper half of the windows displays the days of a month. Each range of dates when someone is unavailable is indicated by a bar. To get a better overview, the view can be switched to a two-months display. The lower half of the window is the legend for the upper half.

Both users, Joerg and Stephan, can see their own and the foreign bar, the latter being labelled with the user name rather than the local label. With regard to the foreign bar, only the date range is of interest, not the reason why someone is unavailable. Each user can make new entries which are distributed to the other user in real-time. With the help of this application it is very easy to find dates, where all members are available.

To develop such an application 'from-scratch', a developer has to implement many tasks, communication protocols, e.g., have to be integrated, shared data have to be managed. The application should offer awareness widgets. All these services have to be developed in addition to the main task, the calendar function. This might overwhelm a developer.

QuickStep helps a developer to concentrate on the application-specific details; communication and data primitives as well as predefined awareness widgets can be used from the platform. In the following chapters, we present the platform in more detail.

4.2 The QuickStep Communication Infrastructure

The sample application above requires a communication link between the handhelds. In principle, the devices could be connected directly. Unfortunately, the computational power of handheld devices is currently too low to handle communication in the background. Often, handheld operating systems (e.g. PalmOS) are generally unable to run background tasks, a prerequisite for handling incoming communication requests. Thus, we need an additional computer, which acts as a communication relay between handhelds. This computer, the *QuickStep server*, contains a generic server application which is able to serve arbitrary QuickStep applications.

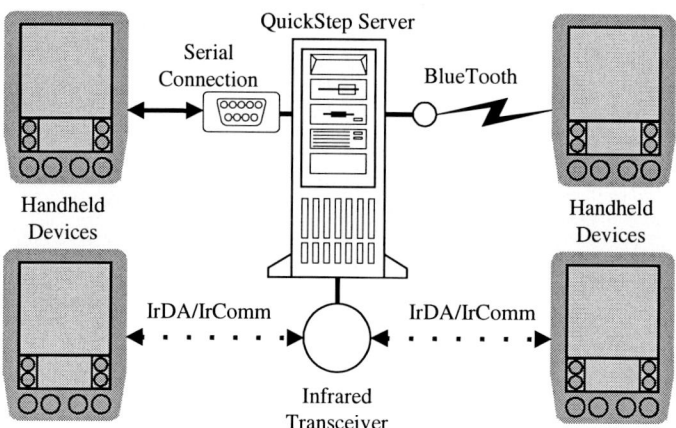

Fig. 2. A QuickStep communication scenario

Figure 2 shows a typical QuickStep communication scenario. In various scenarios the QuickStep approach can be used without setting up an application dependent server. The QuickStep server can be viewed as 'inventory' of a specific environment, e.g. of a meeting room or of 'public' locations like trains or public halls. Once installed, it normally has not to be reconfigured or administered. The server runs without an operator and does not need a user interface, thus can work 'invisibly' behind a panel.

The network connection works either in a wireless way (e.g. via an infrared or radio connection) or via serial cables. Wireless communication protocols are, e.g.,

BlueTooth and IrDA/IrComm. Typical handheld devices already provide a serial port and a built-in infrared transceiver. In addition, a TCP/IP communication stack is integrated into most handheld operating systems.

4.3 Group Management

Groups of collaborating users are not defined explicitly in QuickStep. All users connected to a specific QuickStep server at the same time and using the same QuickStep application form a collaborative session. This concept allows to run a server without defining groups centrally. It is possible for a user to join a group without having explicit permission from existing users. Since a mechanism for anonymizing data is integrated into the platform, a user cannot spy out private data (see below).

QuickStep is mainly created to support synchronous collaboration. In contrast to desktop computers, handhelds are not permanently switched on. During collaboration, the handheld may be switched off because of the auto-power-off mechanism. In addition, handheld network connections tend to be unstable, thus unwanted disconnections are possible. Following the strict definition of synchronous collaboration, anytime a member is disconnected, she or he would automatically leave a running session. To overcome this problem, we introduce the notion of *relaxed synchronous collaboration* for group members who collaborate synchronously, but may infrequently be disconnected from the network for short periods of time. Relaxed synchronous collaboration is placed between (strict) synchronous and asynchronous collaboration. As in asynchronous scenarios, shared data have to be stored during disconnections, but data manipulations are happening much more frequently.

QuickStep does not provide services for leaving a session. When a user disconnects, the server first assumes a temporary disconnection. Only if a user is disconnected for a longer time (e.g. an hour), the server removes that user from the session. The period of time, a user has to be disconnected until a leave operation is performed, is defined by the corresponding application.

4.4 Managing Data

Usually, data inside handheld devices are well-structured and record oriented. Common operating systems for handhelds have built-in services to store and retrieve data records. PalmOS supports an entity called *database* [1] (not to be confused with the classical database). A palm database is a persistent collection of records. Each record has a unique identifier, which allows its identification, but its content is opaque to the operating system. Constructing and interpreting records solely depends on the corresponding application.

The database is a common programming abstraction in handheld applications, thus the ideal abstraction for collaborative applications as well. QuickStep follows the same paradigm when collecting and distributing data. The QuickStep application programming interface (API) has similar database functions as the handheld operating systems. An application developer can use well-known services to handle application specific data. Data stored in QuickStep databases are automatically distributed among a session by the QuickStep platform. Similar to native database services, the actual content of records is not of interest for the distribution mechanism and can only be interpreted by the application. Especially, the QuickStep server does not know the record structure.

When planning data distribution, many contradicting requirements have to be taken into consideration. Many platforms described above have complex mechanisms to detect and resolve conflicts caused by concurrent data manipulations. In our opinion, such mechanisms cannot be used inside handheld devices. Our concept for solving conflicts is simply to avoid them: it is not possible to concurrently manipulate data. For this, each record of data can only be changed by the handheld device which originally created the record. Copies residing on other handheld devices can only be viewed. To modify data which were created by another user, one has to make a private copy, which is treated as a new record.

4.5 Mirroring and Caching

The computation power of handhelds and network bandwidths are considerably low compared with desktop environments. The transfer of processing tasks to a server would relieve handheld devices of heavy computation. On the other hand, it is not possible to transfer large sets of data between handhelds and a server. To reduce network traffic and to perform as many computations as possible on a server, we developed a combined mirroring and caching mechanism. Figure 3 shows the architecture.

The main entities are the following:
- Each handheld has its own *local database* which contains the application's records. Only the owner can add, change or remove local records.
- The QuickStep server has a copy of each local database, the *mirror database*. The mirror database is incrementally updated each time a handheld device is connected to the server.
- To allow viewing data during a disconnection, a local copy of other users' mirror database entries exists on the handhelds, called the *cache database*. Since the amount of data of all mirror databases might be too big for the handheld, a *selector* set by the application reduces the number of cache entries.
- An application accesses the local database and the cache database via the *database proxy*. The proxy provides a similar interface as a conventional database.

The *anonymizer* and the *lifetime supervisors* are related to privacy mechanisms, which we will describe later.

The selector can, e.g., specify the range of days the calendar tool currently displays or a category label in a memo tool. With the help of the selector, only records are loaded and updated which are currently displayed. This approach results in a dilemma: on one hand the set of records which match a specific selector should be computed by the server, not by the handhelds, on the other hand, the selector may be highly application dependent, i.e. hardly to be handled by a generic server.

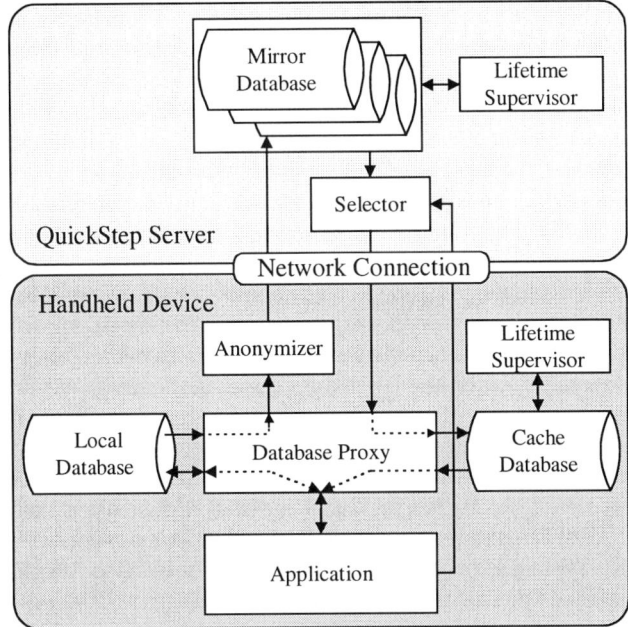

Fig. 3. The QuickStep architecture

To address this problem, we identified two selector types which match most applications: the *number range selector* and the *string match selector*. Both selector types are predefined in the QuickStep server. The number range selector can be used for all kind of records which are ordered by a numeric value. A good example are date entries in the calendar tool presented above. To each entry, a number can be assigned, e.g. the day index. An entry matches a specific number range selector, if the corresponding index is within the selected range. In the calendar application, the current view is defined by a range (*from date...to date*). This range is sent to the server, which in turn only sends records which are within this range. The string match selector is used to match records which have a string value attached. This value has not to be unique inside the database. The string match selector can be used to select all memos of a specific category.

To maintain consistency of the mirror database, a logging mechanism is included into the platform. Every local record in the database has a unique identifier which can be used to identify records in the server's mirror database. When the application removes, adds or changes a record, the corresponding change is logged locally. Whenever the handheld is reconnected to the QuickStep server, the changes are transferred to the server, which updates the corresponding mirror database. Applying changes incrementally ensures that the amount of transferred data is low, even when the handheld database has many entries.

4.6 Private Data

For users, privacy is an important requirement. We decided not to transfer any private data across the network. For this, every record can be marked as private (the default value). Private records reside only in the handheld and will not be transferred under any circumstances.

Non-private records are not transferred until an anonymizing process relieves them from personal fields. Since the record structure is opaque to the underlying system, the anonymizing function has to be provided by the application. In the calendar application, e.g., the anonymizing function blanks out the labels of appointments and transfers the dates only.

As an additional concept, each record has a 'time to live' entry, after which a record is deleted automatically from the QuickStep server and other handheld devices. This approach guarantees a user that her or his data are not available for ever on other computers (even in anonymized form). The time to live entry can be either *session*, *min*, *hour*, *day*, or *forever*. If the value is *session*, the corresponding record will be immediately removed from the server and handheld caches when the corresponding handheld is disconnected. The other values indicate the time, a record will reside after disconnection. The lifetime is controlled by lifetime supervisors (see Figure 3) which exist on the handheld devices and on the QuickStep server.

4.7. Context and Group Awareness

A user who collaborates with the help of the QuickStep platform wants to know about the context she or he is currently working in. For this, a QuickStep application can integrate a 'context' button with opens a frame.

The context frame is the central instance for all context-related information:
- What is the current connection state (connected or disconnected)?
- To which server is the handheld currently connected (server name, organisation)?
- Where is the server located?
- Who can be called in case of problems (e.g. network failures)?
- Which users currently form the session and what are their connection states?

Except for the user list, the context information is fixed and has to be configured once when setting up a QuickStep server. The user list is automatically computed and constantly updated.

The context information is important when a user enters an unknown location. Consider a scenario where a huge building is equipped with a number of QuickStep servers (e.g. one per floor). Each QuickStep server provides information about the current location and thus can be used as a beacon for navigating inside the building.

For collaborating users, the connection state is very important. If a user is disconnected, all changes applied to data cannot be viewed by other users. Thus, information about the connection state should be available on the main window of an application. We designed an integrated button and state indicator (see Figure 1, lower right button). This widget allows to connect and disconnect to a QuickStep server and indicates the current state with the help of a small icon.

States can be:
- Disconnected: the button allows to reconnect.
- Connected: the button allows to disconnect.
- All members of a session are connected: this means that all data which can be viewed are up to date. As in the connection state, the button allows to disconnect.
- Error: the QuickStep platform is in an unexpected state, e.g., because of a corrupted local database. Neither connecting nor disconnecting is allowed.

The button/state indicator as well as the context frame are predefined awareness widgets and can be integrated in an application with the help of the QuickStep library. In addition, an application can retrieve state and context information via the QuickStep API and can react on events (e.g. joining a session or disconnecting from a network), thus helping an application developer to create his or her own awareness widgets.

4.8 Realisation Aspects

When realising QuickStep, we decided to use the programming language Java. The QuickStep platform consists of two parts, the QuickStep server application and the handheld platform. We developed the server application with Sun's Java Development Kit for desktop computers.

For handheld devices, especially for PalmOS, three Java platforms for handhelds are currently available: KVM (http://java.sun.com/products/kvm/), Spotless (http://www.sun.com/research/spotless/) and Waba (http://www.wabasoft.com/). KVM has currently no network APIs and Spotless tends to be unstable. We decided to use Waba. Waba provides all services we need, runs stably, and offers a virtual machine and a runtime library. To compile Waba applications, a common Java compiler from any desktop Java Development Kit can be used. Waba has the great advantage of supporting both, PalmOS devices as well as Windows CE devices.

Although Waba covers a wide area of classes and methods, two kinds of services are still missing. First, Waba does not support threads. As a work-around, Waba offers so-called *timers* which can periodically call a predefined method. Unfortunately a method call is only performed, when no other instruction is being executed. Waba does not support real background operations.

Another missing service is the server socket. Waba only allows to open a socket connection to another server. A handheld device cannot offer a socket service itself. This affects how communication is established between two parties. The handheld device always has to be the initiating part of a communication. As a consequence, it is not possible to connect two handheld devices without having a server in-between.

One further drawback of Waba is that rather than using native widgets, all user interface widgets are re-implemented because of two reasons: there does not exist a common set of widgets which is available on all supported operating system platforms. Thus such a set has to be provided by Waba. Secondly, PalmOS does not allow the dynamic creation of native dialogue widgets, the usual way dialogues are created in Java. Since all widgets are handled by Waba, they cost a considerable amount of valuable object memory. In addition they react slightly differently compared to the native PalmOS widgets.

An important problem of Waba is the memory usage under PalmOS. The memory allocation mechanism of PalmOS restricts the entire object heap to 64k, even if the handheld device has a total of 2MB of RAM. Since Waba makes heavy usage of dynamic memory, it is currently not possible to develop bigger applications with Waba.

4.9 More Examples

In addition to the calendar, tool we developed several applications to verify and improve the QuickStep platform. We now briefly describe two of them.

The brainstorming tool (Figure 5a) allows to add ideas to a collaborative list. An idea is presented by a short description, usually one line of text. All collected ideas are presented in a scrollable list box.

Usually, data of collaborative applications are dynamic. The business card collector (Figure 5b) has a completely different character. A personal business card is typically stored once and never changed. When one enters a public location, e.g., a conference, the application presents a list of all other users who published their business cards. A user can view these cards and collect interesting cards in a persistent area.

a) The brainstorming tool   b) The business card collector

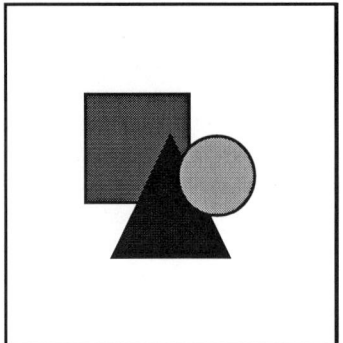 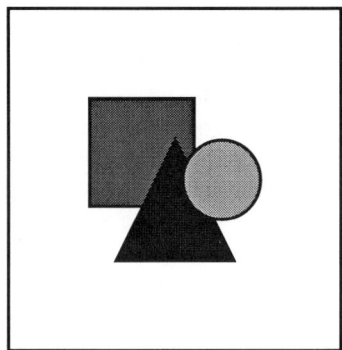

Fig. 4. More QuickStep sample applications

5 Conclusion and Future Work

The QuickStep approach allows to develop mobility and collaboration aware applications and has been especially designed for handheld devices. A generic QuickStep server relieves the handheld devices from heavy tasks and stores data during disconnection. The QuickStep server operates without human intervention and can serve arbitrary QuickStep applications without modification. A server offers contextual information, which can be used by handheld applications.

Data distribution is handled by a caching and mirroring mechanism. Since data are copied across an untrusted network and stored on other handheld devices, mechanisms to ensure privacy are very important. We strongly believe that a platform can only gain acceptance, if users are convinced that their personal data are kept private.

The QuickStep platform is implemented on a Java for handhelds and fully operable on Palm and Windows CE devices. However, more complex application have memory problems, thus we are currently working on a porting for the PalmOS platform in C.

References

1. Bey C., Freeman E., Mulder D., Ostrem J.: Palm OS SDK Reference, 3Com, http://www.palm.com/devzone/index.html, Jan. 2000
2. Boling D.: Programming Windows CE, Microsoft Press, 1998
3. Ellis C. A., Gibbs S. J., Rein G. L.: Groupware - some issues and experiences, Communications of the ACM, Vol. 34, No. 1, Jan. 1991, 39-58
4. Joseph A. D., Tauber J. A., Kaashoek M. F.: Mobile Computing with the Rover Toolkit, IEEE Transactions on Computers, Vol. 46, No. 3, March 1997 337-352
5. Kistler J. J., Satyanarayana M.: Disconnected Operation in the Coda File System, ACM Transaction on Computer Systems, Vol. 10, No. 1, Feb. 1992, 3-25
6. Lotus Development Corporation: Lotus Notes, http://www.lotus.com/home.nsf/welcome/lotusnotes
7. Munson J. P., Dewan P.: Sync: A Java Framework for Mobile Collaborative Applications, special issue on Executable Content in Java, IEEE Computer, 1997, 59-66
8. Myers B. A., Stiel H., Gargiulo R.: Collaboration Using Multiple PDAs Connected to a PC, Proceedings of the ACM 1998 conference on Computer supported cooperative work, 1998, 285-294
9. Noble B., Satyanarayanan M., Narayanan D., Tilton J. E., Flinn J., Walker K.: Agile Application-Aware Adaptation for Mobility, Proceedings of the 16th ACM Symposium on Operating System Principles, Oct. 1997, St. Malo, France
10. Stabell-Kulø T., Dillema F., Fallmyr T.: The Open-End Argument for Private Computing, Proceeding of the First International Symposium on Handheld and Ubiquitous Computing, Karlsruhe, Germany, Sept. 1999, Springer, 124-136
11. Tasker M., Dixon J., Shackman M., Richardson T., Forrest J.: Professional Symbian Programming: Mobile Solutions on the EPOC Platform, Wrox Press, 2000
12. Terry D. B., Theimer M. M., Petersen K., Demers A. J.: Managing Update Conflict in Bayou, a Weakly Connected Replicated Storage System, Proceedings of the fifteenth ACM symposium on Operating systems principles, Copper Mountain, CO USA, Dec. 3-6, 1995, 172-182

Smartcards: How to Put them to Use in a User-Centric System

Tage Stabell-Kulø

Department of Computer Science
University of Tromsø
Tromsø, Norway
tage@cs.uit.no

Abstract. Unlike many other classes of hardware, smartcards do not have the ability to communicate securely with the user. Deprived of means to keep the owner informed, the positive properties of smartcards are difficult to utilize. We explore the area at the border between smartcards and other, more powerful (and thus more useful), machines. On the other side of this border we find the Personal Digital Assistant (PDA).

In our view, to be useful as an extension of the users' private sphere, a machine must at least have enough functionality and resources to create trustworthy digital signatures (to speak for the user, as it were). A less resourceful machine can merely act as a memory prothesis, helping the owner remembering addresses and phone numbers.

Smartcards are designed to be tamper resistant, and as such they seem ideal as a minimal machine. However, trustworthy digital signatures can not be created by smartcards alone, simply because the user does not know what is given to the card for signing.

In order to be trusted—that is, being able to make trustworthy digital signatures—a smartcard must be supported by some infrastructure outside the card proper. We explore what must be included in such an infrastructure, and demonstrate that trustworthy digital signatures can in fact be made using a standard smartcard.

We argue that based on this fact, nontrivial distributed systems can be constructed by utilizing smartcards; a nontrivial system is one where holders of smartcards are "first class citizens". Asserting that a smartcard can act as a trusted machine gives new opportunities for designers of user-centric systems.

Assuming that smartcards are here to stay, finding ways to apply them in constructive manners is prudent.

1 Introduction

In designing modern distributed systems, we face two forces that pull in opposite directions. One is users' desire to include computers into their private sphere. Be it for a simple task such as keeping a diary up-to-date or a more complex one such as keep digital money. The other is users' desire for privacy.

Systems that aim to reach users in their private sphere must be prepared to span more than one administrative domain. A crucial issue in such systems is that it must be possible for them to uniquely identify users. It must be possible for service providers (and others) to determine from whom a request or statement originates. In fact, we dare to say that any system, aiming at being ubiquitous or not, in which users can not make proper identifiable statements is probably trivial to build because they only have to concern themselves with performance issues. In particular, without deterministic identification of statements (requests) charging for services becomes (at best) difficult.

Modern distributed systems are not confined to a predetermined setting. Users have access to networking everywhere; both in friendly environments (for example at home) and possibly unfriendly (an Internet café). In order to be a "first class citizen" also in settings where the infrastructure is controlled by others, the user must be able to make statements without having to trust the infrastructure; a statement is some data, an ASCII string for example, accompanied by a digital signature. It is the signature that sets statements aside from other strings claiming to originate from the user. Public key technology is but one mean to achieve signatures. In any case, a statement can only be made on a trusted machine. This is so because a user can neither verify a signature's (cryptographic) validity, nor whether a signature is on a some data at hand.

It is fairly obvious that when the user is armed with a laptop-type of machine he trusts, he can construct his message and sign it by whatever means he prefers on the laptop. The Trusted Computing Base (TCB) is confined to the laptop itself. The signed statement can then be released to a possible hostile environment for transport to its destination. After signing, the statement can safely be disseminated because it is protected by some cryptographic property. Denial of service is always possible, but any alteration of the statement can be detected.

Not only laptops, but also most contemporary palmtop, such as the Palm Pilot, can be used to sign statements; the performance of a palmtop is not up to that of a laptop, but hardware with cryptographic functionality can easily be added to most such devices. It is worth noting that some cryptographic technologies, RSA in particular, requires substantial computational resources, but that many alternatives exists; systems based on the algebraic properties in elliptic-curves to name but one. A palmtop would be used in the same manner as a laptop: Show the string on the screen, and create the signature. Conceptually, a palmtop is identical to a laptop in this manner. They belong to the same "class" of hardware, because each has both a screen and (some form of) input channel. The smartcard belongs to a different class. The distinguishing aspect is that a smartcard does not have a secure channel to (and from) the user. In other words, there seems to be a conceptually important border dividing the smartcard (and comparable devices) from "real" computers. In the context of security, a border between machines that can securely cerate a digital signature, and those that can not, is an important concept.

For system designers, the mere existence of such a border implies that systems which aims at including smartcards will ultimately be less versatile than those that do not. It is apparent that in one sense, what constitutes the border is the lack of a secure channel. When using a smartcard, all messages to or from the card must pass through some machinery, and the machinery (whatever it might constitute) can alter the message at will. In other words, trusting a smartcard is in itself not enough to create a digital signature. Focusing on the convenience of the smartcard, it is prudent to ask whether it is at all possible to build an infrastructure to compensate for the lack of an communication channel. That is, designing an infrastructure that spans any number of administrative domains but makes no assumptions on the trustworthiness of the terminal the user might be using when asking for a string to be turned into a signed statement by his card. One contribution of this paper is a description of how this can be done. Another, more interesting, is to firmly establish that digital signatures can be made with all kinds of computers, including smartcards. In other words, we claim that the border sketched above does not exist

It is common to issue smartcards to users in order to ensure that users are kept at the fringe of the system; normally, holders of smartcards are at the mercy of the system. MODUS OPERANDI is to request the user to insert his card, surrender his so-called "secret" PIN, and await the verdict delivered by (remote) system components far beyond reach. Seen in this light, the most important ramification of our results is that we can demonstrate how systems can be constructed where holders of smartcards are "first class citizens". It is also possible to construct a system where a user can retain their (digital) identity, as defined by their encryption keys, over a wide range of equipment. As will be shown, it is possible to use smartcards to construct digital signatures without having to surrender a secret PIN to an untrusted terminal.

The rest of the article is structured as follows: In Section 2 the setting is described in more detail, and it is explained why smartcards in themselves makes the user less autonomous. Then an online service is described that, together with a secret number and a one time pad, enables users to create digital signatures on strings. The description is technical in nature to convince the reader about its correctness. Based on our method, we turn in Section 3 to a discussion centered around trust and trust relations. It is shown how a user by means of the solution we have described can take control over his own signatures. Related work is discussed in Section 4. Conclusions are drawn in Section 5.

2 Overview

It is difficult to digitally sign data in a hostile environment, even armed with a smartcard that can create digital signatures by means of some public-key technology [4]. To see why, assume a user U sitting in front of a machine M with the smartcard residing in a smartcard reader connected to M. If U wants to sign some message X, he has no means to verify that M actually gives X to his card; Neither can he prevent M from retaining his PIN, nor that M presents multiple messages to the card to sign. The consequence is that U can not use the card without trusting M just as much as he trusts the integrity of the card itself. But if he trusted M, he could use it to sign rather than involving a smartcard in the first place. When cards are used to create digital signatures, the card is normally used to ensure that the *user* is under control (he must bring his card, and can only use machines chosen by the owner of the system), rather than enabling the user to build a versatile digital personality.

There are many settings where one desires to sign data with a smartcard, where the environment might be hostile. For example a point-of-sale terminal, or during a visit to an "Internet café". Using a computer laboratory at a university is another example. In general, any environment where one does not want to include the terminal in the TCB, for whatever reason [13].

The problem is that there is no authenticated "channel" from the card to the user. The card is unable to "tell" the user what it has been asked to sign, and the user can not verify that the message X has been received for signing; the problem is well known [1,5,14].

In general, data integrity relies on either secret information or authenticated channels [8]. In other words, when using smartcards without any authenticated channels, some sort of secret information is needed. It might be worth noting that we are only interested in creating digital signatures. The user U is unable to encrypt anything with his smartcard without trusting M because all messages to the card must pass through M. That is, secrecy can not be obtained at all in the setting we describe (unless, as before, the user trusts the machine M, in which case the problem of encryption becomes trivial). This is in itself an limiting factor on the systems we can build with smartcards.

The general setting is that the user U has some data, an email perhaps, that he wants to sign, using the secret key stored in his card. He would instruct the software running on M to send the data to the smartcard reader, insert his card, and having the signature returned in order to be attached to the email. The problem is that M might give any data it desires to the card, and the card will sign it. Unless U can verify public-key signatures in his head, he has no means to judge whether M is trustworthy or not.

Only U knows what the card is expected to sign, because only he knows what he intended to have signed; the fact that M also happens to know is of no relevance to us because M is not trusted by the user. The user must thus be involved in the verification of the signature at the "message meaning" level. Or, in other words, no solution to this problem can be envisioned without involving the user in some way, after the signature has been made. In a realistic scenario, we can rule out the possibility of U verifying the signature himself. This implies that a third party must verify the signature. Such a third party should take the form of an online service, in order to better enable the user to timely know about the signature's validity. This, however, raises a new obstacle: How can this online service, called O, communicate with U over a channel that provides integrity? Our contribution is a working method to solve this particular problem; the solution consists of three parts, an on-line service, a small One-Time Pad (OTP) and a shared secret.

An OTP is a perfectly secure method for encryption. Assume the principal A desires to send the message $\{1, 2, 3, 1\}$ to B. If A and B share the encryption

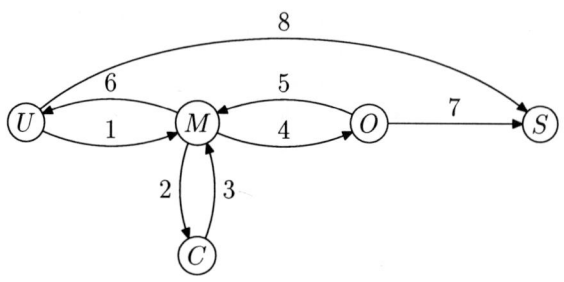

Fig. 1. The protocol run

key 5 (and the algorithm is to add with the secret key), the encrypted message becomes $\{6,7,8,6\}$. Without knowing the number 5 it is impossible to derive the original message; in this example there are few possibilities, but the argument is nevertheless valid. The problem is that it is evident that the first and last component are equal. If, however, A and B share a number of "pads" with numbers (all of them secret), where the first reads $\{4,5,1,7\}$, for example, the first encrypted message becomes $\{10,6,9,8\}$; it is no longer possible to know anything about the contents of the original message. Furthermore, if a pad is only used once (hence the name One-Time Pad), perfectly secure encryption has been achieved. One-Time Pad is an old invention, details can be found in [7,8].

We are now ready to describe how data can be digitally signed by means of a smartcard in a hostile environment (details are given in Section 2.1). We use the notation from the BAN logic [2]; the messages are shown in Figure 1.

- The machine M is not trusted. Thus, M is not the logical sender or recipient of any message (even though the actual hardware will be used to send messages). From a logical point of view, M is part of the communication infrastructure. In this light, the only principals of interest are the user U, his smartcard C and the on-line service O (to be described below).
- The user has some data X, which typically is a string of characters (i.e., a text). U inserts his card (into the smartcard reader attached to M) and instructs M to transfer the data to the card.

$$\text{Message 1: } U \to M : X$$
$$\text{Message 2: } M \to C : X$$

- The card accepts the message and signs X, creating $\{X\}_{K_C^{-1}}$. Notice that the card has no means to verify that X actually originates from U. Two questions must be answered:
  1. Is the signature valid?
  2. Has the correct data been signed?

The online service can be used to verify the signature's validity; the signed data is sent to O.

$$\text{Message 3: } C \to M : \{X\}_{K_C^{-1}}$$
$$\text{Message 4: } M \to O : \{X\}_{K_C^{-1}}$$

- The crux of our solution is that O can send back to U a transformation f of the data it has verified. Assume that U and O share a *small* secret OTP and a secret number (see the Appendix for an example). After verifying the signature on X, O will create two new message as follows.
  Using the OTP, a new message $Z = f(X)$ is constructed, and sent to U.

$$\text{Message 5: } O \to M : Z$$
$$\text{Message 6: } M \to U : Z$$

Z is the message X transformed for integrity under the OTP. We will discuss this transformation below.

Furthermore, if the signature is valid, O constructs a certificate asserting this fact. The certificate is sent to a public server of some sort. We call this server S, its existence is only for convenience and might very well be O itself. A random number Y is associated with each OTP (again, please consult the Appendix). Y is known only to U, but $H(Y)$ is known also by O. If O finds that the signature is valid, O will sign a certificate stating this fact; the certificate will include $H(Y)$. By releasing Y, U proves that he accepts the signature.

$$\text{Message 7: } O \to S : \{C, X, H(X, H(Y))\}_{K_O^{-1}}$$

- When Z is received by U, he can without much effort (and without using M to anything but display Z) verify that $Z = f(X)$. Since Z is a transformation of X, U can conclude that the content was what he intended to sign, and that his trusted server O has verified the signature. U now releases Y by sending it to S.

$$\text{Message 8: } U \to S : Y$$

To sum up, the online service verifies the signature made by the smartcard, and the user acknowledges the actual text by releasing Y.

Messages 5 and 6 contain the string of digits O constructed based on its copy of the OTP. Since the OTP is secret, the string is X combined with a secret. In BAN such a construction is denoted as $\langle X \rangle_{OTP}$.

2.1 The One-Time Pad

We assume that U does not have any significant computational resources at hand (the machine M can not be trusted). Since it is unreasonable to assume that any user can verify digital signatures without the help of a computer, we must thus construct a secure channel from O to U, on which a message can be sent. That is, U needs to receive from O some information that convinces him that the correct text was signed by the smartcard. This information must be a function of the message X in order for U to know that the correct text has been signed. In addition, U must be convinced that the message he receives comes from O. Taken together, the channel we are about to construct must provide authentication (since authentication implies integrity [8]). Clear-text attacks are indeed a threat since M knows X.

If, on the other hand, X was unknown to M then U and O could share a list L of random numbers, each number L_i of L being as long as X. O would verify the signature on X, calculate $Z = X + L_i$ and send the result to U. U would be able to calculate $Z - L_i$ and verify that the card had signed X. This cipher would be perfectly secure [9].

In our system, each OTP contains two small tables. The first contains random numbers, as one would use to create a one-time pad. However, in our case we are not striving for secrecy (X is known to M anyway) but rather for integrity. We achieve this goal incorporating an additional table. It is a permutation of the characters; we denote this a *substitution table*.

We now describe the OTP used by U and O. In the current implementation, the alphabet available to U are all the upper-case characters, space (denoted as '␣'), dot ('.'), the digits and the two symbols $ and @; 40 characters in all. These characters are matched with a table of random numbers, assigning a random number to each character. Appendix 1 shows two examples of tables; each has six rows:

Letter: The alphabet available to users
Subst: The substitution table; each character from the alphabet is replaced by the corresponding number from the substitution table.
X: In this row the user writes his message
OTP: The number representing each character is added (modulo 40) to the corresponding element in the One Time Pad.
Z: The result.
Y: A secret number, see below.

When U receives Z from O, he would want to verify the result. In order to do so, he proceeds as follows.

1. Count the number of characters in the message, and prepend this number (as a string) to the message.
2. Write the string in the table (in the row marked X) above the random numbers.
3. For each character, add the ordinality of the character (taken from the substitution table) with the random number. The addition must be done modulo 40 (the number of characters).

An example of a table which is filled in is shown in the Appendix. The string "GIVE TAGE@ACM.ORG $500." is encrypted for authentication.

If U sees that Z indeed is the correct transformation of X, he will release Y. The certificate generated by O contains $H(Y)$, but Y is only known to U. In other words, by releasing Y, U makes it known that he supports the certificate issued by O.

A more detailed discussion on the protocol, together with an analysis of the different certificates of delegation that is required in order for outsiders to convince themselves about the validity of the signature, can be found in [11].

3 Trust

Creating a digital signature is all about trust. As described in Section 2, signing becomes a problem when the communication channels leading to and from the smartcard is controlled by some other entity. If we discard solutions where the smartcard and infrastructure control the user (and not the other way around), we notice that creating a "stand alone" solution requires a PDA with a display on which the message to be signed can be shown to the user for verification. A smartcard with a display and a single "OK" button would suffice.

In a distributed setting, the online server O is a *trusted third party* in that the user U trusts it to act according to the protocol (i.e., not to certify that a signature is good if it is not). On the other hand, O is not able to deceive U without colluding with the machine M. When O and M collude, M can feed a false message to the card and let O send an erroneous message back to the user. The important issue is that acting in isolation, O can not deceive U. In the same manner as O can not deceive U alone, neither can S, nor C. We can conclude that no principal is in a situation to make U release Y, without colluding with some other principal.

The online server O is central to the security of the system. If it colludes with M, signatures can be created without U's consent. However, it is to be expected that O is under the control of the user. That is, the user can have O placed in a trusted environment (at home, for example) since there is no reason why the online server need to be part of an infrastructure controlled by others. That is, U need not trust an infrastructure controlled by others, such as X.590 [3].

We have not discussed the security of the smartcard itself, but simply asserted that it is a tamper proof device. Concern might be raised against our solution in that the combination of the card and a set of one-time pads represents a threat; losing them together would make the finder able to sign messages. However, access to the card might be secured with a PIN as is done with contemporary cards. This way, theft would not represent a threat.

4 Related Work

In general, we know of no other system where smartcards are used to place the user in control (as opposed to control the user). Storing encryption keys is a prime application for smartcards, but, as we have argued, it places users at the fringe of the system. As an example, smartcards can be integrated into Kerberos [6].

Our solution is basically a Message Authentication Code (MAC). MACs are well covered in the literature, see for example [10,8,12]. However, most MACs are computationally intensive; they are surjective, and require some computation to be secure (mapping one language onto a smaller one while being a one-way function).

The use of unconditionally secure MACs are described in [12, Chapter 10] with the use of orthogonal arrays (OAs). These OAs seems, however, to be infeasible to work with for human beings compared to substitution tables and OTPs that only require the use of elementary arithmetics. Authentication by means of a secret one-time pad is an old invention [7].

5 Conclusion

Smartcards are commonly used to ensure that users are firmly placed at the fringe of the system. Lacking communication channels to the user, the system is in full control of the situation. The rôle assigned to users is one where he presents his PIN whenever requested to do so. In our view, such a rôle is rather old fashioned. The challenge is to make it possible to enjoy the benefits of tamper resistant hardware with a standardized form factor, while building user-centric systems.

In our view, the crux of controlling one's own private computing environment, is the ability to create digital signatures in a secure manner. We have shown that users can achieve secure authentication of messages signed with a smartcard even in hostile environments, using a partial trusted verification server together with a substitution table and a one-time pad. The applicability of the proposed solution lies in that short messages with small character sets.

Admittedly, the solution is cumbersome, and of limited use as it is. However, it proves that, from a security point of view, there is no border separating smartcards from more powerful machines. Or, in other words, user-centric systems can be built also if one wants to place secrets on smartcards.

Now that a method for creating digital signatures has been shown to exist, more work is needed to further explore how smartcards can be included in modern, distributed systems.

Acknowledgments. Faculty, students and staff affiliated with the PASTA laboratory in Tromsø have, by their relentless nagging, made this article both necessary and possible. Per Harald Myrvang contributed both to the techniques (see [11] for details), and to their presentation.

One of the anonymous referees provided us with substantial feedback; we hope you notice that we have applied almost all your suggestions.

References

1. M. Abadi, M. Burrows, C. Kaufman, and B. Lampson. Authentication and delegation with smart-cards. *Science of Computer Programming*, 21(2):93–113, October 1993.

2. M. Burrows, M. Abadi, and R. Needham. A Logic of Authentication. *ACM Transactions on Computer Systems*, 8(1):18–36, February 1990.
3. CCITT. Information Technology — Open Systems Interconnection — The Directory: Authentication Framework. CCITT Recommodation X.509, ISO/IEC 9594-8, December 1991.
4. H.enry Dreifus and T.homas Monk. *Smart Cards - A Guide to Building and Managing Smart Card Applications.* IEEE Computer Press, 1997. ISBN 0-471-15748-1.
5. H. Gobioff, S. Smith, J. D. Tygar, and B. Yee. Smart Cards in Hostile Environments. In *Proceedings of the Second USENIX Workshop on Electronic Commerce*, Oakland, CA, November 1996.
6. P. Honeyman and N. Itoi. Smartcard integration with Kerberos V5. In *Proceedings of the Usenix workshop on smartcard technolog*, Chicago, May 1999.
7. D. Kahn. *The Codebreakers: The story of secret writing.* Macmillan Publishing Company, New York, USA, 1967.
8. A. J. Menezes, P. C. van Oorschot, and S. A. Vanstone. *Handbook of applied cryptography.* The CRC Press series on discrete mathematics and its applications. CRC Press, 2000 Corporate Blvs., N.W., Boca Raton, Florida 33431, USA, 1997. ISBN 0-8493-8523-7.
9. C. E. Shannon. Communication theory of secrecy systems. *Bell System Technical Journal*, 28:656–715, October 1949.
10. G. J. Simmons, editor. *Contemporary Cryptology: The Science of Information Integrity.* IEEE Press, 1992. ISBN 0-87942-277-7.
11. T. Stabell-Kul , R. Arild, and P. H. Myrvang. Providing authentication to messages signed with a smart card in hostile environment. In *Proceedings of the Usenix workshop on smartcard technology*, pages 93–99, Chicago, May 1999.
12. D. R. Stinson. *Cryptography: Theory and Practice.* CRC Press, Inc., 1995. ISBN 0-8493-8521-0.
13. US Department of Defence. *Trusted Computer System Evaluation Criteria*, 1985. DOD 5200.28-STD.
14. B. Yee and D. Tygar. Secure Coprocessors in Electronic Commerce Applications. In *Proceedings of The First USENIX Workshop on Electronic Commerce*, New York, New York, July 1995.

Appendix

Example OTP and Substitution Table

Letter	0	1	2	3	4	5	6	7	8	9	A	B	C	D	E	F	G	H	I	J	K	L	M	N	O	P	Q	R	S	T	U	V	W	X	Y	Z	␣	.	$	@
Subst	05	27	13	32	03	21	16	22	00	08	26	06	04	07	18	39	30	15	19	09	37	23	24	38	17	25	14	20	10	02	31	33	34	35	12	01	36	28	11	29
X																																								
OTP	31	25	08	32	02	16	38	18	19	13	17	01	37	38	20	24	00	33	10	01	24	34	37	11	01	05	08	14	15	29	03	03	18	39	30	05	10	22	24	14
Y																																								
Z	04	17	38	11	35	34	34	20	05	03	35	30	23	02	04	12	17	13	00	37	35	15	02	16	29															

X = 0x8bde94b630f1504b

Y = 0x8bde94b630f1504b

Using Dynamic Mediation to Integrate COTS Entities in a Ubiquitous Computing Environment

Emre Kıcıman and Armando Fox

Stanford University
{emrek,fox}@cs.stanford.edu

Abstract. The original vision of ubiquitous computing [14] is about enabling people to more easily accomplish tasks through the seamless interworking of the physical environment and a computing infrastructure. A major challenge to the practical realization of this vision involves the integration of commercial-off-the-shelf (COTS) hardware and software components: consider the awkwardness of such a mundane task as exporting a textual memo written on a Palm Pilot to a Microsoft Word document. It is not enough to overcome the protocol and data format mismatches that currently impede the interoperation of these entities: for the user experience to be truly seamless, we must provide a framework for the *dynamic* connection of such endpoints on demand, to support the ad-hoc interactions that are an integral part of ubiquitous computing. To this end, we offer a dynamic mediation framework called Paths. A Path consists of dynamically instantiated, automatically composable operators that bridge datatype and protocol mismatches between components wishing to communicate. Because operator composability is inferred from the type system, adding support for a new type of endpoint requires only incremental work; because the control and data flow for Paths are largely decoupled from the communicating endpoints, it is easy to connect COTS or legacy components. We describe the Paths architecture, our prototype implementation, and our experience and lessons based on several production applications built with the framework, and outline some continuing work on Paths in the context of the Stanford Interactive Workspaces project.
Keywords: Ubiquitous Computing, Automatic Mediation, Service Composition, Ad-hoc Applications, Software Infrastructure

1 Introduction

Ubiquitous computing is about enabling people to more easily accomplish tasks through the seamless interworking of the physical environment and a computing infrastructure [14]. This "seamless interworking" implies some level of cooperation among the various devices and software in the environment.

Today, however, most of these devices and software cannot cooperate with each other, simply because they cannot communicate with each other. This stems from a variety of technical causes, but the fundamental cause is that these devices and software simply were *not designed to communicate* with each other. The devices and software were built at different times, for different purposes, and have different capabilities. These problems are especially pronounced when trying to integrate commercial-off-the-shelf (COTS) components and legacy systems into a ubiquitous computing system.

We have two goals: first, to provide a system for connecting heterogeneous, COTS and legacy devices and software, and second, to allow new devices and software to be integrated into the system easily. Our approach is to step away from the tightly-coupled model of direct communication and instead enable loosely-coupled communication through a third party. In this model, two endpoints communicate through a mediating infrastructure rather than communicating with each other directly. This infrastructure *automatically* discovers and places relevant mediators between the two endpoints to compensate for communication mismatches. A loosely-coupled model of communication enables communication between devices and software that were not originally designed to communicate with each other.

1.1 For Example ...

An *interactive workspace* is an emerging type of ubiquitous-computing environment. Such a space typically contains a number of highly heterogenous, multimodal I/O devices: large screen displays, smart whiteboards, projectors, speakers, microphones, wireless pointing devices, etc. In addition, participants in a meeting or other collaborative activity in such a space bring with them a variety of personal devices: PDA's, laptops, cellphones, active badges, etc.

Consider a meeting held in an interactive workspace. As the meeting begins, the meeting organizer displays an agenda (stored on his own laptop) on one of the large screens. During this meeting, the attendees discuss various important points and make decisions, sharing information to clarify and elucidate their respective points of view.

A few attendees have prepared notes and information to share. This information might be in the form of text, graphics or visualizations, spreadsheet data, etc. They pass out electronic copies to the other attendees, who view the information with whatever devices and software they have at hand. Other attendees share unprepared, impromptu data. During discussions, they find or are reminded of relevant documents or elucidating information. Some attendees create documents during the meeting itself. They author these documents using whatever device/software at hand is most appropriate; perhaps a smart whiteboard, perhaps a plain piece of paper (using a scanner to import it into the digital environment).

Looking at this scenario, we see it requires two properties of ubiquitous computing environments:

- Support for Heterogeneous Entities: A ubiquitous computing environment has to support a wide variety of devices, from smart whiteboards to active

badges. The environment also has to support not just "permanent" devices, but PDAs and other personal equipment that people bring with them. Additionally, when these entities are legacy or COTS products, or simply not under the environment's administrative control, they cannot be adapted to the environment. The environment must adapt itself to the entity.
 – Ad-Hoc Communication Between Entities: None of the devices in this scenario were useful individually. Their purpose was to create and disseminate information. They had to communicate with each other to be useful. Though this scenario explicitly required communication between the entities in the system, the principle holds true in ubiquitous computing systems in general: "No computer is an island" [5].

The difficulty with supporting ad-hoc, any-to-any communication in this environment is the communication mismatches between the heterogeneous entities. Any two entities are likely to speak different communication protocols, understand different data formats, and have different user interaction models. Compensating for all of these differences using existing techniques is not feasible.

1.2 Existing Approaches for Communication

Ockerbloom has contributed a very useful analysis of the problem of converting data among various formats [6]. Some of the approaches being used today to mitigate this problem are:

 – Standards: one common approach to solving the problem of incompatibility is to create standard protocols, data formats and behaviors for interacting entities. Though standards are useful, we argue that it is infeasible in ubiquitous computing, where potentially all devices and software must be able to cooperate/interoperate. Additionally, standards alone cannot address the problem of nonstandard legacy systems.
 – Content Negotiation: a more flexible approach is to add a content-negotiation phase to the communications protocol. However, content negotiation presupposes widely-adopted standards for both data formats and negotiation protocols, and also places a burden on devices to understand multiple sorts of data (not always the case with small devices).
 – Polyglot Entities: today, many entities are built understanding multiple datatypes and protocols. These entities can communicate with a larger number of other devices and software, but are still fundamentally limited in their ability to communicate with unknown systems.
 – Least Common Denominator Data Formats: using a least-common-denominator datatype and protocol, such as ASCII or HTML over HTTP, often causes a loss of important information that can not be represented in this simple form.

None of these existing solutions satisfactorily addresses the problem of legacy devices and software, or of incompatible COTS products. Nor do they allow arbitrary ad-hoc communication between two devices: both devices must have been built a priori speaking the same protocols.

2 Paths: A Mediation Infrastructure

To address these problems, we have designed and implemented a prototype mediation infrastructure as a part of *Paths*, a general framework for composing mediators distributed across a network of machines. Using this prototype, we have implemented several applications to support improved integration of devices and software, including legacy and COTS entities, in a ubiquitous computing environment.

The mediation infrastructure consists of a set of mediators that transform data, a set of representatives that speak the native protocols of endpoints, and a coordinator that discovers and initializes paths of mediators to connect endpoints. Mediators can be added to the infrastructure dynamically, simply by announcing their existence to the coordinator. Representatives can be added to the infrastructure in a similar fashion.

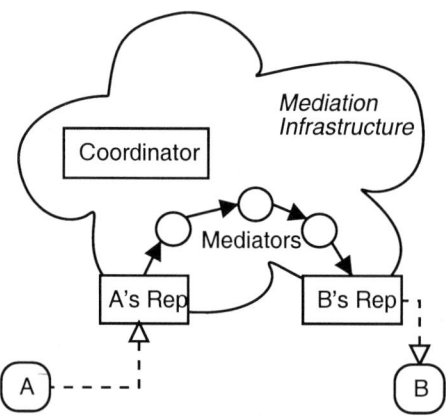

Fig. 1. The Mediation Infrastructure

Communication through a mediating infrastructure avoids the problems associated with existing approaches detailed in Sect. 1.2. There are two prerequisites for entities to communicate through this infrastructure:

- There must exist representatives in the infrastructure capable of communicating directly with each of the endpoints. This representative speaks an endpoint's native communications protocol, and forwards data between the endpoint and any mediators.
- There must exist some series of mediators in the infrastructure, which together can transform data from its source format to the format required by the destination. These mediators bridge the data format mismatches between two entities.

Both of these prerequisites are requirements placed on the infrastructure and not on the communication endpoints. This means that after adding the relevant representatives and mediators to the infrastructure, it is possible for existing devices and software to communicate with each other. This system requires no modification of the endpoints, and enables a third party to "wrap" them into a ubiquitous computing environment.

In addition, the mediation infrastructure also makes it possible to integrate new devices into the environment with only incremental work. Instead of needing a bridge between every existing device and the new device, we only need a bridge between some data format already understood in the mediation infrastructure and the new device. Once we have done this, existing mediators will be able to handle converting this data to formats understood by existing devices.

2.1 Mediators

Mediators are infrastructure services that transform data from one datatype to another. They generally have a single input and a single output. Datatype descriptions are associated with both their input and output. The fundamental semantics of their functionality are completely described by the strongly-typed interfaces of their inputs and outputs. These mediators may be full-fledged autonomous services, or small pieces of mobile code instantiated on demand.

We can connect two mediators together, running them in sequence, if the datatype of one mediator's output matches the datatype of the second mediator's input. By composing mediators one after the other (into a path) we can create more complex transformations. For example, we can chain a mediator which transforms text into a GIF file with a mediator which transforms a GIF file into a JPEG file. These mediator compositions are responsible for bridging the data format mismatches between entities.

2.2 Representatives

Representatives are gateway services between the mediation infrastructure and endpoints. They speak an endpoint's native protocol and data format, and forward that communication into the mediation infrastructure. There is a single representative for each kind of endpoint. As a special case, it is possible for a device to be its own representative in the mediation infrastructure. In our architecture, representatives are responsible for bridging protocol mismatches.

Representatives can either initiate communications with an endpoint, accept communication requests from endpoints, or both. When communicating with its representative, an endpoint does not need to have knowledge of the mediation infrastructure, or of the identity of the other end of the communication. For example, a "dumb" device such as a microphone can send an audio stream to a text editor without knowing what happens to the stream after it leaves the microphone. This is the property that enables us to fully integrate legacy devices and COTS products into a ubiquitous computing environment.

2.3 Setting Up Communication and Mediation

There are two phases to setting up a Path: determining which two endpoints to connect and determining a sequence of available mediators that bridges the mismatches between the endpoints.

Choosing the Endpoints. One general issue of communications in a ubiquitous computing environment is "who talks to whom?" That is, which endpoints should be connected together? Our mediating infrastructure does not make this decision itself, nor does it dictate which entity makes this decision. Therefore, we have adopted a flexible control model: a separate controller entity decides which endpoints in the environment should communicate with each other, and notifies the appropriate representatives and the coordinator to establish the communication (as a special case, the controller may be the end-points or their representatives). This decision is made in some out-of-band manner, such as in response to a request by a person, or some set of conditions in the environment. For example, the communications between various applications and displays in an interactive workspace could be controlled using a separate user interface, rather than through the applications or displays themselves.

Automatic Composition of Mediators. Usually no single mediator provides the exact transformation required to connect two endpoints. In this situation, we must compose multiple mediators in sequence to provide the transformation. In the general case, a human must decide how to compose this mediation. However, when the requirements the endpoints have on their inputs and outputs are completely described in terms of their datatypes, we can automate the composition process. By simply finding a path of mediators that transform from data of the type produced by the source to that required by the destination, we will have bridged the datatype mismatch between the endpoints.

The process of finding a path of mediators can be conceptualized as a graph search. The vertices of the graph are the datatypes. Mediators are the edges connecting the datatypes they transform between. Automatic composition of mediators is thus reduced to finding a least-cost path between two vertices in a graph.[1].

The effectiveness of automatic composition depends in turn on how effective the type system is at describing the assumptions endpoints make on the data they receive. We discuss some of the work we have done to extend traditional type systems to better support automatic composition in Sect. 5.2.

3 Paths Prototype

We have implemented this mediation infrastructure as part of Paths, a general composition framework for autonomous services in a network of machines.

---

[1] Unfortunately, the implementation of automatic composition is more complicated, due to the existence of parametric types and polymorphic operators.

A Path is a pipe/filter stream through a graph of operators and connectors. Operators perform computations on data. Connectors transport data between machines. Operators and connectors interface with one another via queues. Data packets are packaged in the form of Application Data Units (ADUs). An ADU is the smallest unit of data independently processable by an operator [1].

Advantages of using stream-based computing, instead of an RPC interface, include the ability to support unbounded data, such as real-time audio and video, and the potential to provide progressive and incremental computation on large datasets [13]. For example, lengthy speech recognition processes can begin executing before the audio stream has finished.

We use XML-based description languages to describe datatypes, operators, connectors, and paths. The Paths prototype is written in Java, but the entities connected by Paths need not be in Java—the only requirement is that it must be possible to write a Java-based representative that can communicate with the entity. In Sect. 4 we describe several specific representatives we have built to connect legacy applications to our interactive workspace.

3.1 Operators and Connectors

An operator consists of a piece of code that performs some transformation and an XML description of its input and output types. An operator may have zero or more inputs and outputs (for example, a data source has zero inputs but one or more outputs). These inputs and outputs are strongly typed and govern how the operator can be composed with other operators. The operator's XML description also includes information on where to get the code (e.g., a URL) and how to run it.

Operators play a number of roles:

- Mediators perform datatype transformations, such as GIF to JPEG or XML to HTML conversions. These operators are the mediators in our mediation infrastructure.
- Semantic processors perform some operation on data that does not change the type of the data, e.g., mathematical computation, sorting or filtering. The dividing line between mediators and semantic processors depends on the descriptiveness of the type system. Semantic operators provide higher-level functionality not represented within our mediation infrastructure.
- Aggregators and Disseminators perform fan-in and fan-out functions within a path. Since our mediation infrastructure currently supports only pairwise communication, it does not use aggregators and disseminators. In the future, they will be used to provide support for treating multiple endpoints as a single, virtual endpoint (e.g., combining two displays to create a larger viewing area).
- Data sources and data sinks are operators which have only a single output or input. From the viewpoint of a path, these operators are generating and consuming data, respectively. In the mediation infrastructure, these data sources and data sinks are the representatives of the true endpoints of the communication, the devices and software.

Connectors, unlike operators, are type-neutral pieces of code described by their transport characteristics. Some of the characteristics that might describe a connector include its reliability, latency, in-order delivery, QoS, and security levels. By default, we currently use a reliable ordered bytestream connector, implemented using TCP. In the future, we plan to allow the controller entity in our mediation infrastructure to decide what sorts of connectors to use based on the purpose of the communications channel; for example, a path manipulating real-time streaming data might prefer an unreliable ordered connector, to avoid retransmissions that violate real-time constraints.

3.2 Path Creation

Path creation is the process of turning a logical path description into an instantiation of a path. The first phase of path creation handles assigning operators onto physical hosts and adding any necessary connectors. The second phase of path creation dispatches the path description to appropriate hosts. Finally, the last phase of path creation instantiates the operators and connectors. After this, the path is ready to accept data.

The process of creating a path is itself implemented as a path, with each of the phases of path creation being encapsulated within an operator. The advantage of implementing the path creation as a path is the flexibility we have to add new functionality to the path creation process.

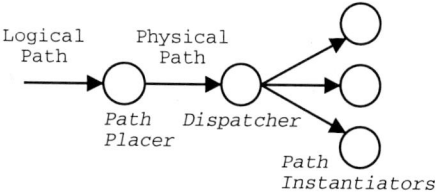

Fig. 2. The Path Creation Path

The first extension we have added to the path creation process is Automatic Path Creation (APC), by prepending an extra operator to the beginning of the path creation path. APC is a generic term for taking a high-level query and generating a path from it. The sort of APC that we have implemented is a Partial-Path APC. A partial path is a path description containing mismatches between adjacent operators. Partial-Path APC takes this description and generates a logical path by mediating between the mismatched operators. This logical path is then turned into an instantiation of a path via the original path creation process.

Our automatic mediation problem in the mediation infrastructure is a special case of Partial-Path APC. The generation of the partial path query is the rendezvous problem discussed in Sect. 2.3. Once we have determined which representatives to connect, we generate a partial path query consisting of two operators connected together. These operators model the source and destination representatives, with the appropriate datatype specifications on their inputs and outputs. Applying APC to this partial path query discovers a mediation path between the two representatives.

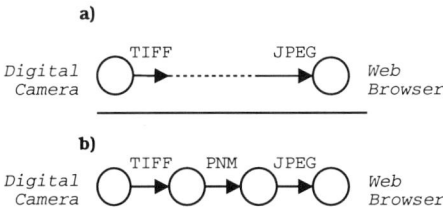

Fig. 3. a) a partial-path query between a digital camera and a web browser; b) the result of the query, a full path between the digital camera and a web browser.

4 Applications

We have developed a number of services using the Paths prototype and Automatic Mediation. Here, we present three applications with particular relevance to ubiquitous computing, and the lessons we learned while developing them.

4.1 Room Control Service

As an initial exploration of Automatic Mediation, we implemented an any-to-any messaging service that enabled users to send and receive messages from potentially any networked device. On top of this system, we implemented a multimodal Room Control service for audio/visual and other resources in several classrooms and conference rooms in Soda Hall, UC Berkeley's Computer Science building. The end devices we connected to this system include a desktop computer GUI, microphone and speakers, a cell phone, and a Palm Pilot.

Users can use graphical, text, or speech based user interfaces to send messages to one another and to programmatic entities (such as the Room Control). When users send a message, it is routed through an automatically generated path of mediators to transform the data from its original data format to the format required by the receiver. These mediators include straightforward data format conversion mediators (GSM audio to PCM audio) as well as more complicated mediators such as speech-to-text and a rule-based text command interpreter. The latter two are interesting because they may inject context-based semantics into the transformation procedure. In Sect. 5.1 we discuss a classification of

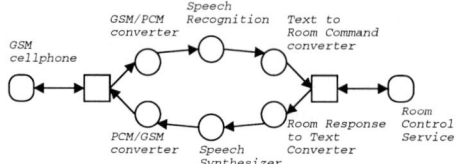

Fig. 4. Communication between a cellphone and the Room Control Service.

mediators that has emerged from our experience using Paths to build several applications.

This system was implemented as part of the ICEBERG and Ninja projects at U.C. Berkeley [12,4]. It leveraged existing software, such as the speech recognizer and IP telephony infrastructure, and was completed in only a few person-months of work. Extending the system has been equally easy. For example, adding support for sending messages from the Palm Pilot required only two hours of work.

In the process of building this system, we made significant advances in our understanding of paths and our requirements of them. We found that support for parametric types and polymorphic operators (described in Sect. 5.2) greatly increases operator reusability and flexibility.

4.2 Dada (Data–Application and Device–Application Decoupling)

In the Dada project, we explored the use of the Paths framework for flexible data representation, manipulation and display in interactive workspaces. The goal of Dada was to decouple data/application and device/application dependencies, and give the user the ability to display and manipulate data in an ad-hoc fashion. In particular, Dada allows a user to select what data to view, what semantic processors to apply to this data, and on which device to display the results. Once the user makes these choices, Dada initializes a Path from the appropriate data source, through the chosen semantic processors, and to the display device, using automatic mediation to resolve mismatches between the chosen services. As the data processing completes, the user sees the results on the chosen display, and, if applicable, can manipulate and interact with these results.

We chose to work within the domain of architectural design and construction planning because this domain requires multiple integrated views of and interactions with project data from a variety of sources. The Stanford Interactive Workspaces Project provided the environment and infrastructure for the implementation of Dada [10]. The data sources included 3D models of buildings, time schedules and cost estimates for construction of these buildings, encoded in various XML-compliant markup languages and stored in databases. These data were interlinked, with parts of buildings, scheduled work tasks, and cost items being associated with each other. The device types we supported were large wall-mounted displays and a table display, all capable of showing 2D and 3D data. The table display required its contents to be rotatable so that data may be read from any side of the table.

Some of the more interesting semantic processors we wrote for Dada implemented application-level functionality within the Path itself. These semantic processors manipulated the data flowing through them in response to user actions. These user actions were propagated to the semantic processors using control messages flowing along the reverse path. To ensure decoupling of semantic processors and the devices displaying actions to the user, the semantic processor packages the control message associated with a user action. In this way, the control message is acting as a callback function. Additionally, downstream operators can transform and even replace these user actions as they are sent to the device, then "undo" this transformation as the control messages flow back up the path.

One example of such a semantic processor we wrote was a data-agnostic operator for Cut&Paste functionality. These operators associate Cut&Paste actions with data objects as they flow through them. Upstream in the path, a mediator renders these associated actions into a device-specific UI description language. Thus, users see live data that they can manipulate and move between displays.

Another interesting mediator converted data for display on the table. It transformed 3D data into rotatable data by wrapping it in a simple user interface for controlling rotation. When the user triggered a rotation action, this mediator applied the appropriate rotation.

Because these semantic processors are both data-agnostic and application-agnostic, it was easy to integrate them into the transformational path. From building the Dada prototype, we gained valuable experience in using Paths and mediators to render user interfaces and dynamic data. Specifically, we gained insights into the requirements dynamic data and user actions had on control messages.

4.3 Global Clipboard

The Global Clipboard is a multi-machine, cross-platform clipboard with history. Its purpose is to support transfer of data between heterogeneous, *legacy* applications and devices within an interactive workspace by automatically transforming data among appropriate formats. Target platforms include MS Windows applications and Palm Pilot devices, among others. Target application domains for mediators include image and text document transformations. The prototype global clipboard is currently under development.

Users copy data into the global clipboard just as they would copy data into the normal system clipboard (e.g., by pressing Control-C). A daemon running on each participating machine intercepts the copy operation and forwards a copy of the data to our global clipboard system. When a user pastes data into an application, our daemon again intercepts the request, adds context information about the requesting application and the datatypes that application can accept, and forwards it to the global clipboard. The global clipboard fulfills the paste request by transforming the data currently in the clipboard into one of the formats understood by the application.

By interposing our mediation layer in the clipboard, we are extending an already-familiar metaphor by enabling users to transfer data between applications that otherwise could not understand each other's data formats at all; for example, for cutting and pasting between Microsoft Word and a Palm Pilot memo directly on the Palm Pilot device.

5 Discussion

In Sect. 4, we presented three applications that use the Paths mediation infrastructure. Here we discuss some of the lessons we learned about our mediation infrastructure while implementing those prototypes.

5.1 Classification of Mediators

Through our experience writing and using mediators in applications, we have discovered a classification of mediators based on the effect they have on the semantic richness of the data they transform.

 - Negative-Delta Mediators perform lossy transformations which lose data, structure, and/or semantic information. Examples of this sort of transformation include converting an image from a lossless to a lossy encoding; and transforming XML into HTML, losing the semantic meaning of the original data. They are similar to prior work at lossy encodings to adapt Internet content to small devices [2].
 - Zero-Delta Mediators perform non-lossy transformations between equivalent formats. This includes converting an image between two lossless encodings, and converting from a less expressive encoding to a more expressive one (e.g., converting ASCII text to Rich Text Format).
 - Positive-Delta Mediators perform a type transformation where some semantic knowledge (context information, etc.) is required to perform the transformation. These mediators are effectively injecting semantic information from domain- or context-specific knowledge into the data as they transform it. For example, Dey and Abowd's CyberDesk [7] uses positive-delta mediation to attach semantic properties such as "this is an email address" to strings that otherwise have no semantics of their own.

This classification of mediators is useful in approximating the degree of information loss that occurs during a transformation. Each negative-delta mediator causes some information to be lost. Positive-delta mediators can re-inject information. However, there is no guarantee that they will re-inject the *same* information that was lost by a negative-delta mediator. Therefore, to guarantee that the existing semantic information is perfectly preserved through a transformation path, all mediators in the path must be zero-delta or positive-delta mediators. In general, the acceptability of negative-delta mediators in a transformation depends on how the transformed data is to be used (e.g., people viewing data can often tolerate more semantic loss than a computer program can).

5.2 Extending the Type System

As we noted in Sect. 2.3, the descriptiveness of the type system in our mediation infrastructure has a great effect on the usability of automatic composition of mediators. In order to better describe the data in our systems, we have built a simple, extended type system. Here are the three extensions we made to better describe our data:

- Attributes are ¡key,value¿ pairs representing some specific metainformation. For example, our speech recognizer requires that its audio input is not only in PCM sound format, but that is also sampled at 8000Hz. Therefore, the type description of its input includes the attribute ¡samplerate, 8000Hz¿.
- Type Relationships, such as a "contains" or "represents" relationship, describe relationships between types that are awkward to capture with simple subtypes or "is-a" relationships. For example, an aggregator that generates a list of images has an output datatype of "List" with the addition of a "contains" relationship to the "image" datatype.
- WILDCARD and UNKNOWN values are used when an attribute or relationship field does not yet or cannot have a specific value. An attribute or relationship value of "wildcard" means the associated field will match whatever is required. An "unknown" value means no assumptions or assertions can be made about the value of the field.

These data type descriptions are made in a language-neutral format. The type requirements of endpoints are made external to the endpoint. This means we can describe the requirements of third-party entities without modifying them.

It is important to highlight that there is a tradeoff between how descriptive and complete a type system is, and how unwieldy and difficult the type system is to use. As more semantic information is encoded in the type system, the potential for "false negatives" when comparing two datatypes increases. As part of our current research, we are investigating the nature of this tradeoff.

We are continuing to experiment with our extended type system to evaluate its efficacy. Other type systems that may provide enough descriptive power for our purposes include Spreitzer and Begel's Flexible Types [9].

5.3 Path Lifetime

In our applications, we have experimented with both long-lived and short-lived paths. Short-lived paths are simple and straightforward, and are appropriate for sessionless message-based communication (i.e., no expectation that multiple messages will follow). Both the Room Control Service and the Global Clipboard use short-lived paths to perform their communication and transformation. The main disadvantage of using a short-lived path is the cost of tearing down and setting up a new path for every message sent.

Long-lived paths can handle a wider variety of applications than short-lived paths. They are more appropriate for session-oriented applications, including streaming media applications and applications that maintain other session state. An example of such an operator might be a "moving-average" operator that tracked the value of a variable throughout the duration of a session. We used long-lived paths in Dada to support the long-lived user interaction sessions.

5.4 User Interaction

Our mediation infrastructure provides a progammatic interface to ease development of cross-device applications and ad-hoc applications, but does not enforce any particular interaction mechanisms upon end users. Instead, Paths leaves the presentation of a user interface to a higher-level task-aware entity.

In our prototype applications, we have just begun to study the problem of user interaction with groups of heterogeneous devices. Our Room Control service built application-aware client programs on each of our supported device which provided the user with a high-level of control. In Dada, we took advantage of general-purpose viewers to generate and render simple user interfaces directly on the client devices. In the Global Clipboard, we hid most of the user interface behind an existing interface, the native system clipboard. In each of these cases, we chose to implement significantly different user interaction mechanisms, but were able to use the same Paths mechanism.

6 Related Work

Our work was first motivated in the context of composing Internet services, particularly by work in using web proxies to adapt to client variations [2]. We are still actively working in this area, in collaboration with the Ninja and Iceberg projects at UC Berkeley.

The Compose Group at Carnegie Mellon University has done much work in the area of component composition in the context of software architectures [3, 8]. With respect to their terminology, Paths matches the "pipe/filter model" of software architecture.

Sun's combined effort with Java and Jini is also trying to address the problem of communication in a ubiquitous computing environment [11]. However, they are applying the standards-based approach, and defining a homogeneous system to which entities must conform. We have explicitly attempted to enable communication among COTS and legacy applications and devices.

In the area of ubiquitous computing, our work is most closely related to the context-aware systems designed by the Future Computing Environments group at Georgia Institute of Technology [7]. The type converters or context interpreters described in the context of CyberDesk are the equivalent of our mediators. That work uses type converters primarily to generate context information that can be used as a trigger. We see our work as complementary to theirs and can envision ways in which both systems might be enriched if they could be integrated. Since integration with other systems is one of primary goals, we do not expect this to be particularly difficult.

7 Conclusions

Ubiquitous computing requires a seamless interworking of heterogeneous entities, including legacy entities that is not feasible to implement using current technologies.

The mediation infrastructure described in this paper enables ad-hoc, loosely-coupled communication between heterogeneous, potentially legacy and COTS, entities that were not originally designed to communicate with each other. It compensates for mismatches between communicants through the automatic composition of mediators. Due to the use of composable mediators, support for new entities can be added with only incremental work. We have implemented a prototype of this infrastructure and built a number of applications using it.

Continuing work on the mediation infrastructure includes research into the tradeoffs related to the descriptiveness of the type system, and the use of this mediation infrastructure for supporting dynamically transformed or generated user interfaces, and multimodal interfaces.

Acknowledgements. Early work on Paths began at UC Berkeley; we would like to thank Prof. Eric Brewer for introducing us to the conceptual Paths model, Prof. Randy Katz for his guidance, and especially Prof. Anthony Joseph for his feedback and advice during the development of the Room Control Service. The Room Control Service prototype was implemented with Barbara Hohlt of UC Berkeley. The Dada prototype was implemented with John R. Haymaker, Martin Jonsson and Shankar Ponnekanti at Stanford University. We thank Steve Gribble, Andy Huang, and Michelle Munson for providing us with valuable feedback on this paper. This material is based on work supported under an STMicroelectronics Stanford Graduate Fellowship and a National Science Foundation Fellowship.

References

1. Clark, D., and Tennenhouse, D. Architectural Considerations for a New Generation of Protocols. *Proceedings of ACM SIGCOMM '90*, Sept. 1990, pp. 201-208.
2. Armando Fox, Steven D. Gribble, Yatin Chawathe, Eric A. Brewer. Adapting to Network and Client Variation Using Active Proxies: Lessons and Perspectives. *IEEE Personal Communications (invited submission)*, Aug 1998. Special issue on adapting to network and client variability.
3. David Garlan, Robert Allen, and John Ockerbloom. Architectural Mismatch, or, Why it's hard to build systems out of existing parts. *Proceedings of the 17th International Conference on Software Engineering,* April 1995.
4. Steve Gribble, Matt Welsh, Eric A. Brewer, and David Culler. The MultiSpace: an Evolutionary Platform for Infrastructural Services. In *Second USENIX Symposium on Internet Technologies and Systems (USITS '99)*, Aug 1999.
5. Andrew C. Huang, Benjamin C. Ling, John Barton, and Armando Fox. Running the Web Backwards: Appliance Data Services. *WWW-9*, Amsterdam, May 2000.
6. John Ockerbloom. Mediating Among Diverse Data Formats. *PhD Thesis, Carnegie Mellon University,* Jan 1998.

7. Daniel Salber, Anind K. Dey and Gregory D. Abowd. The Context Toolkit: Aiding the Development of Context-Enabled Applications. *In the Proceedings of the 1999 Conference on Human Factors in Computing Systems (CHI '99)*, Pittsburgh, PA, May 15-20, 1999. pp. 434-441.
8. M. Shaw, R. DeLine, V. Klein, T.L. Ross, D.M. Young, G. Zelesnik. Abstractions for Software Architecture and Tools to Support Them. *IEEE Transactions on Software Engineering, Vol. 21, No 4*, April 95.
9. Mike Spreitzer and Andrew Begel. More Flexible Data Types. *In Proceedings of The Eighth IEEE International Workshops on Enabling Technologies: Infrastructure for Collaborative Enterprises*, June 1999.
10. Stanford Interactive Workspaces Project. http://graphics.stanford.edu/projects/iwork/
11. Sun Microsystems. Jini Connection Technology Overview. *whitepaper. http://www.sun.com/jini/overview/overview.ps*
12. Helen J. Wang, Bhaskaran Raman, et al. ICEBERG: An Internet-core Network Architecture for Integrated Communications. *Submitted to IEEE Personal Communications.*
13. J. A. Watlington and V. M. Bove, Jr. Stream-Based Computing and Future Television. *Proc. 137th SMPTE Technical Conference*, pp. 69-79, 1995.
14. Mark Weiser. The computer for the 21st century. *Scientific American*, 265(3):94–104, September 1991

EVENTMANAGER: Support for the Peripheral Awareness of Events

Joseph F. McCarthy and Theodore D. Anagnost[1]

Center for Strategic Technology Research (CSTaR)
Andersen Consulting
3773 Willow Road
Northbrook, IL 60062 USA
mccarthy@cstar.ac.com

Abstract. EVENTMANAGER is a tool that supports peripheral awareness by enabling users to be notified when events of interest take place within their workplace environment. Our initial implementation of the tool allows users to specify events based on people and their locations within the physical environment, e.g., the event of Joe entering his office. We describe the context of the environment in which the tool is used, the event specification language, the features embodied in the interfaces and some potential extensions for future versions of the tool.

1 Introduction

A number of researchers have created tools designed to provide a peripheral awareness [Bly, *et al.*, 1993] of the activities of their colleagues. Some tools use video and/or audio information (using cameras, microphones, displays and speakers) – sometimes filtered – to provide awareness of the activities of other people [Dourish & Bly, 1992; Lee, *et al.,* 1997; Hudson & Smith, 1996]. Others have used more abstract or symbolic representations to provide this awareness [Ishii & Ulmer, 1997; Wisneski, *et al.,* 1998; Pedersen & Sokoler, 1997]. All of these tools rely on users' monitoring the displays or other representations – possibly at intervals – if they are interested in a particular activity or event.

EVENTMANAGER takes a different approach: rather than requiring users to continuously or repeatedly monitor "displays" that provide awareness information, we have built a tool that permits users to specify an event of interest involving people and locations. Users can then turn their attention to other tasks until they are notified that the event has occurred. For example, EVENTMANAGER enables users to be notified if or when:

- Joe arrives at work in the morning
- Eric and Jim are both in The Lab
- Ted returns to his office
- Anatole leaves the meeting
- The conference room is empty

---

[1] Second author's current address: theodore.anagnost@med.ge.com.

If I need to ask Anatole a question, but he is now in a meeting, and I know he has another meeting immediately following this one, I can ask EVENTMANAGER to notify me when he is leaving one meeting and on his way to the next, presenting an opportunity to intercept him in the hallway. Without EVENTMANAGER, I would need to interrupt the current meeting, camp outside the meeting room until Anatole comes out, or wait until his meetings are over and he returns to his office to check for messages. Of course, if we had video cameras throughout the environment, I could monitor them to look for my opportunity, but this could require a great deal of attention over time.

In general, EVENTMANAGER provides opportunities to informally meet with one or more people [cf. Nakanashi, *et al.*, 1996] through an event specification language and interface through which I can specify one or more contexts in which I think such opportunities might exist. For example, if I need to ask Ted a question, I could ask EVENTMANAGER to notify me when he returns to his office, or if I need to talk with both Eric and Jim, I could ask EVENTMANAGER to notify me when they are both in The Lab. This approach is reminiscent of event-action specifications used for software-related objects and processes [Krishnamurthy & Rosenblum, 1995; Rosenblum & Wolf, 1997], but our tool applies to events that occur in the physical world rather than the digital world.

Peripheral awareness mechanisms can be characterized along two dimensions that define how much attention they require. One dimension is the attention *effort*, i.e., the amount of attention required each time the user wants to update his or her awareness. The other dimension is the number of attention *samples*, i.e., the number of times a user has to turn his or her attention to the awareness mechanism to gain or maintain awareness.

Most previous work in the area of peripheral awareness has focused on mechanisms that require low effort per sample, e.g., a quick glance at an awareness display (e.g., ACTIVEMAP [McCarthy & Meidel, 1999]), but may require multiple samples to monitor for specific events of interest. EVENTMANAGER, by contrast, requires a higher degree of effort to initially specify an event of interest, but then eliminates the need for subsequent attention sampling. While the low effort per sample mechanisms are clearly better for general awareness of activities in an environment, we believe EVENTMANAGER represents a better approach to providing awareness of specific, definable activities within an environment.

EVENTMANAGER works within the context of an intelligent environment [Coen, 1998], i.e., a physical space that can sense and respond appropriately to the people and activities taking place within it. One consequence of work in this area is a shift in perspective regarding human-computer interaction: rather than viewing people as *users* of computer systems, it becomes more appropriate to view people as *inhabitants* of computer-imbued spaces. In particular, EVENTMANAGER presumes that the environment can sense the locations of its inhabitants [Want, *et al.*, 1992; Harter & Hopper, 1994], and respond to the person who specified the event wherever he or she may be within the environment.

This paper will describe our EVENTMANAGER tool. We first describe the context within which EVENTMANAGER operates; we then present the EVENTMANAGER event specification language and its associated interfaces; we conclude with a discussion of some of our plans for extending the EVENTMANAGER.

2 Environmental Context

The environmental context in which we have designed and built the EVENTMANAGER is the physical space occupied by the Center for Strategic Technology Research (CSTaR®), a 16,000 square foot section of the second floor of Andersen Consulting Technology Park, in Northbrook, IL, USA. The CSTaR area includes 40 individual offices, four laboratories, two large conference rooms (the Group Discussion Lab, or GDL, and a VideoConference room), two small conference rooms, a break area with kitchenette and vending machines, three furnished open areas used for informal meetings and numerous hallways. There are approximately 30 members of the CSTaR group in Northbrook,[2] including researchers, programmers, technical writers and administrative staff.

We have installed an ArialView™ Awareness System [Arial Systems Corp.] within the CSTaR area, consisting of a network of over 70 ceiling-mounted nodes each housing an infrared sensor, radio frequency receiver and audio speaker, and a set of badges that transmit infrared identification signals every two seconds.[3] In addition to this hardware, the ArialView system includes components to process the signals and maintain badge location information in a Microsoft SQL Server 7.0 database, and a web browser interface for accessing and administering this information.

Some members of CSTaR have voiced privacy concerns about wearing a badge that allows them to be located in real-time or tracked over a period of time. Fortunately, we work in a profession in which our location does not reveal a great deal about our work (or play) activities: time spent in a colleague's office could represent an intensive exchange of project-related ideas, or a heated debate over whether a president committed impeachable offenses. One of the appealing features of a badge system is that anyone who objects to being located or tracked can simply not wear a badge; cameras and microphones are not so easy to avoid (though one can presumably at least control the devices installed in one's office).

We believe that most people are willing to relinquish some degree of privacy for what they perceive as a compensating benefit. For example, most people in the United States are willing to let grocery stores track their purchases via some kind of preferred shopper's card in exchange for small discounts received when they present the card to the cashier. It remains to be seen whether the members of CSTaR will perceive enough benefits from our suite of intelligent environment applications to warrant their continued wearing of badges.[4]

---

[2] There are six members in another CSTaR group in Palo Alto, CA, USA, but their workspace is not yet incorporated into the environment(s) served by EVENTMANAGER.

[3] The ArialView system is similar in many respects to the Olivetti Active Badge System [Want, et al., 1992; Harter & Hopper, 1994], except that the current ArialView badges have a single two-position slider switch rather than two buttons, and the ArialView sensor nodes include RF receivers and speakers.

[4] See Harper [1992], for a more thorough discussion of acceptance issues with respect to the use of badges in a research lab context.

3 The EVENTMANAGER Tool

There are two interfaces for managing events in the EVENTMANAGER. The *event management interface* allows the user to create, modify, delete, activate or deactivate events.[5] The *event specification interface*, invoked from the event manager interface, allows the user to create or modify a single event, based on our event specification language. When an event's *conditions* are satisfied, the EVENTMANAGER has a number of *actions* it can use to inform the user. Each of these components is described in more detail below.

3.1 Event Management Interface

Figure 1 shows the primary interface to the EVENTMANAGER. The *inactive* events listed in the top frame have been specified by the user at some time, but are not currently being monitored by the system. The *active* events in the lower frame are specified events that are currently being monitored. Each event is assigned a *name* by the user, and has an associated *description* based on the primitives available in the event specification language. The active events shown in the lower frame also show how much time has elapsed since each event was activated.

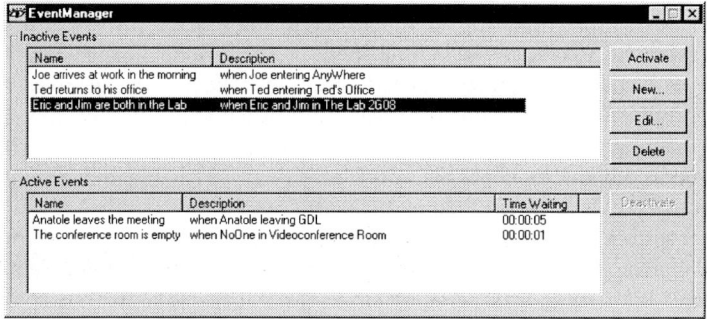

Fig. 1. EVENTMANAGER's Primary Interface

There are four buttons on the right side of the primary interface:
- *New*: create a new event via the event specification interface
- *Edit*: view/modify an existing event via the event specification interface
- *Activate*: add the selected event(s) to the list of active events
- *Delete*: delete the selected event(s)

There is also a *Deactivate* button on the lower right side of the interface, used to deactivate an event before its conditions have been satisfied.

---

[5] We will simplify our description of the tool by referring to *event specifications* as *events*, except in contexts where event specifications in the tool may be confused with events in the physical environment.

3.2 Event Specification Language and Interface

Figure 2 shows the Event Specification Interface to the EVENTMANAGER. The interface allows a user to specify any event within the constraints of our event specification language. Each event specification in our language has the general form:

when <*person*>+ is/are <*relationship*> <*location*>+ then <*action*>+

Where
- <*person*> is one or more members of the research group (the selection of multiple people is interpreted as a conjunction), or exactly one of the following special cases:
  - **SomeOne**
  - **NoOne**
- <*relationship*> is one of the following:
  - **entering**
  - **leaving**
  - **in**
  - **alone in**
  - **not in**
- <*location*> is one or more offices, conference rooms, open areas or hallways in the CSTaR area (the selection of multiple locations is interpreted as a disjunction), or exactly one of the following special cases:
  - **AnyWhere**
  - **NoWhere**
- <*action*> is one or more actions to take when the event occurs; this topic is covered in more detail below.

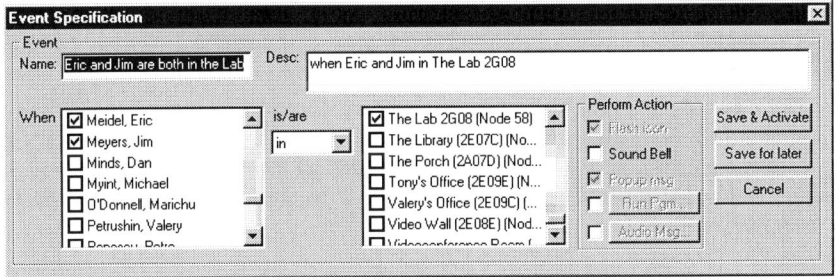

Fig. 2. EVENTMANAGER's Event Specification Interface

Using this simple interface, we can specify the sample events listed in Section 1:
- when Joe is entering AnyWhere
- when Eric and Jim are in The Lab
- when Ted enters Ted's Office
- when Anatole is leaving The GDL
- when NoOne is in The GDL

The interpretation of a selection of two or more people as a conjunction (rather than a disjunction) was chosen because of our expectation that users would be more interested in knowing when two or more people are together in a location than in knowing when any one of a set of people is in a location. Another reason for this interpretation is that the latter class of events can be encoded by multiple single-person event specifications, e.g., "when Ted or Joe is in The Lab" can be represented by the two event specifications "when Ted is in The Lab" and "when Joe is in The Lab." Note that the interpretation of multiple selected people as a disjunction would not allow for alternate representations of conjunctions, i.e., we would not be able to specify the event of when Ted and Joe are both in The Lab at the same time.[6]

In addition to specifying one or more people, a single relationship, and one or more locations, the event specification interface requires users to *name* each event. There is also a *description* associated with each event, which is generated automatically from the selections made of the person(s), relationship and location(s). The name field was included to allow users to specify shorter identifiers for their events.

There are a variety of actions that the EVENTMANAGER can take once the conditions of an activated event specification have been satisfied:

- *Flash Icon*: EVENTMANAGER is part of a suite of awareness tools, collectively known as POCKETWATCH. When the main POCKETWATCH application is running, it has a special icon in the Windows 95/98/NT taskbar tray. This icon flashes whenever an event from the user's active event list takes place.
- *Sound Bell*: The computer's bell can be sounded to notify the user.
- *Pop-up Msg*: The user can ask for EVENTMANAGER to pop-up a small message-box window that lists the name of the event that has taken place.
- *Audio Msg*: The ArialView system provides the capability to send any arbitrary text message through a speech synthesizer and out to the speaker included in any of our ceiling-mounted nodes. One option for the user to be notified is to play a message that can be directed to wherever the user (or another inhabitant) is within the environment. This is a particularly useful option for notification since it provides users with an awareness of events of interest even when they are away from their offices.
- *Run Pgm*: We expect that a number of other people will want to extend the functionality of EVENTMANAGER in a variety of ways. One way we can permit some extensions early on, is to allow people to run any arbitrary application whenever an event takes place. We will discuss some of the ways that we plan to extend the EVENTMANAGER in the next section.

After creating or modifying an event specification, the user has three options:
- *Save & Activate*: adds the specified event to the list of active events
- *Save For Later*: adds the specified event to the list of inactive events
- *Cancel*: discards the specified event

---

[6] The specification of two or more locations within a single event is interpreted as a disjunction because in our experience, people can not be in more than one location at any given time.

4 Future Work

We currently envision a number of dimensions along which we want to extend the EVENTMANAGER. These include extensions to the event specification language, adding additional sensor information to augment the ArialView system, adding a synchronization capability for notifications, and adding new notification mechanisms.

4.1 Event Specification Language Extensions

We would like to enable users to specify a broader range of events, e.g., "when Eric is in The Lab, but Jim is not in The Lab," or "when three or more people are gathered together in any open area." One way we might do this is to specify ways to combine atomic events, such as those now enabled by the primary interface, using logical operators (AND, OR and NOT). Another potential direction is to allow variables and quantification, along the lines of predicate calculus representation.[7]

The current event specification language and interface only permit specification of discrete events. We would like to add the capability to include time intervals in the specification. This would enable us to specify events such as "when Anatole is alone in his office for more than 5 minutes," to distinguish this from when Anatole stops in his office to pick something up. We are also considering the addition of scheduling information to our event specifications so that a user can specify a time to activate and/or deactivate any event, or to create a regularly scheduled event, e.g., "when Joe arrives at work every day."

4.2 Integration with Other Information Resources

The current version of EVENTMANAGER relies entirely on information provided by our ArialView badge system. While this enables us to locate people throughout the environment, it doesn't tell us much about what they are doing. If we had access to information about whether someone was typing on their computer keyboard or whether their telephone was being used, we might be able to specify an event such as "when Anatole is alone in his office for more than 5 minutes and is not on the telephone."

It would also be useful to integrate calendar and scheduling information, particularly when someone is not locatable within the environment (due to a hidden badge, attendance at a meeting in a part of the building not covered by sensors, or being offsite). For example, if Anatole's schedule indicates that he will be in Palo Alto for three days, EventManager might notify a user who is specifying an event that involves Anatole returning to his office.

---

[7] We should note that expanding the expressiveness of the specification language might yield undesirable consequences. If everyone specifies an event "when ten or more people are in The GDL" to await a critical mass of meeting attendees to arrive at our weekly seminar, we could experience deadlock, as everyone waits for everyone else to arrive. Of course, the seminar speaker might counter such a condition by specifying harassment events to send directed audio reminders to anyone not yet in the seminar room.

4.3 Notification Synchronization

The current implementation of EVENTMANAGER provides immediate notification when a specified event occurs. However, the environmental state can change before the notification has been observed. For example, I might be away from my office when a pop-up messagebox announces that "Anatole is available in his office." Upon returning to my office, I may see this message and then walk over to Anatole's office. Unfortunately, he may no longer be available.

One possible solution is to incorporate a mechanism that automatically updates the pop-up message box when the state changes, e.g., "Anatole *was* available in his office." Another possible solution is to provide a capability to manually refresh the notification, e.g., a button that causes EVENTMANAGER to check the state of the system to confirm whether the condition indicated by the notification is still valid.

4.4 New Notification Mechanisms

Although we have included a catch-all notification mechanism in our current interface – the capability to run any arbitrary program when a specified event occurs – we'd like to investigate other mechanisms for notification to include in our default set. We are particularly interested in investigating the use of "tangible" notification mechanisms [Ishii & Ulmer, 1997; Wisneski, *et al.,* 1998] and other abstract or symbolic methods [Pedersen & Sokoler, 1997] for alerting users when events occur.

5 Conclusion

We have designed and built EVENTMANAGER, a tool that enables users to specify events of interest involving people and locations within an intelligent environment. The user is then notified if or when those events take place. We have considered a number of possible extensions, and are looking forward to feedback from our users to better understand how we might best expand the capabilities of this awareness tool.

References

1. Arial Systems Corp. ArialView™ Awareness System. http://www.arialsystems.com.
2. Sara A. Bly, Steve R. Harrison and Susan Irwin. 1993. Media Space: Bringing People Together in a Video, Audio, and Computing Environment. *Communications of the ACM,* 36(1), January 1993, pp. 28-47.
3. Michael Coen (Ed.). 1998. *Papers from the 1998 AAAI Spring Symposium on Intelligent Environments.* March 1998, Technical Report SS-98-02, AAAI Press.
4. Paul Dourish and Victoria Bellotti. 1992. Awareness and Coordination in Shared Workspaces. In *Proceedings of the ACM 1992 Conference on Computer Supported Cooperative Work (CSCW '92).* 330-337.

5. Paul Dourish and Sara Bly. 1992. Portholes: Supporting Awareness in Distributed Work Groups. In *Proceedings of the ACM 1992 Conference on Human Factors in Computer Systems (CHI '92)*.
6. Richard H. R. Harper. 1992. Looking at Ourselves: An Examination of the Social Organisation of Two Research Laboratories. In *Proceedings of the ACM 1992 Conference on Computer Supported Cooperative Work (CSCW '92)*. 330-337.
7. Andy Harter and Andy Hopper. 1994. A Distributed Location System for the Active Office. *IEEE Network* 8(1): 62-70.
8. Scott E. Hudson and Ian Smith. 1996. Techniques for Addressing Fundamental Privacy and Disruption Tradeoffs in Awareness Support Systems. In *Proceedings of the ACM 1996 Conference on Computer Supported Cooperative Work (CSCW '96)*. 248-257.
9. Hiroshi Ishii and Brygg Ulmer. Tangible Bits: Towards Seamless Interfaces between People, Bits and Atoms. In *Proceedings of the ACM 1997 Conference on Human Factors in Computer Systems (CHI '97)*. 234-241.
10. Balachander Krishnamurthy and David S. Rosenblum. 1995. Yeast: A General-Purpose Event-Action System. *IEEE Transactions on Software Engineering*, 21(10), October 1995, pp. 845-857.
11. Alison Lee, Andreas Girgensohn and Kevin Schlueter. 1997. NYNEX Portholes: Initial User Reactions and Redesign Implications. In *Proceedings of the ACM 1997 International Conference on Supporting Group Work (GROUP '97)*.
12. Joseph F. McCarthy and Eric S. Meidel. 1999. ActiveMap: A Visualization Tool for Location Awareness to Support Informal Interactions. In Hans W. Gellersen (Ed*.) Handheld and Ubiquitous Computing*. Proceedings of the First International Symposium (HUC '99), Karlsruhe, Germany, September 1999. Lecture Notes in Computer Science, Vol. 1707. Springer – Verlag, Heidelberg. 158-170.
13. Hideyuki Nakanashi, Chikara Yoshida, Toshikazu Nishimura and Toru Ishida. 1996. FreeWalk: Supporting Casual Meetings in a Network. In *Proceedings of the ACM 1996 Conference on Computer Supported Cooperative Work (CSCW '96)*. 308-314.
14. Elin Ronby Pedersen and Tomas Sokoler. AROMA: Abstract Representation of Presence Supporting Mutual Awareness. In *Proceedings of the ACM 1997 Conference on Human Factors in Computer Systems (CHI '97)*. 234-241.
15. David S. Rosenblum and Alexander L. Wolf. 1997. A Design Framework for Internet-Scale Event Observation and Notification. In *Proceedings of the Sixth European Software Engineering Conference / ACM SIGSOFT Fifth Symposium on the Foundations of Software Engineering*.
16. Roy Want, Andy Hopper, Veronica Falcao, and Jonathon Gibbons. 1992. The Active Badge Location System. *ACM Transactions on Information Systems* 10(1): 91-102.
17. Mark Weiser and John Seeley Brown. 1997. The Coming Age of Calm Technology. In *Beyond Calculation: The Next Fifty Years of Computing*. Peter J. Denning and Robert M. Metcalfe, Eds. Springer Verlag. 75-85.
18. Craig Wisneski, Hiroshi Ishii, Andrew Dahley, Matt Gorbet, Scott Brave, Brygg Ulmer and Paul Yarin. 1998. Ambient Displays: Turning Architectural Space into an Interface between People and Information. In Norbert A. Streitz, Shin'ichi Konomi and Heinz-Jurgen Burkhardt (Eds.) *Cooperative Buildings - Integrating Information, Organization and Architecture*. Proceedings of the First International Workshop on Cooperative Buildings (CoBuild '98), Darmstadt, Germany (February 25-26, 1998). Lecture Notes in Computer Science, Vol. 1370. Springer - Verlag, Heidelberg. 22-32.

Safety and Comfort of Eyeglass Displays

Erik Geelhoed[2], Marie Falahee[1], and Kezzy Latham[1]

[1] School of Life and Health Sciences, Aston University, Birmingham B4 7ET, UK.
M.Falahee@aston.ac.uk
[2] Hewlett-Packard Laboratories, Bristol, BS34 8QZ. U.K.
erik_geelhoed@hp.com

Abstract. An eyeglass display features two micro displays and both eyes are presented with the same image. This configuration is safer than virtual reality helmets, which give rise to severe vision problems and nausea. They are also safer than monocular displays, which impair judgement of distance, speed and size. Current eyeglass display products are occluded and are likely to produce vergence lock, a potential health hazard. We suggest that eyeglass displays should allow good peripheral vision and should be used in relatively light environments to counteract vergence lock.

1 Introduction

In most wearable computer research programs Head Mounted Displays (HMD) have played a prominent role, e.g. [1], [2]. Applications feature helmet style systems to facilitate augmented reality or immersion in Virtual Reality (VR) environments. Use of the rather cumbersome and heavy HMD is at odds with the need for ultra portable, wearable or otherwise "unconsciously" worn systems. In addition there are some serious health and safety issues that need to be addressed . In this report we describe eyeglass displays as a much lighter alternative for HMD. In addition we present results from health and safety studies of eyeglass displays use , carried out at Hewlett Packard research laboratories.

A number of studies have demonstrated changes to the visual system [3], [4], [5], [6] and reported symptomatic changes such as increased nausea, dizziness and headaches, and eyestrain [7], [8], [9], [10] as a result of using HMDs for VR immersion. These adverse effects are similar to those reported for other three-dimensional / stereoscopic display appliances, such as flight simulators [11], night vision goggles [12], stereo-microscopes [13], and monocular displays [14]. Monocular displays, such as those developed for use by Apache helicopter pilots, have also been shown to result in distortions of size, distance, and motion perception [14].

The symptoms which result from using VR appliances are similar to the symptoms of motion sickness, and both are generally thought to be caused by conflicts between the information received by two or more sensory systems [15]. In the case of immersive VR, conflict is caused by either the time lag for the virtual scene to be updated following a head movement, or the impression that the world is moving visually whilst no physical movement of the body is occurring (known as visually-induced motion sickness), or both [5].

An eyeglass display is an appliance featuring two micro displays and both eyes are presented with the same flat (two dimensional) image. The virtual screen is a simulation of a computer screen or a TV. The simpler configuration of eyeglass displays means that they tend to be smaller and lighter than VR helmets. Because of the enhanced portability of eyeglass displays, they may be very suitable for use with some mobile computing applications (e.g. notebooks), for example, offering the user a lightweight, more private alternative to their computer screen. Eyeglass displays also have potential value for home entertainment (e.g. viewing DVD / videos; playing computer games). Although exactly which applications / tasks are (not) suitable for use of eyeglass displays is an empirical matter which has yet to be addressed in the research literature, we believe that eyeglass displays have a role to play in the realm of Handheld and Ubiquitous Computing (HUC).

Given the mounting list of alarming reports on the adverse effects of VR helmets and similar applications, it is essential to explore the possibility that eyeglass displays may be prone to similar problems. However, this has been the focus of very few researchers. Furthermore, the results of the few existing relevant studies (reviewed below) are inconsistent, and we have no theoretical framework in which to place their findings. What the researchers are agreed on, though, is that, compared to the effects of virtual reality helmets, the effects of eyeglass displays are mild. There are two main themes that run through the publications. These are: vergence lock and nausea.

When you stare at a particular point in space for a prolonged period of time, there is a slight tendency towards rigidity in vergence, called *vergence lock*. This happens sometimes when we are absorbed in a book for a long time [16]. Simply looking away from the book, around us, counteracts vergence lock, and we recover rapidly. When we use eyeglass displays for watching a feature length movie, and eyeglass displays are often occluded, it is true to say, that we do look at the same distance, that is the focal distance determined by the optics of the eyeglass display, for a prolonged period of time, with little opportunity to give our eyes a break by looking around. This is in stark contrast to the highly fluid accommodation and vergence activities of the visual system under normal conditions. There is clear evidence that eyeglass displays give rise to vergence lock in adults and children e.g.[17], [18], [19]. These experiments describe single experimental sessions only and participants recovered rapidly, but these findings raise questions about what would happen if people regularly use (occluded) eyeglass displays. The effects of extended use may be of particular concern for the developing visual systems of children.

Neveu et al [20], could not find strong evidence that the same happens with accommodation, although they found a significant increase in latency to relaxation of accommodation after eyeglass display use, indicating that some rigidity in accommodation might come into play.

Howarth and Costello [5] investigated the occurrence of simulator sickness-type symptoms after one hour of using a HMD which had been configured as a personal viewing system (Vs. a conventional VDU screen) to play a chess game. Their comparison of the HMD and conventional viewing systems is somewhat problematic, however, given that the VDU condition employed a much higher resolution screen than the HMD device. The HMD condition produced a greater frequency of symptom reports than the VDU condition. They also reported that malaise ratings increased steadily throughout the experimental session using the HMD. The authors explain these results in terms of the sensory conflict associated with the HMD device - head movements are not accompanied by changes in the visual scene - however, no measurements of head movement were included in this research design. In contrast, Peli [17] found no indication of nausea in his study, which compared a conventional VDU display with HMD conditions for both monoscopic and stereoscopic viewing. The same task was carried out by participants in all three conditions (30 minutes of playing a computer game). Peli reported no significant differences between the monoscopic HMD use and the VDU. The only significant difference found for the subjective impression of comfort was between the VDU and stereoscopic conditions.

This paper presents results from a series of experiments carried out at Hewlett-Packard Laboratories, Bristol, to investigate the effects of using eyeglass displays for different tasks (reading vs. video watching) on objective and subjective measures of visual functioning, and on subjective reports of sickness and discomfort. Evaluation of a prototype eyeglass display appliance (figure 1) developed at Hewlett-Packard Laboratories highlighting the importance of configuration issues is also included.

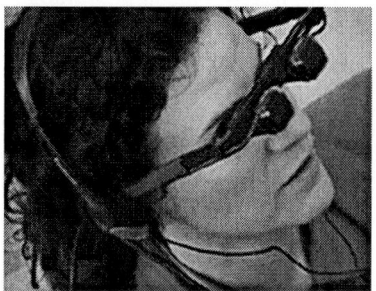

Fig. 1. HP prototype

2 Method

2.1 Measures

We used a variety of measures. For the purpose of clarity I will only describe those measures that had a strong bearing on the results and conclusions.

2.1.1 Questionnaire
We used a standard questionnaire that consists of three sections : 1. What you see, 2. Your eyes feel, 3. Discomfort. The first section (What you see) asks subjects about blurred vision, double vision and speed of focus change. The second section (Your

eyes feel) asks subjects how their eyes feel, e.g. tired, watering, hot, itchy etc., whereas the third section (Discomfort) asks about other sorts of discomfort, e.g. neck and shoulder pains, dizziness and nausea.

2.1.2 Dissociated Phoria

When looking at a target, the eyes are not perfect in pointing in the direction of the target, i.e. some people's eyes over-shoot (exo-phoria), some under-shoot (eso-phoria), few are actually right on the mark (ortho-phoria) (figure 2).

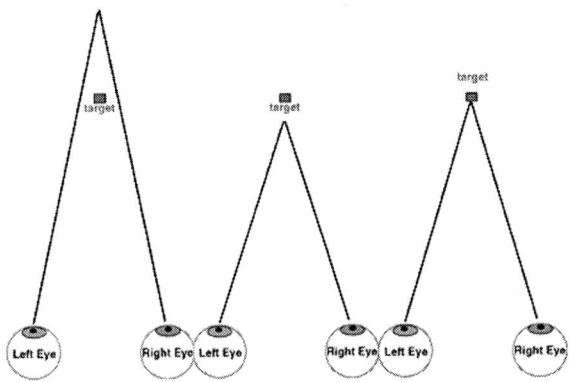

Fig. 2. over shooting, under shooting and on-the-mark exo-phoria, eso-phoria, ortho-phoria

Even though vergence is not perfect, the brain is very good at fusing images (and compensating for imperfections) from the left eye and right eye into one (relatively) clear and sharp picture.

For healthy eyes, when we look around us, the eyes move in tandem. When we cover one eye (e.g. with a pirate's patch) and we look around us with the remaining seeing eye, the covered eye (even though it cannot see anything) still moves in tandem with the one seeing eye. This situation is called dissociated phoria and we can measure this via the Maddox Rod test, [21]. The dissociated phorias measure has proved to be a good indicator for vergence lock.

2.1.3 Inter Pupillary Distance (IPD)

To ensure that subjects' eyeglass displays were configured correctly we measured the distance between the pupils of the left eye and the right eye.

2.2 Participants

Experimentally naïve participants (mean age 30.5 years) were screened by a professional optometrist to make sure that they were visually healthy enough to take part. This did not mean that the visual systems of the people who took part were perfect. In addition we took a "visual profile", screening measures that might predict individual differences in people's reactions to eyeglass display use.

2.3 Apparatus

For the early work we employed the, then state-of-the-art, albeit rather cumbersome, Kaiser Head Mounted Display (HMD). Later, as the much lighter Sony Glasstron eyeglass display became available, we used this to benchmark the prototype against. For listening subjects used very comfortable high quality padded headphones (Sennheiser HMD 25-1).

The Kaiser ProView 30 Head Mounted Display features two VGA resolution adjustable LCD displays. The focal distance was set at optical infinity (5.5 meters). The Sony Glasstron plm s-700 features (emissive) LCD glasses for viewing videos and contains two SVGA quality 0.7 inch LCD displays. The focal distance is set at 1.2 meters. The Glasstron allows some degree of see-through, but this mode was disabled. The optional "blinkers" to make the experience more immersive were not used in the experiment. The optics of Glasstron have a wide exit pupil. This allowed for an eyeglass displays where individual adjustments need not, and indeed, cannot be made. The prototype features (non see-through) reflective LCD micro displays of XGA resolution (1024 * 768 pixels). The focal distance is set at 1 meter. Compared to existing eyeglass displays products which are occluded, the prototype has a small form factor which allows for a generous peripheral vision. Enabling this small form factor (and a low level of illumination) is a much smaller exit pupil than the Sony Glasstron, necessitating individual adjustments of the inter screen distances. The housings of the two screens (optics blocks) were set at a slight angle, resulting in a vergence distance, depending on inter pupillary distance, of between 85 and 90 cm.

3 Three Experiments

3.1 Experiment 1 : Reading vs. Video Watching

Task differences have not been studied in the realm of eyeglass display research. Since video watching and using eyeglass displays for computer tasks are two applications under consideration, this experiment was designed to compare the effects of these two different tasks.

3.1.1 Procedure

Ten volunteers, eight females and two males, took part in three separate sessions, all three lasting under an hour, on different days. The first session aimed to establish a visual profile for each subject, the next two sessions were the experimental sessions, the reading and video watching tasks, balanced for order, i.e. five subjects did the reading task first and five did the video watching task first.

The Flight Begins

As I undertake this extended stay on the Mir Space Station, I am adapting to a lifestyle that can certainly be called unusual, if not bizarre. Perhaps it even defies adequate description. Nonetheless, I would like to attempt to share the experience with friends, colleagues or anyone else who is struck by the fascination for this kind of adventure.

So I hope to find time, over the coming months, to describe the sensations of the flight and some of the events that make this experience so unique. I am hoping then, that this will be the first in a series of letters home that will give people some idea of what it is like to travel and live in space on an orbiting outpost.

The weather had been questionable that day and there was still some uncertainty as to whether or not we would actually go. But a few minutes before launch, all the launch controllers were polled by the launch director

Fig. 3. . Reading task

The reading task consisted of a series of screens of text, Arial 18 point alternately accompanied by a small image in the top left corner measuring 115 * 150 pixels or as a sheet of text only (figure 3). Subjects were asked to read the text aloud while being reassured that this was not a performance task. At the end of every screen the experimenter "turned" the page. The task lasted 20 minutes.

The video watching task consisted of subjects watching an animation consisting of sophisticated computer graphics changing rapidly in a "roller coaster ride" fashion accompanied by music for 20 minutes.

3.1.2 Results

Vergence Lock. Although we only found minor changes we did get some indication that after 20 minutes of exposure there was a tendency for the eyes to be locking into the focal distance of the eyeglass display, i.e. there was a significant, $p = .018$, difference between the pre- and post measures where the dissociated phorias were significantly raised after subjects performing the tasks (irrespective of task or distance) into an exo-phoric direction.

Nausea. Even though the video watching task concerned a virtual roller coaster ride, none of the subjects were experiencing serious nauseous feelings. We included a questionnaire about susceptibility to motion sickness. One or two subjects felt slightly queasy, but they had never had any problems with travel sickness, whereas the subjects who had suffered as a child or were still susceptible to motion sickness did not report any such nauseous feelings. It does not seem likely that there is a link between travel sickness and HMD induced nausea.

Task Differences. The visual symptoms questionnaire demonstrated some mild changes that were, however, significant. Video watching produced increases in watering eyes and dizziness. Comparing video watching to reading we found significant higher scores for video watching with regards to itchy eyes and feelings of drowsiness and a possible trend to have more hot / burning eyes.

Dissociated phorias were more affected by the reading task. Here we must bear in mind that the reading task required subjects to explore all corners of the screen as they went from top left to bottom right. In addition, as the task required subjects to read out loud, the HMD wobbled with the movement of people's jaws. As a consequence there is the possibility that subjects eyes were not entirely lined up to the centre of the lenses. If spherical lenses are not lined up to the centre of the screen, people effectively look through a prism. Since prisms do test the vergence system, the changes in phorias might be as a result of this wobble. A valuable lesson that can be learned from this though is that if we explore possibilities of integrating eyeglass displays with a communicating wearable system (e.g. mobile telephones) this wobble as a result of people talking must be addressed.

Predictors. The symptoms were too mild to find predictors of people predisposed to adverse effects. Neither did the profiling measures provide indicators for (un)successful HMD use. We did find however, that when people are not well, this may be reflected in vision parameters which, as a result of using an eyeglass displays, may exacerbate.

3.2 Experiment 2: A Comparison of the HP Prototype vs. Sony Glasstron

3.2.1 Procedure

Eleven volunteers, seven male, four female watched 20 minutes of video on the Sony Glasstron and then at a later stage they watched 20 minutes of video on the prototype. On both occasions they sat comfortably on a sofa in day light conditions (figure 4). The Sony glasses allowed subjects to see the outside world from the corners of their eyes. Wearing the prototype allowed for even more peripheral vision. Whereas the previous experiment was conducted in a room without windows, testing took place in a room *with* windows which looked out onto a corridor, during normal office hours. In the corridor, regularly there were people walking by the experimental room. Hereby, we aimed to distract subjects so that they would regularly divert their gaze outside of the virtual environment, with the objective of counteracting vergence lock. We took ophthalmic measures (before and after usage) and also carried out a structured interview afterwards discussing likes and dislikes and usage issues.

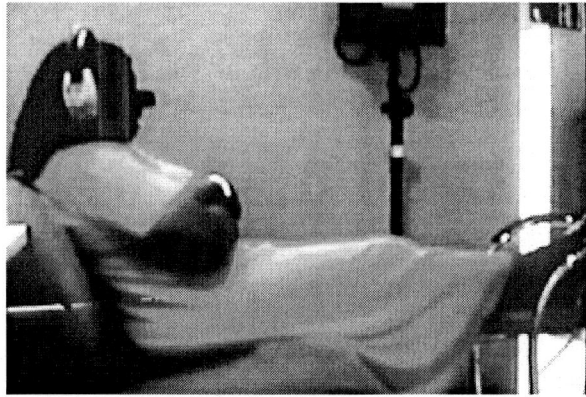

Fig. 4. Comfortably on a sofa

3.2.2 Results

The Sony Glasstron sessions resulted in mild symptom occurrence only. Eyestrain was raised, indicating that people did find the glasses strenuous to some extent. Drowsiness was also increased, not so much as a side effect of nausea (there were no reports of nausea), but probably more as a result of the relaxing influence of immersive video watching. There was no evidence for increased burning eyes overall, although some individuals did experience watering and burning eyes.

Evaluating the Sony Glasstron, we could find no indicators for vergence lock. Given that other researchers did find vergence lock for Sony's eyeglass displays, we speculate that this might be due to the fact our subjects were encouraged to divert their gaze outside of the virtual environment.

The evaluation of the prototype showed, that they too produce few symptoms. Itchy eyes, but not Eyestrain (as was the case with Sony glasses), was raised significantly but the increase was only mild. However there were very strong indicators that the prototype causes vergence lock. At this point, I will discuss the results of the dissociated phoria and fixation disparity measures in more detail.

Dissociated Phorias The dissociated phorias were measured three times at each of two different distances (50cm and 100cm). The graph below (figure 5) shows the (prototype) results for the 50 cm distance. The three trials, trial 1, trial 2 and trial 3, are along the X-axis. The Y-axis shows the mean responses across the eleven subjects. A positive number indicates exo-phoria and a negative number indicates eso-phoria.

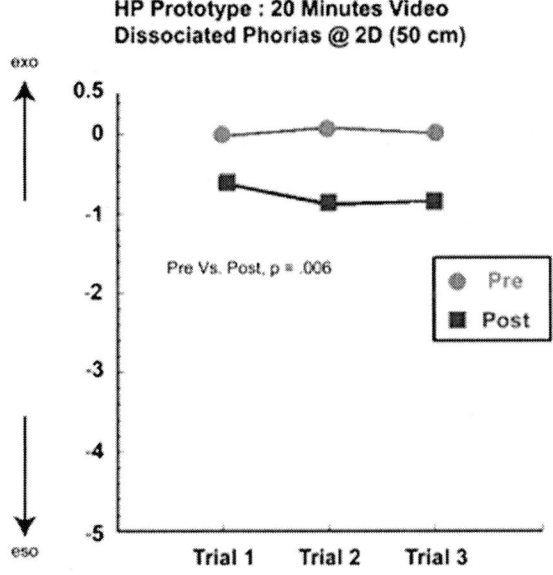

Fig. 5. Mean dissociated phorias at 50 cm

The grey line with round markers signifies the mean dissociated phorias (for the three trials) before testing, and since we had a good mix of exo-phoric and eso-phoric subjects, the mean for the pre-testing measures is close to zero. The darker line with square markers shows the mean dissociated phorias after testing. It is clear from the graph that the means are closer to -1, indicating an overall shift into an eso-phoric direction.

Evaluating the effects of pre-post measurement and trials per distance showed the pre post effects for the 50 cm and also 100 cm (not shown here) distances to be highly significant. For 50 cm this level of significance was $p = .006$ (and for 100 cm this was $p = .022$). The correlation between before and after phoria scores for 50 cm was highly significant, $r = .969$, $df = 10$, $p = .000$. This indicates that by and large all subjects showed a similar change.

User Issues. For both eyeglass displays, prototype and Sony, most people found the experience highly enjoyable and they could see themselves using glasses for watching films or playing games, in situations where people are not required to be social. Some people thought that they could be good to use with a notebook while on the road. But the glasses are not for every one, some people would not want to use them and found them uncomfortable. Although most people were very much immersed in the film, they expressed the wish for a more occluded eyeglass display for that bit of extra immersion. They mentioned that they were highly aware of people walking by in the corridors and they actually found this annoying. They were also pleasantly surprised by the quality of the prototype and the Glasstron display and overall rate it as good as a computer screen and better than a TV screen.

During the sessions all subjects without exception sat very still, hardly changed position. This included an overall lack of head movement. From peoples' comments we deduce that this is not as a result from peoples' unease with the combination of a non-moving image with a moving head, but is more likely to be a consequence of participant's immersion in the film.

3.3 Experiment 3 : Feature Length Video Watching

Going through a similar procedure, seven subjects watched 90 minutes of video on the prototype. Again we found a highly significant eso-shift of dissociated phorias and fixation disparities. Compared to the 20 minute video watching experiment, the magnitudes of the effects were not greater. We also found a mild but significant worsening of accommodation. Interestingly, one subject, who had been ill the previous day, reported a relatively high number of symptoms before testing, which after the video watching were markedly reduced. We mention this, because there have been subjects whose symptoms exacerbated after wearing the glasses.

4 Discussion

Our experiments indicate that eyeglass displays do not produce nausea. However, vergence lock, as a consequence of staring at the same focal distance for a prolonged period of time, can be a serious problem. This problem can be attenuated by providing enough peripheral vision and encouraging people to look away from the virtual environment regularly. We found indications that watching a video on a eyeglass display in a light, distractive environment with good peripheral vision might counteract vergence lock. However, participants expressed a preference for a more immersive, occluded appliance. For (mobile) computer tasks, the opposite, a strong desire to remain aware of what is happening around you, might be true.

The comparison of reading and video watching tasks showed that video watching is more likely to result in itchy and burning eyes and people are likely to become more drowsy as a result of the relaxing nature of the experience. In contrast, reading really forces the eyes to work hard, covering all corners of the screen. One must bear in mind here, that if we do not look through the centre of a lens we effectively look through a prism, which is strenuous for the eyes. Reading might result in not always looking through the centre of the lens. One consequence is, that the different tasks require different optics. For video watching it might be sufficient to have good central vision with less need for clear edges, whereas for every day computer tasks, the whole of the screen including the edges must be absolutely sharp and clear.

Both the prototype and the Sony Glasstron are very well suited for watching video and this is, for most people, very enjoyable. People also judge the virtual displays to be very good, as good as computer monitors and better than TV's. They could see themselves using the glasses in situations where they do not need to be social. Both eyeglass displays produced few symptoms, although our results confirmed that the eyes feel a bit hot and burning, resulting in tearing.

The prototype needed some further refinements. Whereas the Sony glasses produced no significant effects on the visual system, for the prototype we found a pronounced esophoric shift both for the dissociated phoria and fixation disparity measures.

The prototype is characterised by a one meter apparent viewing distance. The small form factor of the prototype allows a clearly visible peripheral field. However, this necessitates a narrow exit pupil requiring adjustment to suit individuals' inter pupillary distance. Together, with the slight canting of the optics block this resulted in a vergence demand of somewhere between 85 and 95 cm, "shoe-horning" as it were subjects into an eso-response. The Sony Glasstron similarly has a 1.2m apparent viewing distance. It differs from the prototype in that the peripheral field is less visible (only from the corners of the eyes), there is a wide exit pupil.

To resolve these conflicts we suggest that the focal distance should be set at 300 cm with the optics block perpendicular to the frame of the glasses. Hereby we overcome the current optical conflicts. Three meters has been suggested by our optometry experts as a comfortable distance for most people. There is a further advantage to setting accommodative and vergence demand to three meters: It is less problematic for presbyopic subjects: almost anyone over the age of about 50 years won't be able to accommodate to the currently required one meter without their spectacles.

5 Acknowledgements:

Barry Bronson, Annelies De Bruine, Andrew Nelson and Phil Stenton

References

1. Weiss, P. : Smart Outfit, Computers worn like clothes may alter the fabric of everyday life Science News Online, 156, No. 21 (1999)
   http://www.sciencenews.org/sn_arc99/11_20_99/bob1.htm
2. Pera, S., Jonker, P.: On positioning for Augmented Reality Systems, In Proceedings of Handheld and Ubiquitious Computing, First international Symposium, HUC'99, Karlsruhe, Germany (September 1999) 327-329
3. Mon-Williams, M., Wann, J. P., Rushton, S.: Binocular vision in a virtual world: Visual deficits following the wearing of a head-mounted display. Opthalmic and Physiological Optics, Vol. 13 (1993) 387-391
4. Rushton, S., Mon-Williams, M. & Wann, J. P.: Binocular vision in a bi-ocular world: New generation of head-mounted displays avoid causing visual deficit. Displays, Vol. 15 (1994) 255-260
5. Howarth, P. A., Costello, P. J.: The nauseogenicity of using a head-mounted display, configured as a personal viewing system, for an hour. (1996)
   http://info.lboro.ac.uk/departments/hu/groups/viserg/disp.htm
6. Costello, P. J., Howarth, P. A.: The visual effects of immersion in four virtual environments. VISERG Internal Report 9604. (1996)
   http://info.lboro.ac.uk/departments/hu/groups/viserg/9604all.htm
7. Regan, E. C.: An investigation into nausea and other side-effects of head-coupled immersive virtual reality. Virtual Reality, Vol. 1 (1) (1995) 17-32
8. Cobb, S., Nichols, S., Wilson, J. R.: Health and safety implications of virtual reality: In search of an experimental methodology. In Proc. FIVEí95 (Framework for Immersive Virtual Environments), University of London, (December 1995)
9. Kennedy, R. S., Lanham, D. S., Drexler, J. M., Massey, C. J., Lilienthal, M. G.: Cybersickness in several flight simulators and VR devices: a comparison of incidences, symptom profiles, measurement techniques and suggestions for research. In Proc. FIVEí95 (Framework for Immersive Virtual Environments), University of London, (December 1995)
10. Kolasinki, E. M.: Simulator sickness in virtual environments. Technical Report 1027, U.S. Army Research Institute for the Behavioural and Social Sciences, Alexandria, VA. (1995)
11. Kennedy, R. S., Fowlkes, J. E., Berbaum, K. S., Lilienthal, M. G.: Use of a motion sickness history questionnaire for prediction of simulator sickness. Aviation, Space and Environmental Medicine, 63 (1992) 588-593
12. Sheehy, J.B., Wilkinson, M.: Depth perception after prolonged usage of night vision goggles. Aviation, Space and Environmental Medicine, Vol. 60 (1989) 573-579
13. Soderberg, I., Calissendorff, B., Elofsson, S., Kanve, B., Nyman, K. G.: Investigation of visual strain experienced by microscope operators at an electronics plant. Applied Ergonomics, (December 1983) 297-305

14. Kotulak, J. C., Morse, S. E.: Oculomotor responses with aviator helmet-mounted displays and their relation to in-flight symptoms. Human Factors, Vol. 37 (4) (1995) 699-710
15. Reason, J. T., Brand, J. J.: Motion Sickness. London: Academic Press (1975)
16. Wilkins, A.: Reading and visual discomfort. In : Willows, D. M., Kruk, R. S., Corcos, E. (eds.) Visual Process in Reading and Reading Disabilities. Hillsdale, New Jersey: Lawrence Erlbaum Associates (1993) 435-456
17. Peli, E.: The visual effects of head-mounted-displays (HMD) are not distinguishable from those of desk-top computer display.In communiqué (1997)
18. GanNichida, T., Ervin, A., Gemmill, M. C., Drack, A., Holt, P. H, Lynn, M.: Relationship between clinical symptom report and ophthalmic function in virtual environment with HMD. Poster presented at the annual ARVO conference, Fort Lauderdale, Florida, (1998)
19. GanNichida, T., Ervin, A., Gemmill, M. C., Drack, A., Holt, P. H, Lynn, M.: Effects of viewing a movie using HMD on paediatric ophthalmic function and symptom report . Poster presented at the annual ARVO conference, Fort Lauderdale, Florida, (1998)
20. Neveu, C., Blackmon, T., Stark, L.: Evaluation of the effects of a head-mounted display on ocular accommodation. Presence, Vol. 7 (3), (1998) 278-289
21. Vaughan, D.G., Asbury, T. & Riordan-Eva, P.. General Ophthalmology (14th Edition). Appleton & Lange. (1995)

Author Index

Abowd, Gregory D.   172
Anagnost, Theodore D.   227

Baldonado, Michelle   100
Binder, Thomas   30
Björk, Staffan   46
Brumitt, Barry   12

Caswell, Deborah   114
Cousins, Steve   100

Dai, Guozhong   63
Debaty, Philippe   114
Dey, Anind K.   172

Falahee, Marie   236
Fox, Armando   211

Geelhoed, Erik   236
Goose, Stuart   143
Guan, Zhiwei   63
Gwizdka, Jacek   100

Havinga, Paul J.M.   85
Holmquist, Lars E.   46

Kanter, Theo   1
Kern, Amanda   12
Kıcıman, Emre   211
Krumm, John   12

Latham, Kezzy   236
Li, Yang   63
Ljungstrand, Peter   46

Marmasse, Natalia   157
Masui, Toshiyuki   72
McCarthy, Joseph F.   227
Meyers, Brian   12

Nilsson, Jörn   30

Oppermann, Reinhard   127

Paepcke, Andreas   100
Pham, Thai-Lai   143

Redström, Johan   46
Roth, Jörg   187

Schmandt, Chris   157
Schneider, Georg   143
Shafer, Steven   12
Siio, Itiro   72
Smit, Gerard J.M.   85
Sokoler, Tomas   30
Specht, Marcus   127
Stabell-Kulø, Tage   200

Unger, Claus   187

Wang, Hongan   63
Wetcke, Nina   30

Lecture Notes in Computer Science

For information about Vols. 1–1844
please contact your bookseller or Springer-Verlag

Vol. 1845: H.B. Keller, E. Plöderer (Eds.), Reliable Software Technologies Ada-Europe 2000. Proceedings, 2000. XIII, 304 pages. 2000.

Vol. 1846: H. Lu, A. Zhou (Eds.), Web-Age Information Management. Proceedings, 2000. XIII, 462 pages. 2000.

Vol. 1847: R. Dyckhoff (Ed.), Automated Reasoning with Analytic Tableaux and Related Methods. Proceedings, 2000. X, 441 pages. 2000. (Subseries LNAI).

Vol. 1848: R. Giancarlo, D. Sankoff (Eds.), Combinatorial Pattern Matching. Proceedings, 2000. XI, 423 pages. 2000.

Vol. 1849: C. Freksa, W. Brauer, C. Habel, K.F. Wender (Eds.), Spatial Cognition II. XI, 420 pages. 2000. (Subseries LNAI).

Vol. 1850: E. Bertino (Ed.), ECOOP 2000 – Object-Oriented Programming. Proceedings, 2000. XIII, 493 pages. 2000.

Vol. 1851: M.M. Halldórsson (Ed.), Algorithm Theory – SWAT 2000. Proceedings, 2000. XI, 564 pages. 2000.

Vol. 1852: T. Thierauf, The Computational Complexity of Equivalence and Isomorphism Problems. VIII, 135 pages. 2000.

Vol. 1853: U. Montanari, J.D.P. Rolim, E. Welzl (Eds.), Automata, Languages and Programming. Proceedings, 2000. XVI, 941 pages. 2000.

Vol. 1854: G. Lacoste, B. Pfitzmann, M. Steiner, M. Waidner (Eds.), SEMPER — Secure Electronic Marketplace for Europe. XVIII, 350 pages. 2000.

Vol. 1855: E.A. Emerson, A.P. Sistla (Eds.), Computer Aided Verification. Proceedings, 2000. X, 582 pages. 2000.

Vol. 1856: M. Veloso, E. Pagello, H. Kitano (Eds.), RoboCup-99: Robot Soccer World Cup III. XIV, 802 pages. 2000. (Subseries LNAI).

Vol. 1857: J. Kittler, F. Roli (Eds.), Multiple Classifier Systems. Proceedings, 2000. XII, 404 pages. 2000.

Vol. 1858: D.-Z. Du, P. Eades, V. Estivill-Castro, X. Lin, A. Sharma (Eds.), Computing and Combinatorics. Proceedings, 2000. XII, 478 pages. 2000.

Vol. 1860: M. Klusch, L. Kerschberg (Eds.), Cooperative Information Agents IV. Proceedings, 2000. XI, 285 pages. 2000. (Subseries LNAI).

Vol. 1861: J. Lloyd, V. Dahl, U. Furbach, M. Kerber, K.-K. Lau, C. Palamidessi, L. Moniz Pereira, Y. Sagiv, P.J. Stuckey (Eds.), Computational Logic – CL 2000. Proceedings, 2000. XIX, 1379 pages. (Subseries LNAI).

Vol. 1862: P.G. Clote, H. Schwichtenberg (Eds.), Computer Science Logic. Proceedings, 2000. XIII, 543 pages. 2000.

Vol. 1863: L. Carter, J. Ferrante (Eds.), Languages and Compilers for Parallel Computing. Proceedings, 1999. XII, 500 pages. 2000.

Vol. 1864: B. Y. Choueiry, T. Walsh (Eds.), Abstraction, Reformulation, and Approximation. Proceedings, 2000. XI, 333 pages. 2000. (Subseries LNAI).

Vol. 1865: K.R. Apt, A.C. Kakas, E. Monfroy, F. Rossi (Eds.), New Trends Constraints. Proceedings, 1999. X, 339 pages. 2000. (Subseries LNAI).

Vol. 1866: J. Cussens, A. Frisch (Eds.), Inductive Logic Programming. Proceedings, 2000. X, 265 pages. 2000. (Subseries LNAI).

Vol. 1867: B. Ganter, G.W. Mineau (Eds.), Conceptual Structures: Logical, Linguistic, and Computational Issues. Proceedings, 2000. XI, 569 pages. 2000. (Subseries LNAI).

Vol. 1868: P. Koopman, C. Clack (Eds.), Implementation of Functional Languages. Proceedings, 1999. IX, 199 pages. 2000.

Vol. 1869: M. Aagaard, J. Harrison (Eds.), Theorem Proving in Higher Order Logics. Proceedings, 2000. IX, 535 pages. 2000.

Vol. 1872: J. van Leeuwen, O. Watanabe, M. Hagiya, P.D. Mosses, T. Ito (Eds.), Theoretical Computer Science. Proceedings, 2000. XV, 630 pages. 2000.

Vol. 1873: M. Ibrahim, J. Küng, N. Revell (Eds.), Database and Expert Systems Applications. Proceedings, 2000. XIX, 1005 pages. 2000.

Vol. 1874: Y. Kambayashi, M. Mohania, A M. Tjoa (Eds.), Data Warehousing and Knowledge Discovery. Proceedings, 2000. XII, 438 pages. 2000.

Vol. 1875: K. Bauknecht, S.K. Madria, G. Pernul (Eds.), Electronic Commerce and Web Technologies. Proceedings, 2000. XII, 488 pages. 2000.

Vol. 1876: F. J. Ferri, J.M. Iñesta, A. Amin, P. Pudil (Eds.), Advances in Pattern Recognition. Proceedings, 2000. XVIII, 901 pages. 2000.

Vol. 1877: C. Palamidessi (Ed.), CONCUR 2000 – Concurrency Theory. Proceedings, 2000. XI, 612 pages. 2000.

Vol. 1878: J.P. Bowen, S. Dunne, A. Galloway, S. King (Eds.), ZB 2000: Formal Specification and Development in Z and B. Proceedings, 2000. XIV, 511 pages. 2000.

Vol. 1879: M. Paterson (Ed.), Algorithms – ESA 2000. Proceedings, 2000. IX, 450 pages. 2000.

Vol. 1880: M. Bellare (Ed.), Advances in Cryptology – CRYPTO 2000. Proceedings, 2000. XI, 545 pages. 2000.

Vol. 1881: C. Zhang, V.-W. Soo (Eds.), Design and Applications of Intelligent Agents. Proceedings, 2000. X, 183 pages. 2000. (Subseries LNAI).

Vol. 1882: D. Kotz, F. Mattern (Eds.), Agent Systems, Mobile Agents, and Applications. Proceedings, 2000. XII, 275 pages. 2000.

Vol. 1883: B. Triggs, A. Zisserman, R. Szeliski (Eds.), Vision Algorithms: Theory and Practice. Proceedings, 1999. X, 383 pages. 2000.

Vol. 1884: J. Štuller, J. Pokorný, B. Thalheim, Y. Masunaga (Eds.), Current Issues in Databases and Information Systems. Proceedings, 2000. XIII, 396 pages. 2000.

Vol. 1885: K. Havelund, J. Penix, W. Visser (Eds.), SPIN Model Checking and Software Verification. Proceedings, 2000. X, 343 pages. 2000.

Vol. 1886: R. Mizoguchi, J. Slaney /Eds.), PRICAI 2000: Topics in Artificial Intelligence. Proceedings, 2000. XX, 835 pages. 2000. (Subseries LNAI).

Vol. 1888: G. Sommer, Y.Y. Zeevi (Eds.), Algebraic Frames for the Perception-Action Cycle. Proceedings, 2000. X, 349 pages. 2000.

Vol. 1889: M. Anderson, P. Cheng, V. Haarslev (Eds.), Theory and Application of Diagrams. Proceedings, 2000. XII, 504 pages. 2000. (Subseries LNAI).

Vol. 1890: C Linnhoff-Popien, H.-G. Hegering (Eds.), Trends in Distributed Systems: Towards a Universal Service Market. Proceedings, 2000. XI, 341 pages. 2000.

Vol. 1891: A.L. Oliveira (Ed.), Grammatical Inference: Algorithms and Applications. Proceedings, 2000. VIII, 313 pages. 2000. (Subseries LNAI).

Vol. 1892: P. Brusilovsky, O. Stock, C. Strapparava (Eds.), Adaptive Hypermedia and Adaptive Web-Based Systems. Proceedings, 2000. XIII, 422 pages. 2000.

Vol. 1893: M. Nielsen, B. Rovan (Eds.), Mathematical Foundations of Computer Science 2000. Proceedings, 2000. XIII, 710 pages. 2000.

Vol. 1894: R. Dechter (Ed.), Principles and Practice of Constraint Programming – CP 2000. Proceedings, 2000. XII, 556 pages. 2000.

Vol. 1895: F. Cuppens, Y. Deswarte, D. Gollmann, M. Waidner (Eds.), Computer Security – ESORICS 2000. Proceedings, 2000. X, 325 pages. 2000.

Vol. 1896: R. W. Hartenstein, H. Grünbacher (Eds.), Field-Programmable Logic and Applications. Proceedings, 2000. XVII, 856 pages. 2000.

Vol. 1897: J. Gutknecht, W. Weck (Eds.), Modular Programming Languages. Proceedings, 2000. XII, 299 pages. 2000.

Vol. 1898: E. Blanzieri, L. Portinale (Eds.), Advances in Case-Based Reasoning. Proceedings, 2000. XII, 530 pages. 2000. (Subseries LNAI).

Vol. 1899: H.-H. Nagel, F.J. Perales López (Eds.), Articulated Motion and Deformable Objects. Proceedings, 2000. X, 183 pages. 2000.

Vol. 1900: A. Bode, T. Ludwig, W. Karl, R. Wismüller (Eds.), Euro-Par 2000 Parallel Processing. Proceedings, 2000. XXXV, 1368 pages. 2000.

Vol. 1901: O. Etzion, P. Scheuermann (Eds.), Cooperative Information Systems. Proceedings, 2000. XI, 336 pages. 2000.

Vol. 1902: P. Sojka, I. Kopeček, K. Pala (Eds.), Text, Speech and Dialogue. Proceedings, 2000. XIII, 463 pages. 2000. (Subseries LNAI).

Vol. 1903: S. Reich, K.M. Anderson (Eds.), Open Hypermedia Systems and Structural Computing. Proceedings, 2000. VIII, 187 pages. 2000.

Vol. 1904: S.A. Cerri, D. Dochev (Eds.), Artificial Intelligence: Methodology, Systems, and Applications. Proceedings, 2000. XII, 366 pages. 2000. (Subseries LNAI).

Vol. 1906: A. Porto, G.-C. Roman (Eds.), Coordination Languages and Models. Proceedings, 2000. IX, 353 pages. 2000.

Vol. 1908: J. Dongarra, P. Kacsuk, N. Podhorszki (Eds.), Recent Advances in Parallel Virtual Machine and Message Passing Interface. Proceedings, 2000. XV, 364 pages. 2000.

Vol. 1910: D.A. Zighed, J. Komorowski, J. Żytkow (Eds.), Principles of Data Mining and Knowledge Discovery. Proceedings, 2000. XV, 701 pages. 2000. (Subseries LNAI).

Vol. 1912: Y. Gurevich, P.W. Kutter, M. Odersky, L. Thiele (Eds.), Abstract State Machines. Proceedings, 2000. X, 381 pages. 2000.

Vol. 1913: K. Jansen, S. Khuller (Eds.), Approximation Algorithms for Combinatorial Optimization. Proceedings, 2000. IX, 275 pages. 2000.

Vol. 1917: M. Schoenauer, K. Deb, G. Rudolph, X. Yao, E. Lutton, J.J. Merelo, H.-P. Schwefel (Eds.), Parallel Problem Solving from Nature – PPSN VI. Proceedings, 2000. XXI, 914 pages. 2000.

Vol. 1918: D. Soudris, P. Pirsch, E. Barke (Eds.), Integrated Circuit Design. Proceedings, 2000. XII, 338 pages. 2000.

Vol. 1920: A.H.F. Laender, S.W. Liddle, V.C. Storey (Eds.), Conceptual Modeling – ER 2000. Proceedings, 2000. XV, 588 pages. 2000.

Vol. 1921: S.W. Liddle, H.C. Mayr, B. Thalheim (Eds.), Conceptual Modeling for E-Business and the Web. Proceedings, 2000. X, 179 pages. 2000.

Vol. 1922: J. Crowcroft, J. Roberts, M.I. Smirnov (Eds.), Quality of Future Internet Services. Proceedings, 2000. XI, 368 pages. 2000.

Vol. 1923: J. Borbinha, T. Baker (Eds.), Research and Advanced Technology for Digital Libraries. Proceedings, 2000. XVII, 513 pages. 2000.

Vol. 1924: W. Taha (Ed.), Semantics, Applications, and Implementation of Program Generation. Proceedings, 2000. VIII, 231 pages. 2000.

Vol. 1926: M. Joseph (Ed.), Formal Techniques in Real-Time and Fault-Tolerant Systems. Proceedings, 2000. X, 305 pages. 2000.

Vol. 1927: P. Thomas, H.W. Gellersen, (Eds.), Handheld and Ubiquitous Computing. Proceedings, 2000. X, 249 pages. 2000.

Vol. 1931: E. Horlait (Ed.), Mobile Agents for Telecommunication Applications. Proceedings, 2000. IX, 271 pages. 2000.

Vol. 1766: M. Jazayeri, R.G.K. Loos, D.R. Musser (Eds.), Generic Programming. Proceedings, 1998. X, 269 pages. 2000.

Vol. 1933: R.W. Brause, E. Hanisch (Eds.), Medical Data Analysis. Proceedings, 2000. XI, 316 pages. 2000.